Question&Answer
COMPANY LAW

Law Express Q&A

Question&Answer

COMPANY LAW

Fang Ma
University of Hertfordshire

Longman
is an imprint of

Harlow, England • London • New York • Boston • San Francisco • Toronto • Sydney • Singapore • Hong Kong
Tokyo • Seoul • Taipei • New Delhi • Cape Town • Madrid • Mexico City • Amsterdam • Munich • Paris • Milan

Pearson Education Limited

Edinburgh Gate

Harlow

Essex CM20 2JE

England

and Associated Companies throughout the world

Visit us on the World Wide Web at:
www.pearson.com/uk

First published 2012

© Pearson Education Limited 2012

ISBN: 978-1-4082-6670-0

British Library Cataloguing-in-Publication Data
A catalogue record for this book is available from the British Library

Library of Congress Cataloging-in-Publication Data
A catalog record for this book is available from the Library of Congress

10 9 8 7 6 5 4 3 2
15 14 13

Typeset in 9/12pt Helvetica Neue by 3
Printed in Malaysia, CTP-KHL

Contents

Acknowledgements   vii
What you need to do for every question in Company Law   viii
Guided tour   x
Guided tour of the companion website   xiii
Table of cases and statutes   xiv

Chapter 1: Incorporation   1
Chapter 2: The *Salomon* principles and the corporate veil   23
Chapter 3: Company constitution   43
Chapter 4: Directors' duties   67
Chapter 5: Corporate governance   105
Chapter 6: Shares and share capital   139
Chapter 7: Loan capital   171
Chapter 8: Shareholder remedies   191
Chapter 9: Corporate insolvency   217

Bibliography   245
Index   251

Supporting resources

Visit the **Law Express Question&Answer** series companion website at
www.pearsoned.co.uk/lawexpressqa to find valuable student learning material
including:

- Additional **essay and problem questions** arranged by topic for each chapter
  give you more opportunity to practise and hone your exam skills.
- **Diagram plans** for all additional questions assist you in structuring and writing
  your answers.
- **You be the marker** questions allow you to see through the eyes of the
  examiner by marking essay and problem questions on every topic covered in
  the book.
- Download and print all **Attack the question** diagrams and **Diagram plans**
  from the book.

Also: The companion website provides the following features:

- Search tool to help locate specific items of content.
- Online help and support to assist with website usage and troubleshooting.

For more information please contact your local Pearson sales representative or
visit www.pearsoned.co.uk/lawexpressqa

Acknowledgements

I would like to thank the team at Pearson, in particular, Zoe Botterill and Gabriella Playford, for their support in completing this book. I am grateful for the comments made by reviewers of this book. I also owe my gratitude to my colleagues and my family for their encouragement and help in writing this book.

Publisher's acknowledgements

Our thanks go to all reviewers who contributed to the development of this text, including students who participated in research and focus groups which helped to shape the series format.

What you need to do for every question in Company Law

HOW TO USE THIS BOOK

Books in the *Question and Answer* series focus on the *why* of a good answer alongside the *what,* thereby helping you to build your question answering skills and technique.

This guide should not be used as a substitute for learning the material thoroughly, your lecture notes or your textbook. It *will* help you to make the most out of what you have already learned when answering an exam or coursework question. Remember that the answers given here are not the *only* correct way of answering the question but serve to show you some good examples of how you *could* approach the question set.

Make sure that you regularly refer to your course syllabus, check which issues are covered (as well as to what extent they are covered) and whether they are usually examined with other topics. Remember that what is required in a good answer could change significantly with only a slight change in the wording of a question. Therefore, do not try to memorise the answers given here, instead use the answers and the other features to understand what goes into a good answer and why.

Before answering any exam question in Company Law, it is essential that you read the question very carefully. Students often make the mistake of not addressing the question which is being asked or misunderstanding the question. Try to avoid giving a general answer by writing everything you know about the topic without reference to the particular issues raised in the question. Most of the topics in company law are interrelated because of the pervasive nature of this subject; it is therefore important to plan your answer, for example, by drawing a simple diagram plan. Good planning helps you clearly structure your answer, identify all the key legal issues that are raised in the question and avoid repetition.

In most instances, you need to consider whether the question concerns a private company or a public company because different rules may apply, in particular in the areas of share capital, loan capital, corporate insolvency and corporate governance. Make sure that your answer is well supported and shows good understanding of the relevant law, not just common sense. It is surprisingly common to come across exam answers with little application of case law or statutes such as the Companies Act 2006 and the Insolvency Act 1986. In relation to case law, students tend to give too much detail of the case facts without appropriate discussion of the important legal principles. It should be noted that the cases discussed in the suggested answers in this book are not the only correct or relevant cases. You can use other cases covered in textbooks or lectures to illustrate the same legal principles. In an exam the full case references are not usually required; mentioning the name of the case and the year when it was decided should be sufficient.

Guided tour

What you need to do for every question in Company Law

What to do for every question – Find out the key things you should do and look for in any question and answer on the subject in order to give every one of your answers a great chance from the start.

Incorporation
1

How this topic may come up in exams

Standard exam questions may ask you to discuss the following issues: the advantages and disadvantages of incorporation compared with partnerships and sole traders, the procedures for setting up a company and the considerations in choosing a company name. A clear understanding of the distinction between private companies and public companies is essential, as well as the change of company status from private to public companies and vice versa. The duties of promoters and the pre-incorporation contracts are also popular topics for examination. You should pay special attention to the personal liabilities of promoters with regard to these contracts.

How this topic may come up in exams – Learn how to tackle any question on this topic by using the handy tips and advice relevant to both essay and problem questions. In-text symbols clearly identify each question type as it occurs.

 Essay question

 Problem question

Attack the question – Attack attack attack! Use these diagrams as a step by step guide to help you confidently identify the main points covered in any question asked.

Answer plans and Diagram plans – Clear and concise answer plans and diagram plans support the planning and structuring of your answers whatever your preferred learning style.

■ Attack the question

Is the person concerned a director of the company?

Yes. Has he breached any of his general duties under ss 170–177 of the CA 2006?

No, director's duties do not apply.

Yes. Has the breach of duty been ratified?

No, the issue of breach of directors' general duties does not arise.

Yes. No further actions.

No. The company may bring an action against the director. Alternatively, a shareholder may bring a derivative action or unfair prejudice petition against the director.

...ter's right to nominate...

...whether Peter can enforce his right in the...
...ary £50,000.

Evaluate whether the clause which has the effect of compul...
shareholder's shares can be added to the articles.

Diagram plan

(1) Alteration of the articles of association (s 21)

(4) Is the compulsory purchase clause valid?

The enforcement of the articles of association

(2) Can Peter... his right to... a dir...

(3) Can Peter rely on the articles to protect his annual salary?

...table version of this diagram plan is available from www.pearsoned.co.uk/...

Answer plan

→ Discuss whether Peter's right to nominate a director can be a...

→ Examine whether Peter can enforce his right in the articles... salary £50,000.

→ Evaluate whether the clause which has the effect of compulsor... shareholder's shares can be added to the articles.

Answer with accompanying guidance –
Make the most out of every question by using the guidance to recognise what makes a good answer and why. Answers are the length you could realistically hope to produce in an exam to show you how to gain marks quickly when under pressure.

Case names clearly highlighted – Easy to spot bold text makes those all important case names stand out from the rest of the answer, ensuring they are much easier to remember in revision and in the exam.

Make your answer stand out – Really impress your examiners by including these additional points and further reading to illustrate your deeper knowledge of the subject, fully maximising your marks.

Don't be tempted to … – Avoid common mistakes and losing easy marks by understanding where students most often trip up in exams.

Bibliography – Use this list of further reading to really explore areas in more depth, enabling you to excel in exams.

QUESTION 3

[5]This paragraph demonstrates how the rule of disclosure was developed at common law since *Erlanger*. The discussion of case law is essential for a sound answer.

[6]After analysing the relevant law, you should apply it to the problem question. The sentence gives advice on the remedies available to the company. It goes beyond the issue of Steve's breach of duties.

would not be sufficient if the original shareholders were not truly independent and the scheme as a whole was designed to defraud the investing public.[5]

The current law appears to require that disclosure be made to an entirely independent board or to the existing and potential members as a whole. As Steve made a secret profit without disclosing to either an independent board or any existing member of the company, he has breached his fiduciary duty as a promoter. Organic Bakery Ltd can rescind the contract with Steve and recover the secret profit.[6]

2. The expense of £10,000 in promoting the company

The next issue concerns whether Kate can recover the expenses in promoting the company.[7] Kate, as a promoter, is not entitled to recover any remuneration from Organic Bakery Ltd for her services unless there is a valid contract in this matter between her and the company. Without such a contract she is not even entitled to recover

[1]Clearly state the key legal issues that you are going to address in your answer.

[2]Some students go straight into examining the law on lifting the corporate veil without explaining the *Salomon* principles. You will lose some marks if the case of *Salomon* is not discussed.

In order to advise the board of directors in Easyclean Ltd as to whether Adrian will be held personally liable for the return of profits and for the breach of the agreement with the company, it is necessary to examine whether and on what basis the corporate veil can be lifted in relation to Pureclean Ltd.[1]

The corporate veil is a metaphor to describe the principle of separate legal personality, as established in **Salomon v Salomon & Co Ltd** [1897] AC 22.[2] A company, once incorporated, is an independent legal entity separate from those who set it up. It can own property (**Macaura v Northern Assurance Co** [1925] AC 619), sue for defamation (**South Hetton Coal Co Ltd v North-Eastern News Association Ltd** [1894] 1QB 133), employ members and outside

✓ Make your answer stand out

- Explain what is meant by a variation of class rights. The courts have drawn an artificial distinction between matters affecting the rights attaching to each share and matters affecting the enjoyment of those rights. Only variation which affects the rights attached to each share attracts the protection of the procedure in s 630.
- In relation to the test of '*bona fide* for the benefit of the company as a whole', discuss *Sidebottom* v *Kershaw, Leese & Co Ltd* [1920] 1 Ch 154 and *Dafen Tinplate Co Ltd* v *Llanelly Steel Co Ltd* [1920] 2 Ch 124.
- Examine the circumstance where a shareholder enters into a shareholder agreement, for example, a voting agreement (*Russell v Northern Bank Development Corp Ltd*

! Don't be tempted to…

- Consider the common law restrictions on the power to alter the articles without reference to the cases of *Shuttleworth* (1927) and *Greenhalgh* (1950).
- Only focus on the common law restrictions imposed by *Allen* v *Gold Reefs of West Africa Ltd* [1900] 1 Ch 656. The statutory provisions must also be discussed in your answer.

Bibliography

Abarca, M. L. de E. (2004), 'The need for substantive regulation on investor protection and corporate governance in Europe: does Europe need a Sarbanes-Oxley?' *Journal of International Banking Law and Regulation* 419

Guided tour of the companion website

 Book resources are available to download. Print your own **Attack the question** and **Diagram plans**.

 Additional **Essay and Problem questions** with **Diagram plans** arranged by topic for each chapter give you more opportunity to practise and hone your exam skills. Print and email your answers.

 You be the marker gives you a chance to evaluate sample exam answers for different question types for each topic and understand how and why an examiner awards marks. Use the accompanying guidance to get the most out of every question and recognise what makes a good answer.

All of this and more can be found when you visit
www.pearsoned.co.uk/lawexpressqa

Table of cases and statutes

▮Cases

AA Mutual International Insurance Co Ltd, Re [2005] 2 BCLC 8 225

Aberdeen Rly Co v Blaikie Bros (1854) 1 Macq 461 72, 88, 97, 102, 109, 161, 200

Adams v Cape Industries plc [1990] BCLC 479 29–34, 36, 38–41

A-G's Reference (No. 2 of 1982) [1984] 2 All ER 216 27, 34

Agnew v IRC (Re Brumark) [2001] 2 BCLC 188 173, 175–77, 182, 183

Allen v Gold Reefs of West Africa Ltd [1900] 1 Ch 656 52, 54, 55, 57, 60

Anglo Petroleum Ltd v TFB (Mortgages) Ltd [2008] 1 BCLC 185 160

Association of Certified Public Accountants of Britain (Association of) v Secretary of State for Trade and Industry [1997] 2 BCLC 307 10

Bacon (MC) Ltd, Re [1990] BCLC 324 189, 242

Bairstow v Queens Moat Houses plc [2002] BCC 91 147, 157

Balston Ltd v Headline Filters Ltd [1990] FSR 385 93

Barclays Bank plc v Stuart London Ltd [2001] 2 BCLC 316 179

Barings plc, Re (No.5) [2000] 1 BCLC 523 85, 86

Barings plc, Re [2002] 1 BCLC 401 71

Bayoil SA, Re [1999] 1 BCLC 62 230

Beattie v E. and F. Beattie Ltd [1938] Ch 708 47, 51, 60, 64

Bentinck v Fenn (1887) 12 App Cas 652 72

Bhullar v Bhullar [2003] 2 BCLC 241 90

Bird Precision Bellows Ltd, Re [1984] Ch 419 206, 210

Bishopsgate Investment Management Ltd v Maxwell (No. 2) [1994] 1 All ER 261 86

Blue Arrow plc, Re [1987] BCLC 585 204

Boardman v Phipps [1966] 3 All ER 721 88, 92

Borland's Trustee v Steel Bros & Co Ltd [1901] 1 Ch 279 142

Bradford Investments plc, Re (No. 2) [1991] BCLC 688 157

Brady v Brady [1988] BCLC 20 148, 160, 162, 165

Bratton Seymore Service Co Ltd v Oxborough [1992] BCLC 693 46

Bray v Ford [1896] AC 44 91, 92

Braymist Ltd v Wise Finance Co Ltd [2002] 1 BCLC 415 21

Brian D Pierson Ltd, Re [2001] 1 BCLC 275 104, 238

Brightlife Ltd, Re [1986] BCLC 418 184

Bristol & West Building Society v Mothew [1998] Ch 1 70, 71, 83, 144

Brownlow v G. H. Marshall Ltd [2000] 2 BCLC 655 206, 210

Brumark, Re. See Agnew v Commissioner of Inland Revenue

Burland v Earl [1902] AC 83 213

Bushell v Faith [1970] AC 1099 50–2, 65

Cade (JE) & Son Ltd, Re [1991] BCC 360 204

Cardiff Savings Bank, Re, Marquis of Bute's case [1892] 2 Ch 100 84

Carlen v Drury (1812) 1 Ves & B 154 76

Charterbridge Corp Ltd v Lloyds Bank Ltd [1970] Ch
62 76, 77, 79, 101, 200

Charterhouse Investment Trust Ltd v Tempest Diesels
Ltd [1986] BCLC 1 160, 164

Chaston v SWP Group plc [2003] 1 BCLC 675 149,
160, 164

Chatterley-Whitfield Collieries Ltd, Re [1948] 2 All ER
593 169

Citco Banking Corp NV v Pusser's Ltd [2007] 2 BCLC
483 56

City Equitable Fire Insurance, Re [1925] Ch 407 70,
84, 85–6

Clark v Cutland [2003] 4 All ER 733 207, 214

Coleman Taymar Ltd v Oakes [2001] 2 BCLC
749 100

Commissioners of Inland Revenue v Adam & Partners
Ltd [2001] 1 BCLC 222 220

Company (No. 00477 of 1986), Re A [1986] BCLC
376 205, 206

Company (No. 005134 of 1986), Re A, ex p Harries
[1989] BCLC 383 53, 75

Continental Assurance Co of London plc, Re [2007] 2
BCLC 287 238

Cook v Deeks [1916] 1 AC 554 71, 88, 92, 110

Corbenstoke Ltd, Re (No. 2) [1990] BCLC 60 230

Cotronic (UK) Ltd v Dezonie [1991] BCLC 721 21

Cumbrian Newspapers Group Ltd v Cumberland and
Westmoreland Herald Newspaper and Printing Co
Ltd [1986] 2 All ER 816 59

D'Jan of London Ltd, Re [1994] 1 BCLC 561 84, 99

Dafen Tinplate Co Ltd v Llanelly Steel Co Ltd [1920] 2
Ch 124 57, 61, 62

Daimler v CTR [1916] 2 AC 307 31

Dalby v Bodilly [2005] BCC 627 153, 205

Daniels v Daniels [1978] Ch 406 195

DHN Food Distributors Ltd v Tower Hamlets LBC [1976]
3 All ER 462 30, 40

Dimbleby v National Union of Journalists [1984] 1 WLR
427 31

Dorchester Finance Co Ltd v Stebbing [1989] BCLC
498 71, 99, 109

Downsview Nominees v First City Corp [1993] AC
295 225

Dyment v Boyden [2005] 1 BCLC 163 149, 159, 164

Ebrahimi v Westbourne Galleries [1973] AC 360 204,
206, 209

Edwards v Halliwell [1950] 2 All ER 1064 195

Eley v Positive Life Association (1876) 1 Ex D 88 46,
47, 52, 60, 64

Emma Silver Mining Co v Lewis (1879) LR 4 CPD
396 14

English and Colonial Produce Co, Re [1906] 2 Ch
435 15

Erlanger v New Sombrero Phosphate Co (1878) 3 App
Cas 1218 14, 15, 17, 18

Estmanco (Kilner House) Ltd v GLC [1982] 1 WLR
2 195

Evans v Rival Granite Quarries Ltd [1910] 2 KB
979 174

Exchange Banking Co, Re, Flitcroft's case (1882) 21 Ch
D 519 157

Exchange Travel (Holdings) Ltd, Re [1996] 2 BCLC
524 189

Foss v Harbottle (1843) 67 ER 189 47, 48, 56, 109,
194, 195, 198, 199, 212

Franbar Holding Ltd v Patel [2008] BCC 885 144, 197,
201, 215

Fulham Football Club and Others v Cabra Estates plc
[1994] 1 BCLC 363 71, 81, 109, 137

Gallagher (NT) & Son Ltd, Re [2002] 2 BCLC 133 222

Gencor ACP Ltd v Dalby [2000] 2 BCLC 734 35, 90

Gilford Motor Co v Horne [1933] Ch 935 27, 30, 35, 39

Gluckstein v Barnes [1900] AC 240 14, 18, 19

Great Wheal Polgooth Co Ltd, Re (1883) 53 LJ Ch
42 16

Greenhalgh v Arderne Cinemas Ltd [1950] 2 All ER
1120 52, 55, 61

Greenhalgh v Mallard [1943] 2 All ER 234 57, 63

Greenwell v Porter [1902] 1 Ch 530 65

Gwembe Valley Development Co Ltd v Koshy [2004] 1
BCLC 131 97

Heald v O'Connor [1971] 2 All ER 1105 165

Hickman v Kent or Romney Marsh Sheepbreeders
Association [1915] 1 Ch 881 43, 45, 47, 48, 50,
51, 59, 62–4

Hogg v Cramphorn [1967] Ch 254 70, 75, 109

TABLE OF CASES AND STATUTES

House of Fraser plc v ACGE Investments Ltd [1987] AC 387 170

Howard Smith Ltd v Ampol Petroleum [1974] AC 821 70, 75, 77, 144, 153, 161

Howard v Patent Ivory Manufacturing Co (1888) LR 38 Ch D 156 21

Hutton v West Cork Railway Company (1883) LR 23 Ch D 654 79, 135

Hydrodan (Corby) Ltd, Re [1994] BCC 161 70

Iesini v Westrip Holdings Ltd [2009] EWHC 2526 (Ch) 197, 202

Industrial Development Consultants Ltd v Cooley [1972] 2 All ER 162 89, 92

IRC v Wimbledon [2005] 1 BCLC 66 221

Island Export Finance Ltd v Umunna [1986] BCLC 460 93

It's a Wrap (UK) Ltd v Gula [2006] 2 BCLC 634 147

Item Software (UK) Ltd v Fassihi [2005] 2 BCLC 91 90

JJ Harrison (Properties) Ltd v Harrison [2002] 1 BCLC 162 161, 165

Jones v Lipman [1962] 1 WLR 832 30, 34, 39

Keenan Bros Ltd, Re [1986] BCLC 242 176, 185

Kelner v Baxter (1866) LR 2 CP 174 15, 16, 18–20

Kenyon Swansea, Re [1987] 3 BCC 259 205

Kiani v Cooper [2010] EWHC 577 197, 202

Kleanthis v Paphitis and Ors [2011] EWHC 2287 197

Kyrris v Oldham [2004] 1 BCLC 305 224

Lee v Lee's Air Farming Ltd [1961] AC 12 5, 27, 34

Legal Costs Negotiators Ltd, Re [1999] BCC 547 204, 209

Leyland Daf, Re [2004] 1 BCLC 281 233

Little Olympian Each-Ways Ltd, Re [1995] 1 BCLC 636 205

Lomax Leisure Ltd v Miller [2008] 1 BCLC 262 230

London School of Electronics Ltd, Re [1986] Ch 211 210

Macaura v Northern Assurance Co [1925] AC 619 5, 26, 34

MacDougall v Gardiner (1875) LR 1 Ch D 13 195, 213

Mackenzie and Co Ltd Re [1916] 2 Ch 450 169

Macro (Ipswich) Ltd, Re [1994] BCC 781 205

MCI WorldCom Ltd, Re [2003] 1 BCLC 330 230

Mission Capital plc v Sinclair [2008] BCC 866 144, 161, 197, 201, 215

Movitex Ltd v Bulfield [1988] BCLC 104 98

MS Fashions Ltd v BCCI SA (No. 2) [1993] 3 All ER 769 234

MT Realisations Ltd v Digital Equipment Co Ltd [2003] 2 BCLC 117 164

Natal Land Co & Colonization Ltd v Pauline Colliery and Development Syndicate Ltd [1904] AC 120 17, 20

National Telephone Co, Re [1914] 1 Ch 755 167

National Westminster Bank plc v Hones [2002] 1 BCLC 55 242

National Westminster Bank plc v Spectrum Plus Ltd [2005] 2 BCLC 269 175–7, 182–6

New British Iron Co, Re, ex p Beckwith [1898] 1 Ch 324 60

New Bullas Trading Ltd, Re [1994] 1 BCLC 485 182, 183

Newborne v Sensolid (GB) Ltd [1954] 1 QB 45 16, 17, 20

Noble (A) & Sons Ltd, Re [1983] BCLC 273 210

Noel Tedman Holdings Pty Ltd, Re [1967] Qd R 561 27

Norman v Theodore Goddard [1991] BCLC 1028 84

O'Neill v Phillips [1999] 1 WLR 1092 203, 205, 207, 209, 214

Official Receiver v Doshi [2001] 2 BCLC 235 238

Omnium Electric v Baines [1914] 1 Ch 332 18

Ooregum Gold Mining Co of India v Roper [1892] AC 125 155

Ord v Belhaven Pubs Ltd [1998] BCC 607 40

Ossory Estates plc, Re [1988] BCLC 213 157

Paramount Airways Ltd, Re [1992] 3 All ER 1 103, 144

Patrick and Lyon Ltd, Re [1933] Ch 786 237

Pavlides v Jensen [1956] Ch 565 195

Pender v Lushington (1877) 6 Ch D 70 47, 59, 64

Percival v Wright [1902] 2 Ch 421 70, 74, 79, 83, 88, 135, 199

Peso Silver Mines v Cropper (1966) 58 DLR (2d) 1 94

Phonogram Ltd v Lane [1982] QB 938 16, 17, 20

Power v Sharpe Investments Ltd [1994] 1 BCLC 111 188

Prudential Assurance Co Ltd v Newman Industries Ltd (No. 2) [1982] Ch 204 195, 213

Puddephatt v Leith [1916] 1 Ch 200 64
Punt v Symons & Co Ltd [1903] 2 Ch 506 60, 65

Queensland Mines Ltd v Hudson (1978) 52 ALJR
399 94
Quin & Axtens Ltd v Salmon [1909] AC 442 46, 48,
49

Ratners Group plc, Re [1988] BCLC 685 147, 169
Rayfield v Hands [1958] 2 All ER 194 143
Regal (Hastings) Ltd v Gulliver [1942] 1 All ER 378 71,
89, 92, 109, 200
Regentcrest plc v Cohen [2001] 2 BCLC 80 76, 101
Ricketts v Ad Valorem Factors Ltd [2004] 1 BCLC
1 239
Roots v Williamson (1888) 38 Ch D 485 143, 144
Rose, Re, Rose v IRC [1952] 1 All ER 1217 144
Royal Trust Bank v National Westminster Bank plc
[1996] 2 BCLC 682 184
Russell v Northern Bank Development Corporation Ltd
[1992] BCLC 1016 57, 62, 63, 65, 66

Salomon v Salomon & Co Ltd [1897] AC 22 5, 11, 14,
18, 23, 25–39, 237
Saltdean Estate Co Ltd, Re [1968] 3 All ER 829 169
Saul D Harrison & Sons plc, Re [1994] BCC 475 205
Shuttleworth v Cox Bros & Co (Maidenhead) Ltd [1927]
2 KB 9 55, 56, 61
Sidebottom v Kershaw, Leese & Co Ltd [1920] 1 Ch
154 57, 61, 62
Siebe Gorman & Co Ltd v Barclays Bank Ltd [1979] 2
Lloyd's Rep 142 176, 182–4, 186
Smith & Fawcett Ltd, Re [1942] 1 All ER 542 71, 76,
79, 109, 135, 143, 144, 153, 161, 200, 210
Smith v Croft (No. 2) [1988] Ch 114 195, 213
Smith, Stone & Knight Ltd v Birmingham Corp [1939] 4
All ER 116 6, 30, 35, 36, 39
South Hetton Coal Co Ltd v North-Eastern News
Association Ltd [1894] 1 QB 133 27, 34
Southern Counties Fresh Foods Ltd, Re [2008] All ER
(D) 195 (Nov) 81, 137
Southern Foundries (1926) Ltd v Shirlaw [1940] 2 All
ER 445 53, 60
Spectrum Plus Ltd, Re. See National Westminster Bank
plc v Spectrum Plus Ltd
Stainer v Lee [2010] EWHC 1539 (Ch) 197, 202

Stimpson v Southern Landlords Association [2009]
EWHC 2072 (Ch) 197, 202

Teleomatic, Re [1994] 1 BCLC 90 179
Trevor v Whitworth (1887) 12 App Cas 409 146, 148,
163
Trustor AB v Smallbone [2001] 2 BCLC 436 35, 39
Twycross v Grant (1877) 2 CPD 469 14, 18

Wallace v Universal Automatic Machines [1894] 2 Ch
547 174
Wallesteiner v Moir [1974] 3 All ER 217 31, 36
Wallerstein v Moir (No. 2) [1975] QB 373 197, 215
Webb v Whiffin (1872) LR 5 HL 711 235
Whaley Bridge Printing Co v Green (1880) LR 5 QBD
109 17
White v Bristol Aeroplane Co Ltd [1953] Ch 65 152,
168
William C Leitch Bro Ltd, Re [1932] 2 Ch 71 237
William Gaskell Group Ltd v Highley [1994] 1 BCLC
197 185
Williams v Natural Life Health Foods [1998] 1 BCLC
689 5
Wilson v Kelland [1910] 2 Ch 306 176, 180
Wood v Odessa Waterworks Co (1889) 42 Ch D
636 47, 59, 60, 64
Woodroffes (Musical Instruments) Ltd, Re [1986] Ch
366 174
Woolfson v Strathclyde Regional Council (1979) 38 P
&CR 521 6, 31
Wragg Ltd, Re [1897] 1 Ch 796 155, 158

Yorkshire Woolcombers Association, Re [1903] 2 Ch
284 174, 183, 185

◼ Statutes

Companies Act 1862 25
Companies Act 1929
s 45 163
Companies Act 1948
s 210 204
Companies Act 1980
s 75 204

TABLE OF CASES AND STATUTES

Companies Act 1981 163
  s 155–158 163
Companies Act 1985
  s 36 20
    (3) 16
  s 103 157
  s 113 157
  s 121 65
  s 459 204
Companies Act 2006 ix, 3, 4, 11, 16, 56, 67, 70, 79,
    91, 92, 94, 97, 107, 109, 129, 133, 134, 142,
    145, 147, 149, 162–4, 190, 193, 202, 212, 215,
    236
  s 3(2) 4, 8
    (3) 4
    (4) 4
  s 4(1) 8
    (2) 9
  s 7 8, 9
  s 8 8, 9
  s 9 8, 11
  s 10 8
  s 11 8
  s 12 8
  s 13 8
  s 14 8
  s 15 8, 10
  s 16 8
  s 17 46, 51
  s 18 9
  s 21 43, 46, 49, 50, 52, 54, 58–60, 63, 64, 66,
    121, 152, 168
  s 22 54, 66
  s 25 54, 56
  s 33 43–6, 48, 51, 59, 62, 64, 143
  s 51 13, 16, 17, 20, 21
    (1) 16
  s 53–65 8, 10
  s 66 8, 10, 11
  s 67 8, 10
  s 68 8, 10
  s 69 8, 10, 11
  s 70–76 8, 10
  s 77 8, 10, 11
  s 78 8, 10, 11
  s 79–96 8, 10

s 125 143
s 154 70
s 168 49, 50, 65, 121, 206, 209
s 170 67–70, 74, 82, 86, 88, 104, 109, 115, 150,
    159, 199, 237, 244
  (1) 70, 88, 199
  (3) 79
  (4) 72, 79, 88, 199
s 171 36, 53, 67–71, 73–5, 77, 82, 86, 88, 104,
    109, 115, 142, 144, 150, 159, 161, 170, 199,
    237, 244
s 172 36, 53, 61, 67–74, 76–82, 86–8, 90, 100,
    101, 104, 109, 115, 135, 137, 142, 144, 150,
    153, 159, 161, 170, 190, 196, 199–201, 210,
    237, 240, 244
  (1) 77, 80, 81, 136, 137
    (a)–(f) 74, 77
  (3) 101
s 173 67–71, 74, 82, 86, 88, 104, 109, 115, 150,
    159, 161, 199, 237, 244
s 174 67–71, 74, 82–6, 88, 95, 96, 99, 104, 109,
    115, 150, 159, 161, 199, 237, 244
  (1) 86
  (2)(a) 83
    (b) 83
s 175 36, 61, 67–71, 74, 82, 86–95, 100, 104,
    109, 115, 150, 159, 161, 190, 199, 200, 210,
    237, 244
  (1) 87, 92
  (2) 89
  (3) 104
  (4) 71, 87, 89, 93
    (a) 89
    (b) 89
  (5) 89, 93
    (a) 94
    (b) 94
  (6) 89, 93, 200
s 176 67–70, 72, 74, 82, 86, 88, 94–102, 104,
    109, 115, 150, 159, 199, 200, 244
  (4) 99
s 177 67–70, 72, 74, 82, 86, 88, 94–102, 104,
    109, 115, 150, 159, 199, 200, 244
  (1) 96
  (5) 96, 97
  (6) 96

(a) 97
(b) 97
(c) 97
s 178 90, 98
s 182 72, 94–6, 98–102, 104, 199, 200
(5) 96
(6) 96
s 183 100
s 190 96, 98–102
(3) 98
s 191 96, 98, 100–2
s 192–196 96, 98, 100, 101
s 239 72, 77, 87, 90, 91, 201
(2) 93
(4) 94
s 250 69
s 252 94
s 260 77, 81, 109, 122, 128, 136, 142, 153, 159,
161, 170, 192, 193, 198, 199, 207, 212, 215
(3) 195, 212, 213
(5)(c) 212, 214
s 261 77, 81, 109, 128, 142, 153, 159, 161, 192,
193, 196, 198, 199, 207, 212, 213, 216
s 262 77, 81, 109, 128, 142, 144, 153, 159, 161,
192, 193, 198, 199, 207, 212, 216
s 263 77, 81, 109, 128, 142, 144, 153, 159, 161,
192, 193, 198, 199, 207, 212, 216
(2) 93, 194, 196, 201, 213
(a) 202
(3) 194, 196, 199, 201
(b) 202
(f) 215
(4) 194, 196, 199, 201
s 264 77, 81, 128, 192, 193, 198, 199, 207, 212
s 271 9
s 281 9
s 282 50, 75
s 283 52, 54
s 284 50
s 336 9
s 420 132
s 421 132
s 422 132
s 541 142
s 544 143
s 550 75, 153

s 551 53, 150, 151, 167
s 561 53, 75, 150, 151
s 562–568 151
s 569–573 152
s 580 149, 155
s 582 155
s 585–587 1514, 156
s 588 155, 156
s 589 155, 156, 158
s 590 156
s 592 156
s 593 149, 154, 156, 157
s 606 156, 157
s 607 156
s 617 151
s 630 50, 52–4, 56, 57, 59, 66, 150, 152, 167, 168
(1) 168
(4) 168
s 633 152
(2) 168
(5) 168
s 641 146, 147
(a) 169
s 642 146, 147, 169
s 643 146, 147, 170
(4) 147, 169
s 644 146
s 645 146, 147, 169
s 646 146, 147, 169
s 647–657 146
s 658 146, 148
' (2) 148
s 659 148
s 677 146, 148, 158, 159, 163, 164
s 678 146, 148, 158, 162, 163
(1) 159, 160, 162, 164
(2) 148, 159, 160, 162, 164
(3) 164
s 679 146, 158, 163
(1) 164
s 680 146, 148, 158, 161, 163, 165
s 681 146, 158, 163, 166
s 682 146, 158, 163, 166
s 683 146, 158, 163
s 684 146, 148
s 685–689 146

TABLE OF CASES AND STATUTES

s 690–737 146

s 755 8

s 761 9, 29, 31

s 763 9

s 768 143

s 771 142, 143

 (2) 143

 (3) 143

s 829 146

s 830 146, 147, 154, 155, 157

s 831–846 146

s 847 146, 157

s 849–853 146

s 860 177, 178, 185, 187

 (4) 179

 (7) 178

s 870 178, 181, 186, 186

 (1) 179

s 873 177, 179, 181, 187

s 874 187

 (1) 179

 (3) 179

s 993 237

s 994 48, 53, 61, 75, 77, 81, 109, 122, 142, 145, 153, 159, 161, 168, 170, 192, 202–4, 207, 208, 211–15

 (1) 204

 (2) 203, 208, 212, 214

s 995 203, 207, 211

s 996 145, 203, 206, 207, 210–12, 214

 (2) 210

  (b) 161

  (c) 210, 215

  (e)

s 1099 11

s 1100 11

s 1282 233

Company Directors Disqualification Act 1986

 s 6 86, 104, 240

 s 7–9 86

 s 10 190

Enterprise Act 2002 224, 227

Financial Services and Market Act 2000 123

Insolvency Act 1986

Part 1 218, 223

 s 1 218, 219, 220

  (1) 220

s 2 218

 (2) 220

 (3) 220

s 3 218, 219

 (3) 220

s 4 218, 219

 (1) 220

 (4) 220

 4(6) 220

s 4A 218, 219

 (2) 221

 (3) 221

 (6) 221

s 5 218, 219

 (2) 221

s 6 218, 219

 (1) 221

 (2) 221

 (4) 222

s 6A 220

s 7 218, 219

 (2) 222

 (3) 222

 (4) 222

s 73(1) 228

s 84 218, 228

 (1)(b) 228

s 89 228

 (4) 228

 (5) 228

s 91–97 227

s 98 227, 229

s 99–106 227

s 107 228, 235

s 115 233

s 122 207, 218, 227, 228, 229

 (1)(g) 192, 211, 231

s 123 229

s 124(1) 229

 (2) 229

s 127 230, 241, 244

s 143 230

s 165 231

s 167 230

s 168(5) 230

s 175 233
s 176A 234, 235
s 176ZA 233
s 189 235
s 212 101, 103, 244
s 213 28, 29, 31, 104, 237, 244
s 214 28, 29, 32, 85, 190, 237, 238, 244
    (3) 104, 238
    (4) 83, 211, 238
s 216 237, 239
    (2) 239
    (3) 219, 239
    (4) 239
s 238 100–4, 241, 242, 243, 244
    (3) 103, 241, 242
    (4) 102, 241, 242
    (5) 103, 241, 243
s 239 172, 177, 178, 188, 181, 185–8, 190
    (4) 189
    (5) 189
    (6) 189
s 240(1)(a) 241
    (2) 102, 241, 242
s 245 172, 174, 176–8, 180, 181, 185–8
    (2) 181, 188
    (4) 188
s 249 180, 188, 243
s 251 233
s 423 101, 103, 241, 243, 244
s 435 243
Sch 1 226
Sch 6
paras 9–12 234
Sch A1 218, 222
Sch B1 224, 226
para 1 224
para 2 224
para 3 218, 224, 225
para 4 225
para 11 225
para 12 225
para 14 224
    (2) 224
    (3) 225
para 18(3) 226

para 20 226
para 42 224, 226
para 43 224, 227
para 49 227
para 51 227
para 74 224, 226
Limited Liability Partnerships Act 2000 3, 4
Limited Partnerships Act 1907 3, 4
    s 4 4
Partnership Act 1890 3, 4
    s 1 4
    s 5 4

European Union
Directive 68/151/EEC (First Company Law Directive)
    (OJ L65/8, 14 March 1968)
    Art 7 16, 20
Directive 77/91/EEC (Second Company Law Directive)
    (OJ L26/1, 31 January 1977)
    Art 23 163

United States
Sarbanes–Oxley Act 2002 111, 113, 114
    s 302 113
    s 906 113

Statutory Instruments
Insolvency Act 1986 (Prescribed Part) Order 2003 (SI
    2003/2097)
    Art 3 234
Insolvency Rules 1986 (SI 1986/1925) 240
    r 1.18 221
    r 1.19 221
    r 1.20 221
    r 1.29 222
    r 4.73 232
    r 4.90 234
    r 4.228 239, 240
    r 4.229 239
    r 4.230 239
    r 12.3 233
    r 13.12 232
Directors' Remuneration Report Regulations 2002 (SI
    2002/1986) 131–2

Incorporation

1

How this topic may come up in exams

Standard exam questions may ask you to discuss the following issues: the advantages and disadvantages of incorporation compared with partnerships and sole traders, the procedures for setting up a company and the considerations in choosing a company name. A clear understanding of the distinction between private companies and public companies is essential, as well as the change of company status from private to public companies and *vice versa*. The duties of promoters and the pre-incorporation contracts are also popular topics for examination. You should pay special attention to the personal liabilities of promoters with regard to these contracts.

■ Attack the question

What are the advantages and disadvantages of incorporation compared with sole traders and partnerships?

⬇

What are the procedures for setting up a company?

⬇

What are the differences between a private company and a public one? How does a private company become a public one and *vice versa*?

⬇

What are the duties and liabilities of promoters before the incorporation?

A printable version of this diagram plan is available from www.pearsoned.co.uk/lawexpressqa

📝 Question 1

Discuss the advantages and disadvantages of companies compared with other types of business organisations such as sole traders and partnerships.

Answer plan

→ Explain the features of sole traders.

→ Examine the nature of partnerships, including ordinary partnerships, limited partnerships and limited liability partnerships.

→ Analyse the special features of companies and focus on the principles of separate legal personality and of limited liability.

Diagram plan

	Sole Traders	Ordinary Partnerships	Limited Partnerships	Limited Liability Partnerships	Companies
Key Legislation	General law of contract	Partnership Act 1890	Limited Partnerships Act 1907	Limited Liability Partnerships Act 2000	Companies Act 2006
Individual's (partner or member) liabilities in respect of business debts	Unlimited	Each partner is jointly and severally liable	Limited liability for limited partners and unlimited liability for general partners	Limited to the amount as they have agreed	Depending on the type of companies
Separate legal personality?	No	No	No	Yes	Yes

A printable version of this diagram plan is available from www.pearsoned.co.uk/lawexpressqa

Answer

[1]This sentence sets out the general outline of your answer.

Companies are popular forms of business organisations, alongside sole traders and partnerships. Each has its own distinct features and is suitable for a particular type of business.[1]

[2]This comment is useful because it compares a sole trader and a company in relation to the filing and registration requirements.

A sole trader is a one-person business where an individual makes a contract in his own name. There are no legal filing requirements and therefore it has the advantage of privacy.[2] The individual who acts

[3]This phrase is important here because it shows a sharp contrast between a sole trader and a company limited by shares.

[4]Use this sentence to show the examiners where you are going with your answer. This is a broad essay question on various types of business organisation. To gain a higher mark for this type of standard question, you need to show a clear understanding of different types of partnership, in particular, the limited partnership and LLP.

[5]This is the main difference between a partnership and a company and therefore it should be included in a good answer.

[6]This shows that you understand the nature of a partnership and the use of this type of business in practice.

[7]The discussion of limited partnerships is essential here because it demonstrates your sound knowledge of the different types of partnerships. This is often missing in a good exam answer.

[8]Pay attention to the requirement of the general partner without limited liability in addition to the partners with limited liability. This is the basic feature of a limited partnership.

[9]It is very easy to get confused with an LLP because it has the features of both an ordinary partnership and a limited company. An accurate discussion of the features of LLPs makes your answer stand out.

as a sole trader has unlimited liability[3] in respect of the business debts. It is suitable for a one-person business with capital but not for large-scale investment.

There are three main types of partnerships: ordinary partnerships, limited partnerships and limited liability partnerships.[4] Ordinary partnerships are governed by the Partnership Act 1890 unless excluded by the partnership agreement. An ordinary partnership is defined in s 1 as 'the relationship which subsists between persons carrying on a business in common with a view of profit'. In this type of partnership, there must be at least two partners, each of whom becomes an agent of the other (s 5). A partnership does not have a separate legal personality and its assets are owned directly by the partners. Partners personally are parties to the partnership contracts and do not have limited liability in respect of the partnership's debts. Each partner is jointly and severally liable for the debts and obligations of the partnership incurred while he is a partner.[5] The business affairs of a partnership are entirely private and no legal formality or public registration is required. It is therefore suitable for an association of a small number of persons having trust and confidence in each other.[6]

Limited partnerships are governed by the Limited Partnerships Act 1907.[7] In a limited partnership, there are limited partners with limited liability who are excluded from all management functions. Their liabilities for the partnership's debts are limited to the amount of their contribution to it. There must be at least one general partner with unlimited liability[8] who is liable for debts and obligations of the partnership (s 4). Considering these requirements, limited partnerships are relatively rare.

Limited liability partnerships (LLPS), which are a hybrid of partnerships and companies, are governed by the Limited Liability Partnerships Act 2000. An LLP has a separate legal personality from its members. The liability of individual members is limited to such amount as they have agreed internally to contribute to the debts of the LLP.[9] It must be registered at Companies House and file annual reports and accounts. It is much closer to a company than to a partnership except in two aspects. First, the members in an LLP are taxed as if they were partners; secondly, there is no division between members and directors inside an LLP and its members have the same freedom as in an ordinary partnership to decide on their internal decision-making structures.

Companies are governed by the Companies Act 2006 (CA 2006). A company can be limited or unlimited, limited by shares or by guarantee.[10] The most common type of registered company is the company limited by shares where the company's capital is divided into shares and the members' liability is limited to the amount, if any, unpaid on the shares held by them (s 3(2)). In a company limited by guarantee,[11] the liability of its members is limited to such amount as the members undertake to contribute to the assets of the company in the event of its being wound up (s 3(3)). The guarantee companies are widely used by charitable and quasi-charitable organisations such as schools, colleges, museums and galleries. In an unlimited company there is no limit on the liability of its members provided by shares or guarantee (s 3(4)) and therefore it is not usually used for investment purposes.

On incorporation, following a prescribed registration process, a company becomes a separate legal entity, which is distinct and separate from its shareholders. This principle was established by the House of Lords in **Salomon v Salomon & Co Ltd** [1897] AC 22. Lord MacNaghten held that: 'The company is at law a different person altogether from the subscribers to the memorandum; ... the company is not in law the agent of the subscribers or trustee for them.'[12] The company conducts business in its own name, enters into contracts and incurs debts. The assets are in the name of the company, not in the name of its majority shareholder: **Macaura v Northern Assurance Co** [1925] AC 619. The company can sue and be sued: **Williams v Natural Life Health Foods** [1998] 1 BCLC 689. It can employ people including its majority shareholders: **Lee v Lee's Air Farming Ltd** [1961] AC 12. The company has the feature of perpetual succession in the sense that the existence of the company remains even if original members sell their shares. The corporate form may also facilitate borrowing as the lender can obtain an effective security of a floating charge on all the undertaking and assets of the company both present and future or together with a fixed charge on its land. As the use of such form of security is restricted to bodies corporate in practice, a business may be converted to a company solely to raise further capital by borrowing.

[10]This shows that you are aware of the different types of registered company.

[11]This type of company is not as common as companies limited by shares. Some students may fail to include it in their answers.

[12]This is the key case law authority on the principle of separate legal personality. The name of the leading judge and the important judgment are worth learning by heart because they show your specific knowledge of this case.

[13]This is another main advantage of incorporation in addition to the separate legal personality of a company. Clearly outlining this shows your sound knowledge.

[14]A discussion of the problems presents an analytical approach and a balanced view of incorporation. It will help you gain more marks.

In a company limited by shares, the principle of limited liability protects shareholders from personal insolvency.[13] Liability of the members for the company's debts is limited to the amount of their respective shareholdings. This makes it easier for the company to raise capital, as individuals may feel more secure in investing in the company. Another advantage for incorporation is that the word 'Ltd' or 'plc' confers 'prestige, legitimacy and credibility' on the business (Freedman, 1994). The corporate form, however, has some problems associated with it.[14] As Freedman (1994) suggests, the corporate form and its regulatory requirements are burdensome and costly as professional advice is needed to deal with these requirements. The function of limited liability may also be negated by the banks' requiring shareholders to provide personal guarantees for bank loans. In this way shareholders' personal assets could be used to repay any debts owed to the banks or other creditors.

Companies have to be registered with Companies House and their accounts are available for public inspection. Compared with sole traders and partnerships, there is less flexibility, less privacy and more formality after incorporation. Various administrative costs such as filing fees may also be incurred. Despite all these disadvantages, companies have become very popular forms of business. The choice of running a business as a sole trader, partnership or company varies, nevertheless, depending on a number of factors such as the scale of the business, its need for capital, the liability of its members, the internal organisation, privacy and taxation.[15]

[15]This sentence concludes your answer by referring back to the essay question and summarising the issues that need to be considered in choosing a particular type of business organisation.

 Make your answer stand out

- Point out that LLPs are the preferred business formats for solicitors and accountants as they combine the features of corporate personality with partnership structures.
- Briefly discuss the exceptions to the separate legal personality, for example, where an agency relationship exists between a company and its shareholders (*Smith, Stone & Knight Ltd* v *Birmingham Corp* [1939] 4 All ER 116).
- Consider the lifting of the corporate veil where the corporate structure is a mere façade (*Woolfson* v *Strathclyde Regional Council* (1979) 38 P & CR 521).

? Question 2

John and Peter are in a partnership running a furniture removal business. They have heard of the advantages of forming a company limited by shares and decided to incorporate their business. Please advise them on the following matters.

1   The differences between a private company limited by shares and a public one.

2   The procedures for setting up a private company limited by shares.

3   The procedures required for a private company to become a public one.

4   The restrictions on choosing a name for their company.

Answer plan

→ Compare a private company limited by shares with a public one.

→ Discuss the procedures for incorporation.

→ Consider the requirements for altering the status of a private company.

→ Examine the rules on choosing a company name.

Diagram Plan

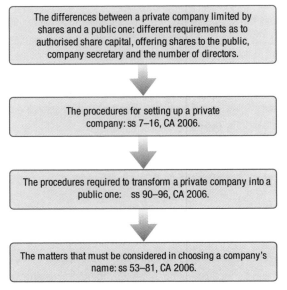

A printable version of this diagram plan is available from www.pearsoned.co.uk/lawexpressqa

Answer

[1]State the main legal issues that will be addressed in your answer.

This question requires a comparison of a private company limited by shares and a public one, a discussion of the legal requirements for setting up a private company, a consideration of the change of the status of a private company and the matters that need to be taken into account when choosing a company name.[1]

1. Private and public companies[2]

[2]Try to adopt a clear structure by using headings which correspond with the legal issues raised in the question.

[3]Explore the common features of both types of companies before discussing their differences. Some students may only focus on their differences. A consideration of their common features shows your sound understanding of the nature of these companies.

Private and public companies limited by shares are two main types of companies. The liabilities of shareholders in both types of companies are limited to the amount, if any, unpaid on the shares held by them: s 3(2) of the Companies Act 2006 (CA 2006).[3] The vast majority of companies are private companies limited by shares, which are defined in s 4(1) which simply states that they are not public companies. A private company can have just one member and there is no minimum capital requirement. It must have the word 'limited' or 'Ltd' at the end of its name (s 59) and cannot offer shares publicly (s 755) or float its shares on the stock market. There is no requirement for annual general meetings; written resolutions can be used in a private company (s 281).

As 'a company whose certificate of incorporation states that it is a public company and the requirements of the Act as to registration as a public company have been complied with'.[4] It is subject to more onerous regulations than a private company. There must be at least two directors (s 154) and a company secretary in a public company (s 271). It must have the words 'public limited company' or 'plc' at the end of its name (s 58). A public company must have at least £50,000 of authorised share capital (s 763) and it cannot start trading without a trading certificate[5] issued by the registrar of companies (s 761). A public company has an unrestricted right to offer shares to the public and these shares may be floated on the stock market. It must hold an annual general meeting (s 336); written resolutions cannot be used in a public company.

2. The procedures for setting up a private company

Section 7 of the CA 2006 states that one or more persons can incorporate, provided it is for a lawful purpose. The following documents must be sent to Companies House: a memorandum of association, the articles of association signed by the subscriber(s), a statement naming the company's first director and company secretary, and a formal declaration that the terms of the statute have been complied with.

A memorandum[6] is a short piece of document which simply records the identity of the original founders of the company and indicates how many shares they took on formation (s 8). The articles of association provide the rules for a company's internal management such as the appointment of directors, transfers of shares and voting rights. Every company must have a set of articles (s 18). The CA 2006 seeks to achieve greater flexibility by providing different forms of model articles so that the terms found within are more applicable to each type of company.[7] The model articles for private companies are very useful, particularly for small businesses who wish to incorporate quickly without going through the time and expense of drafting their own set of articles. John and Peter are therefore advised to adopt most or all of the model articles when drafting their own.[8]

[4]The statutory definition of a public company is an essential part of your answer because it is the basis of your discussion.

[5]Note that a trading certificate is required in addition to a certificate of incorporation. Some students may not notice this requirement.

[6]Although a company's memorandum is no longer part of its constitution, it is still required for the registration with Companies House.

[7]This sentence shows your good understanding of the model articles and the reasons for drafting them. The latter will gain you more marks.

[8]Tie your answer back to the problem question when possible.

9A sound knowledge of the
circumstances where the
registration will be refused
will add credit to your answer
because they go beyond a
description of the simple
procedure for registration.

The registrar at Companies House can refuse to register a company if the terms of the Act have not been met, or the company is being established for an illegal purpose, or when the objectives of a company are contrary to public policy.[9] Once all the required documents are submitted, together with the registration fee, a certificate of incorporation will be issued by the registrar, which is conclusive evidence that there has been compliance with the requirements of the CA 2006 in respect of registration (s 15).

3. From a private company to a public one

John and Peter are advised to initially form a private company limited by shares taking into account the scale of their business and the relatively less regulation compared to a public company. It can be changed into a public company if they need to raise further share capital by offering shares to the public or simply wish to secure a more prestigious status of being a public company.[10] In order to achieve the change of status, the company must be re-registered and a new certificate of registration must be issued which states whether the company is private or public. It must also meet the requirement for the minimum authorised share capital of £50,000. A special resolution is required for the change of the company's status and the registrar of companies must be notified (ss 90–96).

[10]This sentence explains the rationale for the conversion from a private company to a public one. It will gain you more marks than simply stating the procedure.

4. Choosing a company name

The key terms for naming a company are found within ss 53–81 of the CA 2006. A company may not use the name of another existing company (s 66), use offensive language (s 53) or give the impression that it is connected to the Government (s 54). Within 12 months of registration the Secretary of State can order a company to change its name if it is too similar to that of another company (ss 66–67). This time limit can be extended by the Secretary of State if the company name is misleading. In **Association of Certified Public Accountants of Britain v Secretary of State for Trade and Industry** [1997] 2 BCLC 307, Jacob J held that: '...what the court has to do is to decide on the evidence whether the name of the company gives so misleading an indication of the nature of its activities as to be likely to cause harm to the public. It is not sufficient to show that a name is misleading; a likelihood of harm must be shown too.'[11]

[11]The reference to case law makes your answer stand out from others which only state the statutory provisions.

A person may object to a registered name on the ground that it is the same as a name associated with the applicant in which he has goodwill or that it is sufficiently similar to such a name that its use in the United Kingdom would be likely to mislead by suggesting a connection between the company and the applicant (s 69). A company may change its name by a special resolution or by any other means provided by the company's articles (s 77); in any case, a notice must be given to the registrar (s 78). John and Peter would need to take into account the costs involved in relation to financial terms and the goodwill of customers if they decide to change their company's name.[12]

[12]This sentence shows the examiner that you are engaging with the question.

✓ Make your answer stand out

- Discuss the principles of separate legal personality and limited liability by reference to *Salomon* v *Salomon & Co Ltd* [1897] AC 22.
- In relation to company names, consider the ways of avoiding the use of an already existing name by checking the registrar's index of company names (ss 1099 and 1100, CA 2006) and the WebCHeck facility on the Companies House website.
- Outline that the application for registration must state the company's proposed name, its registered office, whether the liability of the members of the company is to be limited, and if so whether it is to be limited by shares or by guarantee, and whether the company is to be a private or a public company (s 9, CA 2006).

! Don't be tempted to...

- Discuss the choice of a company name without explaining certain names which cannot be used, such as the name of another existing company or a name containing offensive language: s 66, CA 2006.
- Include a detailed comparison between companies and partnerships. Although this is important in showing your good understanding of the nature of companies, it should not be discussed in detail here.
- Provide an answer without reference to the statutory provisions in the Companies Act 2006.
- Make generalised statements that may not affect the clients in particular. You should give specific advice which is tailored to the clients' needs.

❓ Question 3

Kate and Steve owned a local bakery and decided to incorporate their business as Organic Bakery Ltd. Steve purchased a warehouse next to the bakery store for £50,000 in May 2009. He then sold it to the company for £80,000 through an estate agent without disclosing his interest in the contract. Kate later discovered that Steve made a secret profit.

Kate and Steve ordered a high-technology oven from Professional Oven Ltd for £20,000. Upon the advice of their solicitors, they signed the agreement 'For and on behalf of Organic Bakery Ltd, as agents only, Kate and Steve'. Kate also signed a document which stated: 'It is hereby agreed that all expenses incurred by Kate in the formation of Organic Bakery Ltd shall be repaid from company funds within six months of the date of incorporation.'

Organic Bakery Ltd was incorporated in October 2009 but shortly went into insolvency. Kate incurred an expense of £10,000 in preparing the formation of the company. The oven was delivered and used but was not paid for.

Discuss:

1. Whether Steve should be held accountable to return the profit made from the sale of the warehouse.
2. Whether Kate should be reimbursed for the expense of £10,000 in the formation of the company.
3. Whether Kate and Steve will be held personally liable for the price of the oven.

Answer plan

→ Identify whether Kate and Steve are considered as promoters of the company.

→ Discuss the fiduciary duties of promoters.

→ Consider whether Steve should be held accountable to return the secret profit made from the sale of the warehouse.

→ Examine whether Kate can claim her expense back from the company.

→ Analyse whether Kate and Steve will be held personally liable for the pre-incorporation contract with regard to the oven purchase agreement.

Diagram plan

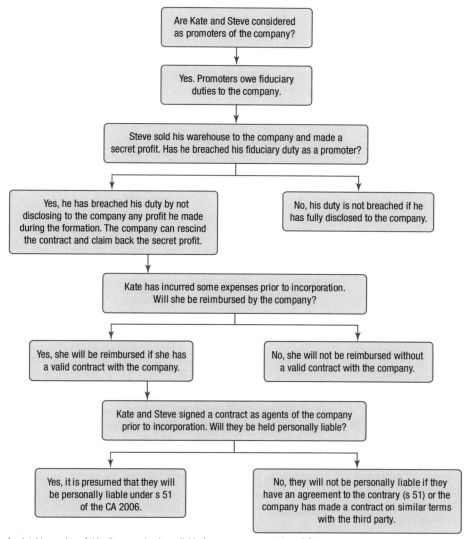

A printable version of this diagram plan is available from www.pearsoned.co.uk/lawexpressqa

Answer

This question raises the issues in relation to the duties of promoters and the legal implications of pre-incorporation contracts. As Kate and Steve have decided to promote a business project through the medium of a company, they are considered as promoters of Organic Bakery Ltd: **Emma Silver Mining Co v Lewis** (1879) LR 4 CPD 396.[1] The word 'promoter' is not defined judicially or in legislation; it is a question of fact as to who constitutes a promoter in a particular case. In **Twycross v Grant** (1877) 2 CPD 469 a promoter is defined as 'one who undertakes to form a company with reference to a given project and to set it going, and who takes the necessary steps to accomplish that purpose'.[2]

[1] Identify who are promoters at the beginning of your answer.

[2] This quotation shows your specific knowledge of the definition of a promoter.

1. Steve's secret profit

A promoter is in a fiduciary relationship with the company at common law. He must not make any secret profit out of the promotion without disclosing it to the company. Any profit which he makes on the promotion and fails to disclose must be returned to the company: **Gluckstein v Barnes** [1900] AC 240. The difficulty lies in deciding whether and how the duty of disclosure is satisfied.[3]

[3] This sentence demonstrates that you appreciate the difficulties in relation to the duties of promoters. It also leads to the discussion in the next two paragraphs.

In **Erlanger v New Sombrero Phosphate Co** (1878) 3 App Cas 1218, a syndicate purchased a mine for £55,000 and formed a company. The syndicate sold the mine to the company for £100,000 without disclosing their interest in the contract. The sale was successfully rescinded by the new board of directors of the company.[4] It was held that it was the promoter's duty to ensure that the company had an independent board of directors and to make full disclosure to it. Failure to disclose all material facts surrounding a contract to the independent board renders the contract voidable at the option of the company.

[4] You should be able to identify that the problem question is similar to the facts in *Erlanger*. The brief summary of the facts shows your good knowledge of this leading case and of its relevance to this question. The detailed facts of this case, however, are not necessary because they will add little to your answer. Many students spend too much time describing the facts of the case and not enough on the application of the relevant legal principles to the problem question.

This rule was considered too strict because an entirely independent board would be impossible in most private companies. In **Salomon v Salomon & Co Ltd** [1897] AC 22 it was accepted that, in the absence of an independent board of directors, a full disclosure to the original shareholders would be equally effective. The House of Lords in **Gluckstein v Barnes** (above), however, held that such disclosure

5This paragraph
demonstrates how the rule of
disclosure was developed at
common law since *Erlanger.*
The discussion of case law is
essential for a sound answer.

6After analysing the relevant
law, you should apply it to
the problem question. The
last sentence gives advice
on the remedies available to
the company. It goes beyond
the issue of Steve's breach
of duties.

7Use a sentence like this
to signpost your answer.
It makes it easier for the
examiners to follow.

would not be sufficient if the original shareholders were not truly independent and the scheme as a whole was designed to defraud the investing public.[5]

The current law appears to require that disclosure be made to an entirely independent board or to the existing and potential members as a whole. As Steve made a secret profit without disclosing to either an independent board or any existing member of the company, he has breached his fiduciary duty as a promoter. Organic Bakery Ltd can rescind the contract with Steve and recover the secret profit.[6]

2. The expense of £10,000 in promoting the company

The next issue concerns whether Kate can recover the expenses in promoting the company.[7] Kate, as a promoter, is not entitled to recover any remuneration from Organic Bakery Ltd for her services unless there is a valid contract in this matter between her and the company. Without such a contract she is not even entitled to recover preliminary expenses or the registration fees: **Re English and Colonial Produce Co** [1906] 2 Ch 435. Although the document signed by Kate purports to bind the company to reimburse her, it has been long established that a company cannot be bound by, or ratify, a contract entered into prior to its incorporation, as the company did not exist at the time of the contract: **Kelner v Baxter** (1866) LR 2 CP 174. Kate therefore cannot recover her expenses as no valid contract exists in this matter between her and the company; however, she could do so if the company, after incorporation, entered into a new contract with Kate on similar terms.

3. The price of the oven

Prior to incorporation, Kate and Steve signed an agreement for the purchase of an oven as 'For and on behalf of Organic Bakery Ltd, as agents only'. The company is now insolvent and unable to pay for the oven. The issue arises as to whether Kate and Steve are personally liable for the purchase price. At common law the legal position of the promoter and the other party seems to depend on the terminology used. If the contract was entered into by the promoter and signed 'for and on behalf of X Co Ltd' the promoter would be personally liable: **Kelner v Baxter** (above). If, however, the promoter signed

[8]Although the distinction is no longer significant in the light of the Companies Act 2006, a discussion of *Kelner* (1886) and *Newborne* (1954) is crucial in showing your sound understanding of the historical development of the promoter's personal liabilities in a pre-incorporation contract.

the proposed name of the company and added his own signature to authenticate it (eg., X Co Ltd, Y Director), there was no contract at all and the promoter would not be personally liable: **Newborne v Sensolid (GB) Ltd** [1954] 1 QB 45.[8] As they signed the contract 'as agents', Kate and Steve would be held personally liable at common law.

This narrow distinction was criticised in **Phonogram Ltd v Lane** [1982] QB 938 by Oliver LJ, who held that the whole of the contract should be looked at rather than just the formula used beneath the signature, in order to determine whether the contract purports to be one directly between the supposed principal and the other party or to be one between the agent himself and the other party. If it is the latter, the promoter would be personally liable at common law, no matter how he signed the document.

[9]This is a very important statutory provision that you should learn during your revision on the topics of promoters' duties and pre-incorporation contracts.

[10]This sentence examines the reasons for the introduction of s 51 in the Companies Act 2006. It will gain you more marks because it goes beyond a simple description of the statutory provision.

[11]This phrase shows that you fully understand s 51 and its legal implications. Although it is presumed under s 51 that promoters are personally liable, you should pay particular attention to 'any agreement to the contrary'.

Following the implementation of Art 7 of the First Company Law Directive by s 36(3) of the Companies Act 1985 and now in s 51 of the Companies Act 2006, the subtle distinction made by **Kelner** and **Newborne** appears to be removed. Section 51(1) of the CA 2006 states that: 'A contract that purports to be made by or on behalf of a company at a time when the company has not been formed has effect, subject to any agreement to the contrary, as one made with the person purporting to act for the company or as agent for it, and he is personally liable on the contract accordingly.'[9] This provision seeks to protect the third party by making promoters personally liable when the company, after incorporation, fails to enter into a new contract on similar terms.[10] Thus, if a person does not contract as an agent or assume personal liability but his signature is appended to that of the company's name to authenticate it as in **Newborne**, he will still be personally liable. In accordance with s 51, Kate and Steve are personally liable to pay for the oven unless there is any agreement to the contrary.[11]

✓ **Make your answer stand out**

■ Examine whether the solicitors are considered as promoters. If solicitors and accountants merely act in a professional capacity and undertake their normal professional duties, they are not considered as promoters: *Re Great Wheal Polgooth Co Ltd* (1883) 53 LJ Ch 42.

- Discuss the circumstances where Kate and Steve would not be personally liable for the purchase contract. In *Natal Land Co & Colonization Ltd* v *Pauline Colliery and Development Syndicate Ltd* [1904] AC 120, it was held that a promoter will avoid personal liability if the company, after incorporation, and the other party substitute the original pre-incorporation contract with a new contract on similar terms.
- Make reference to *Whaley Bridge Printing Co* v *Green* (1880) LR 5 QBD 109 in relation to the meaning of a promoter.

! Don't be tempted to...

- Focus only on s 51 of the Companies Act 2006. You should also discuss the relevant common law and show a good understanding of how the law has developed in relation to the personal liabilities of promoters under pre-incorporation contracts.
- Forget to discuss the company's remedies against a promoter's breach of fiduciary duties. They should be applied to the problem question with reference to case law such as *Erlanger* v *New Sombrero Phosphate Co* (1878) 3 App Cas 1218.

📖 Question 4

Discuss the duties of a promoter and the ways of avoiding his personal liabilities upon a pre-incorporation contract which he may enter into on behalf of the company.

Answer plan

➔ Discuss the meaning of a promoter of a company.

➔ Analyse the fiduciary duties of a promoter and the remedies for a breach of these duties.

➔ Examine the common law and the current legislation in relation to the personal liabilities of a promoter in a pre-incorporation contract.

Diagram plan

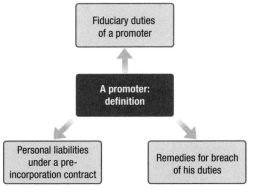

A printable version of this diagram plan is available from www.pearsoned.co.uk/lawexpressqa

Answer

[1]The legal issues are very clear in this essay question. You can go straight into discussing the meaning of a promoter without repeating the question.

A promoter is not defined judicially or in legislation; it is a question of fact as to who constitutes a promoter in a particular case. In **Twycross v Grant** (1877) 2 CPD 469 a promoter is defined as one who undertakes to form a company and set it going.[1] He is not the agent of the company because it has no legal existence before the incorporation: **Kelner v Baxter** (1866) LR 2 CP 174. A promoter is in a fiduciary relationship with the company; he must not make any profit out of the promotion without disclosing it to the company. Thus, there is no absolute prohibition on making a profit – it is the making of secret profit that is forbidden: **Omnium Electric v Baines** (1914) 1 Ch 332. Any profit which he makes on the promotion and fails to disclose must be returned to the company: **Gluckstein v Barnes** [1900] AC 240. The difficulty lies in deciding how this duty of disclosure can be satisfied.

[2]Pay attention to this phrase and the different requirements in the subsequent cases because they demonstrate how the duty of disclosure evolves at common law.

In **Erlanger v New Sombrero Phosphate Co** (1878) 3 App Cas 1218 it was held that a promoter must make full disclosure to an independent board of directors.[2] Failure to do so renders the contract voidable at the option of the company. This requirement was considered as being too strict and impractical because an entirely independent board would be impossible in most companies.[3]

[3]You can further discuss why the requirement of an independent board is impractical in most companies. It will add more credit to your answer.

Subsequently, in **Salomon v Salomon & Co Ltd** [1897] AC 22, it was accepted that in the absence of an independent board of directors a full disclosure to *the original shareholders* would be

[4]This is a House of Lords judgment on the promoter's duty of disclosure and therefore it should be included in your answer.

[5]Explain what a pre-incorporation contract is before exploring further issues. It shows your sound understanding of the basic concept.

[6]This sentence summarises the common law with regard to the liabilities of promoters in a pre-incorporation contract. It also shows where your answer is heading.

[7]You should demonstrate good understanding of both the facts and judgments in *Kelner* (1866) and *Newborne* (1954), which provide excellent illustrations of the common law.

[8]This case is important here because it adopts a different approach to the liabilities of a promoter.

[9]Students are often warned against including detailed case facts in exam answers. A brief account of the facts here shows your good understanding of this case.

equally effective. The House of Lords, however, in **Gluckstein v Barnes** (above) held that such disclosure would not be sufficient if the original shareholders were not truly independent and the scheme as a whole was designed to defraud the investing public.[4] It appears that the disclosure must be made to an entirely independent board or to the existing and potential members as a whole. The disclosure must also be explicit; a partial or incomplete disclosure is insufficient.

A pre-incorporation contract is one which a promoter enters into with a third party before the company is incorporated.[5] At common law, a company cannot be bound by a pre-incorporation contract, neither can it ratify the contract after incorporation. The legal position of the promoter depended on the terminology used.[6] If the contract was entered into by the promoter and signed for and on behalf of the company, the promoter would be personally liable. In **Kelner v Baxter** (above), Kelner sold wine to Baxter who was acting 'on behalf of the proposed company'. The wine was delivered and used but the company went into liquidation before payment. Kelner successfully sued Baxter for the payment. It was held that where a contract was signed by those acting 'as agents' but who had no principal existing at the time, the contract would not be binding and the agents would be held personally liable. If, however, the promoter signed the proposed name of the company and added his own to authenticate it, there was no contract at all. In **Newborne v Sensolid (GB) Ltd** [1954] 1 QB 45, the contract was signed in the name of the company 'Leopold Newborne (London) Ltd' and also signed by the promoter Mr Newborne. It was held that neither the unincorporated company nor Mr Newborne could sue or be sued on the contract which was a complete nullity.[7]

Such narrow distinction was criticised in **Phonogram Ltd v Lane** [1982] QB 938.[8] Mr Lane, the promoter of FM Ltd, accepted a cheque from Phonogram Ltd for £6,000 and signed his name 'for and on behalf of FM Ltd'. The money was to be used to finance the production of an LP; it was repayable if this was not achieved. When the LP was not produced, Phonogram Ltd sought to recover the money from Mr Lane on the ground that the company did not exist at the time of the contract.[9] Oliver LJ held that the whole contract should be looked at rather than just the formula used beneath the signature, in order to determine whether the contract purports to be one directly between the supposed principal and the other party or to be one between the agent himself and the other party. If it is the latter, the promoter would be personally liable at common law, no matter how he signed the document.

In order to address the confusing distinction at common law, the Jenkins Report (1962, para 44) recommended that the agent who acted for the unformed company should be personally liable on the contract.[10] Once incorporated, the company should be able to adopt the contract unilaterally. These proposals were not adopted in the following pieces of legislation and as a consequence a company is still unable to ratify or adopt the contract unilaterally.

[10]The reference to the Jenkins Report demonstrates your wider knowledge and will impress your examiners.

Following the implementation of Art 7 of the First Company Law Directive by s 36 of the Companies Act 1985, which is now in s 51 of the Companies Act 2006, the subtle distinction between **Kelner** and **Newborne** appears to be removed. Section 51(1) of the Companies Act 2006 provides that: 'A contract that purports to be made by or on behalf of a company at a time when the company has not been formed has effect, subject to any agreement to the contrary, as one made with the person purporting to act for the company or as agent for it, and he is personally liable on the contract accordingly.' This provision aims to provide third parties with more security of transactions through an enforceable contract against the promoters rather than the subsequently formed company.

[11]Lord Denning's interpretation of the phrase 'subject to any agreement to the contrary' is essential here because it is directly relevant to this essay question on how a promoter can avoid his personal liabilities.

[12]Some students may forget to discuss this circumstance where a promoter can avoid his personal liabilities under a pre-incorporation contract. The reference to case law strengthens your answer.

Lord Denning in **Phonogram Ltd v Lane** (above) interpreted the phrase 'subject to any agreement to the contrary' as that, in order for a promoter to avoid personal liability, the contract must expressly provide for the exclusion of his liabilities.[11] Thus, a promoter may avoid personal liabilities on a pre-incorporation contract if they are expressly excluded in the contract; or if the company, after incorporation, and the other party substitute the original pre-incorporation contract with a new one on similar terms: **Natal Land Co & Colonization Ltd v Pauline Colliery and Development Syndicate Ltd** [1904] AC 120.[12]

✓ Make your answer stand out

- Point out that the problems in relation to the pre-incorporation contracts are less acute in practice because the majority of companies are bought off the shelf from company incorporation agents.
- Discuss whether a person acting as an agent of an unformed company can enforce a pre-incorporation contract according to s 51 of the CA 2006 – in other words, whether a promoter can sue as well as being sued under a pre-incorporation contract: *Cotronic (UK) Ltd* v *Dezonie* [1991] BCLC 721; *Braymist Ltd* v *Wise Finance Co Ltd* [2002] 1 BCLC 415.
- Consider that a company can enter into a contract post-incorporation, also known as 'novation': *Howard* v *Patent Ivory Manufacturing Co* (1888) LR 38 Ch D 156.
- Refer to academic debates on the personal liabilities of a promoter, such as Griffiths, 'Agents without principals: pre-incorporation contracts and section 36C of the Companies Act 1985' [1993] LS 241; Gross, J. 'Pre-incorporation Contracts' [1971] LQR 367; and Savirimuthu, J. 'Pre-incorporation of contracts and the problem of corporate fundamentalism: are promoters proverbially profuse?' [2003] *Company Lawyer* 196.

! Don't be tempted to...

- Discuss the duties of a promoter without explaining what is meant by a promoter.
- Only focus on the common law. You should also discuss s 51 of the Companies Act 2006 with regard to a promoter's liabilities in a pre-incorporation contract.

The *Salomon* principles and the corporate veil

How this topic may come up in exams

The principles established in **Salomon v Salomon & Co Ltd** [1897] AC 22 are fundamental to English company law. A standard essay or problem question may expect you to comment on the advantages and limitations of these principles. The circumstances where the corporate veil is lifted are often examined in relation to fraud, sham and façade, agency, single economic unit as well as some statutory provisions. You need to appreciate the uncertainties of this area of law and consider proposals for future reforms. The criminal and tortious liabilities of a company may also be subject to examination.

■ Attack the question

📓 Question 1

Limited liability, allowing people to 'trade without committing their personal fortune to a venture, requires a fine legislative balance. The limited company is in danger of being too wide a protection for free enterprise, and of providing a veil for the unscrupulous'. (*The Times,* 'What a Way to Run the DTI', 1 November 1994)

Undertake a critical evaluation of the above statement.

Answer plan

→ Examine the case of *Salomon* v *Salomon & Co Ltd* [1897] AC 22.

→ Discuss the principles of separate legal personality and limited liability.

→ Evaluate how these principles have been upheld by the courts.

→ Consider the criticisms against these principles.

Diagram plan

A printable version of this diagram plan is available from www.pearsoned.co.uk/lawexpressqa

Answer

This question requires an analysis of the principle of separate legal personality of a company and the limited liability of its shareholders. It is commonly accepted that the limited liability is a very important invention in modern times as it allows people to 'trade without committing their personal fortune to a venture'.[1] It can be argued, however, that these principles have caused some problems and are in danger of exploitation.[2]

In **Salomon v Salomon & Co Ltd** [1897] AC 22 Salomon incorporated his business as a limited company with his wife and their five children under the Companies Act 1862. Salomon received fully paid-up shares and debentures of the value of £10,000 for the sale of his business and he subsequently assigned the debentures

[1]This shows that you are engaging with the question at the beginning of your answer.

[2]Clearly state your argument in the introduction so that the examiner knows where you are going with your answer.

[3] Some students may deliberately ignore this aspect of the case, mostly because of a lack of understanding of debentures. A debenture is a document which acknowledges a loan to a company and gives the lender security over the assets of the company. On insolvency the lender can take the assets and recover payment ahead of the unsecured creditors.

[4] It is important to set out the liquidator's allegations against Salomon because they show your detailed knowledge of this case.

[5] Many students go straight to the House of Lords' judgment. You should discuss the decisions of the court at first instance and the Court of Appeal although they were overruled by the House of Lords. They demonstrate that you fully understand the rationale of the House of Lords' judgment.

[6] Try to learn the name of the leading judge and to quote the key judgment. You can also paraphrase it by saying that the company is at law a different person from the subscribers.

to another party.[3] After a year the company became insolvent and was unable to meet the full claims of the unsecured creditors. These creditors argued that the company was merely an agent of Salomon. The liquidator attempted to hold Salomon liable for the debts of the company on the following grounds. First, the whole transaction was a fraud on the company's creditors and therefore Salomon should not be allowed to benefit. Secondly, the company was simply his agent and Salomon should reimburse the unsecured creditors with regard to the debts incurred by the company.[4]

The court at first instance held that the company was merely an agent of Salomon and therefore Salomon, as a principal, was liable for its debts. The Court of Appeal rejected Salomon's appeal and held that Salomon used the company as a device to carry on business in order to defraud creditors.[5] The House of Lords, however, reversed the decisions of the lower courts and held that the company had been fully formed and registered and was not the mere agent for Salomon. He was not liable to indemnify the company against the creditors' claims. It was held that a company is at law a distinct and separate person from the people who set it up. Any fully paid-up shareholder should not be required to pay anymore. Lord MacNaughten stated that: 'The company attains maturity on its birth … The company is at law a different person altogether from the subscribers to the memorandum … the company is not in law the agent of the subscribers or trustee for them. Nor are the subscribers as members liable, in any shape or form, except to the extent and in the manner provided by the Act.'[6] The House of Lords' decision affirms that a company is not the agent of its shareholders, even if it is a one-man company and the control is concentrated in only one shareholder.

The decision in **Salomon** is of vital importance as it encourages individuals to provide money for businesses without the threat of liability if the company becomes insolvent. The courts have confirmed that the company is a separate legal person in various different contexts. It is held, for instance, that property within a company belongs to the company in **Macaura v Northern Assurance** [1925] AC 619. Macaura incorporated a timber company and took out insurance on the timber in his own name instead of that of the company. After the timber was destroyed by fire he tried to rely on his insurance policy. The court held that the only person with an insurable interest in the timber was the company, which was a separate legal entity. The insurance company successfully resisted his claim on the policy. A company can also sue for defamation: **South Hetton Coal Co Ltd _v_ North-Eastern News Association Ltd** [1894] 1 QB 133, employ members and outside individuals: **Lee _v_ Lee's Air Farming** [1961] AC 12; sue directors who steal from them: **A-G's Reference (No. 2 of 1982)** [1984] 2 All ER 216; and continue without its original shareholders or directors: **Re Noel Tedman Holdings Pty Ltd** [1967] Qd R 561.[7]

[7]The reference to the case law authorities is essential to illustrate the courts' support of the _Salomon_ principles.

The original purpose behind the ruling of **Salomon** was to encourage investors to provide money to a business without attracting further risk; however, the **Salomon** principles have been subject to criticisms mainly because they do not provide sufficient protection to creditors. Kahn-Freund (1944)[8] criticises that the **Salomon** decision is calamitous as the courts have rigidly applied the concept of separate corporate entity and it has become very easy to form a company. He incisively argues that the company has often been a means of evading liabilities and of concealing the real interests behind the business.

[8]You should include academic opinions in your answer to show your wider understanding. Kahn-Freund's criticisms are useful to demonstrate the problems caused by the _Salomon_ principles.

Moreover, it can be argued that the principle of limited liability does not play a significant role in under-capitalised small private companies. The protection of limited liability is lost when the company wishes to borrow beyond its capacity. Banks and other creditors generally require that directors or shareholders provide a personal guarantee[9] so that they will be personally liable for the company's debts if it becomes insolvent. In this sense, the advantages of limited liability are restricted.

[9]The requirement of a personal guarantee may defeat the purpose of limited liability. This is a main restriction on the role of the principle of limited liability and therefore it should be discussed in your answer.

Problems also arise when people forming the companies are trying to abuse the principle of limited liability.[10] The **Salomon** decision creates a veil in front of the shareholders, which is a metaphor used to describe the effect of the legal principles of separate legal personality and limited liability. The veil may be lifted by the courts at common law or by statute in some circumstances. For instance, an individual shareholder or a director will be held liable for the company's debts when the corporate structure is a mere sham or façade concealing the true facts.[11] In **Gilford Motor Co _v_ Horne** [1933] Ch 935, the veil was lifted because the company was formed by the defendant as a device to avoid liabilities in breach of

[10]This sentence suggests that this paragraph addresses the issues in relation to 'too wide a protection for free enterprise' and 'a veil for the unscrupulous'.

[11]This sentence shows your understanding of the circumstances when the courts would lift the corporate veil. The discussion here focuses on the most common example of 'fraud, sham or façade' because of time constraint in an exam.

[12]This sentence lists a few examples of statutory provisions whereby the corporate veil will be lifted.

his pre-existing legal duty. The statutory provisions, such as s 213 and s 214 of the Insolvency Act 1986 with regard to the fraudulent and wrongful trading,[12] can deter dishonest or incompetent directors from abusing the **Salomon** principles. Despite the occasions where the veil has been lifted, the courts have gone to great lengths to protect the **Salomon** principles.

[13]The conclusion shows your analytical skills by expressing your views on the issues raised in the question.

In conclusion, the principles of separate legal personality and limited liability play significant roles in promoting company prosperity and economic growth. A fine legislative balance, nevertheless, is required so that they are not abused by the unscrupulous.[13]

✓ Make your answer stand out

- Include more academic opinions in your answer in relation to the criticisms of the *Salomon* principle, such as: Scanlan, G. 'The Salomon principle' (2004) 25 *Company Lawyer* 196; Ottolenghi, 'From peeping behind the corporate veil to ignoring it completely' (1990) 53 *Modern Law Review* 338; Hicks, A. 'Corporate form: questioning the unsung hero' [1997] JBL 306 (on whether it was appropriate that incorporation with limited liability should have become so freely available to small businesses following the *Salomon* decision).

! Don't be tempted to...

- Spell *Salomon* v *Salomon & Co Ltd* incorrectly. Some students write '*Salmon* v *Salmon*'. Make sure you get the name of the leading case right.
- Only address part of the question. Students are generally more familiar with the importance of the *Salomon* principles and the cases which support them. In answering this question, you should pay special attention to the problems that the *Salomon* principles have caused and the criticisms against them.

Question 2

'The general reasoning of the courts in this area [lifting the corporate veil] has been confusing and, at times, contradictory ... It is difficult to start to rationalise the cases except under the broad, rather question-begging heading of policy.' (Marc Moore, 'A temple built on faulty foundations: piercing the corporate veil and the legacy of *Salomon* v *Salomon*' [2006] JBL 180 at 183)

Assess the above statement.

Answer plan

➜ Consider the principles established in *Salomon* v *Salomon & Co Ltd* [1897] AC 22.

➜ Examine the circumstances at common law where the courts lift the corporate veil.

➜ Discuss the statutory provisions according to which the corporate veil will be lifted.

Diagram plan

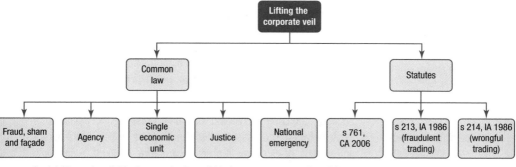

A printable version of this diagram plan is available from www.pearsoned.co.uk/lawexpressqa

Answer

[1]Explain the meaning of the corporate veil at the beginning of your answer. It shows the examiner that you have identified the topic area of this question.

[2]These sentences directly address the question. The phrase 'correctly argued' shows that you are critically analysing the statement in the question rather than providing a narrative account.

[3]This is the key authority on the lifting of corporate veil. You should be familiar with the facts and judgment of this case.

[4]You can structure your answer according to the judgment of this case.

The veil of incorporation is created by the principle of separate legal personality and that of limited liability which are established in **Salomon v Salomon & Co Ltd** [1897] AC 22.[1] A company, once incorporated, is a separate and distinct legal entity from the people who set it up. In a company limited by shares, a member's liabilities for the company's debts are limited to his subscribed shares. The courts are very protective of the **Salomon** principles and only lift the veil in a small number of exceptional cases at common law and by statute. As there are no clear rules or guidelines for lifting the corporate veil, it is correctly argued that this area of law is 'confusing, contradictory and difficult to rationalise'.[2]

The judgment in **Adams v Cape Industries plc** [1990] BCLC 479 has significantly narrowed the ability of the courts to lift the veil.[3] In this case, subsidiary companies were incorporated in the United States so that the parent company in the United Kingdom could avoid future asbestosis claims in the United States. The Court of Appeal reviewed this complex area of law and concluded that the veil could only be lifted in three circumstances.[4]

First, the veil may be lifted when the corporate structure is a mere sham or façade concealing the true facts. It is difficult to clearly define mere façade or decide whether the arrangements of a corporate group involve a façade. In **Adams v Cape**, the Court of Appeal held that the company structure was a façade when it had been used by a defendant to evade limitations imposed on his conduct by law or when it had been used to evade rights which third parties already possessed against him. In **Gilford Motor Co v Horne** [1933] Ch 935, the defendant formed the company as a device to avoid liabilities in breach of his pre-existing legal duty and the veil was lifted. In **Jones v Lipman** [1962] 1 WLR 832 the veil was lifted when the company was set up by the defendant to avoid specific performance in relation to a transfer of land. The court described the company as 'a device, a sham, a mask which he holds before his face in an attempt to avoid recognition by the eye of equity'.[5]

[5]The short quotation of judgment shows your precise knowledge of this case.

Secondly, the court may lift the veil if an express[6] agency relationship exists between a company and its shareholders, or between a parent and subsidiary company in a group structure. Although a company is a separate legal entity instead of an agent of its shareholders, it is possible that there is evidence of day-to-day control and that an agency relationship can be established on particular facts. It is, however, difficult to prove an agency relationship without an express agreement. Some guidance is provided in **Smith, Stone & Knight Ltd v Birmingham Corp** [1939] 4 All ER 116. In order to maximise the amount of compensation, the parent company argued that the subsidiary carried on the business as its agent. It was held that whether there was an agency relationship was a question of fact in each case, such as who was really carrying on the business, who received the profits, who was actually conducting the business, and who was in effective and constant control of the business. As the subsidiary was operating on behalf of the parent company, the court lifted the veil on the basis of the existence of an agency relationship. It can be argued that this is not a true exception to the **Salomon** principles; it is merely an instance where the normal agency principle applies.[7]

[6]Pay particular attention to the requirement of an 'express' agency relationship as opposed to an 'implied' one. Some students may not appreciate the differences between these two.

[7]This comment shows that your answer has adopted an analytical approach.

Thirdly, in relation to the debate on single economic unit, Lord Denning in **DHN Food Distributors Ltd v Tower Hamlets LBC** [1976] 3 All ER 462 argued that a group of companies was in reality a single economic entity and should be treated as one. This view

[8]This is an important House of Lords case in relation to the single economic unit argument. It should be included in a sound answer.

was disapproved by the House of Lords in **Woolfson v Strathclyde Regional Council** (1979) 38 P & CR 521 which held that the veil would be upheld unless it was a façade.[8] Slade J in **Adams v Cape** held that: 'whether or not this is desirable, the right to use a corporate structure in this manner is inherent in our corporate law … The fundamental principle is that each company in a group of companies is a separate legal entity possessed of separate legal rights and liabilities.' The court, however, will ignore the distinction between them and treat them as one on the interpretation of particular statutory or contractual provisions, the meaning of which is disappointingly unclear.[9]

[9]This sentence focuses on the difficulties in applying the judgment in *Adams* v *Cape*; for instance, the meaning of the interpretation of a statute or document is vague and not defined in this case.

There is controversy as to whether the veil can be lifted in the interests of justice. This idea of lifting the corporate veil in pursuit of justice was championed by Lord Denning in **Wallesteiner v Moir** [1974] 3 All ER 217. It is held in **Adams v Cape** that the veil cannot be lifted *merely* in pursuit of justice.[10] Another ground for lifting the veil is where the country is at war and it is in the country's interests to do so: **Daimler v CTR** [1916] 2 AC 307. The application of this category is limited and it is more about politics than law.

[10]Some students are aware of the argument that the veil could be lifted in the interest of justice but fail to appreciate that it has been rejected in *Adams* v *Cape*.

[11]This sentence demonstrates that your discussion has progressed from common law to the statutory provisions.

In addition to the examples at common law, the courts may lift the veil and hold individual shareholders or directors liable for the company's liabilities according to statutory provisions.[11] Section 761 of the Companies Act 2006, for example, requires that the directors of a public limited company be jointly and severally liable to indemnify the other party in respect of any loss or damage suffered by reason of the company's failure to comply with the provision that company should not trade before its registration. According to s 213 of the Insolvency Act 1986 on fraudulent trading, the court may declare that any person, who carries on the business with the intent to defraud the company's creditors, is liable to make such contributions to the company's assets. Lord Diplock in **Dimbleby v National Union of Journalists** [1984] 1 WLR 427 states that the statutory provisions must be in 'clear and unequivocal language'.

The judicial approach towards lifting the corporate veil is still unclear and lacks precise guidance despite the judgments in **Adams v Cape**. The courts appear to proceed on a case-by-case basis in

[12]This paragraph summarises your main arguments and ties your discussion back to the statement in the essay question. The last sentence explores the rationale behind the judicial attitude and will gain you more marks.

deciding whether to lift the corporate veil. The very few number of examples at common law and in statutes reflects the courts' reluctance to ignore the **Salomon** principles, which are the foundations of company law and have promoted the economic growth.[12]

 Make your answer stand out

- Discuss the provisions with regard to the wrongful trading under s 214 of the Insolvency Act 1986. If a director knew, or ought to have concluded, at that time that there was no reasonable prospect that the company would avoid going into insolvent liquidation, he would be liable to make such contribution to the company's assets as the court thinks proper.

- Consider future reforms to clarify this area of law, for instance, evaluate the advantages and disadvantages of having a statutory list of the circumstances for lifting the corporate veil.

- Refer to academic opinions on lifting the corporate veil, such as Linklater, L. 'Piercing the Corporate Veil – the never ending story?' [2006] 27 *Company Lawyer* 65.

! **Don't be tempted to...**

- Forget to discuss *Adams* v *Cape Industries* (1990). This is a very important case in relation to the grounds upon which the veil can be lifted and therefore a detailed discussion of this case must be included in your answer.

- Fail to understand that the single economic unit argument is no longer valid after *Adams* v *Cape Industries*.

- Provide a purely descriptive account of the law on lifting the corporate veil by giving examples under different headings or categories. You should undertake a critical approach towards the uncertainties of this area of law.

❓ Question 3

Adrian was a director of Easyclean Ltd. He diverted the company's business opportunities to Pureclean Ltd, which is wholly owned and controlled by him. All the profits made were paid directly to Pureclean Ltd.

Adrian had an agreement with Easyclean Ltd that he would not compete against it within ten miles of the store premises. One week after his service contract ended, Adrian relocated Pureclean Ltd just one mile away from Easyclean Ltd. When challenged by the board of Easyclean Ltd, Adrian argued that he personally did not receive any profits or compete against the company.

Advise the board of Easyclean Ltd:

1. Whether Adrian will be personally liable for the return of the secret profits which he made while serving as a director; and

2. Whether Adrian will be held liable for the breach of his agreement with Easyclean Ltd.

Answer plan

→ Identify the legal issues in this question: whether the corporate veil in Pureclean Ltd should be lifted.

→ Examine whether and on what grounds Adrian will be personally liable for the return of the secret profits.

→ Discuss whether and on what grounds Adrian will be personally liable for breach of the agreement with Easyclean Ltd.

Diagram plan

The principle of separate legal personality and that of limited liability (the *Salomon* principles)

Lifting the corporate veil:
Adams v *Cape Industries plc* [1990] BCLC 479

Is the incorporation of Pureclean Ltd a fraud, sham or façade?

Is there an agency relationship between Adrian and Pureclean Ltd?

A printable version of this diagram plan is available from www.pearsoned.co.uk/lawexpressqa

Answer

¹Clearly state the key legal issues that you are going to address in your answer.

In order to advise the board of directors in Easyclean Ltd as to whether Adrian will be held personally liable for the return of profits and for the breach of the agreement with the company, it is necessary to examine whether and on what basis the corporate veil can be lifted in relation to Pureclean Ltd.¹

²Some students go straight into examining the law on lifting the corporate veil without explaining the *Salomon* principles. You will lose some marks if the case of *Salomon* is not discussed.

The corporate veil is a metaphor to describe the principle of separate legal personality, as established in **Salomon v Salomon & Co Ltd** [1897] AC 22.² A company, once incorporated, is an independent legal entity separate from those who set it up. It can own property (**Macaura v Northern Assurance Co** [1925] AC 619), sue for defamation (**South Hetton Coal Co Ltd v North-Eastern News Association Ltd** [1894] 1QB 133), employ members and outside individuals (**Lee v Lee's Air Farming** [1961] AC 12) and sue directors who steal from them (**A-G's Reference (No. 2 of 1982)** [1984] 2 All ER 216). Shareholders are protected by the principle of limited liability and are not personally liable for the company's actions or liabilities. The courts are very protective of the **Salomon** principles and only lift the corporate veil in exceptional circumstances.³

³This sentence shows that you are aware of the overall judicial attitude towards lifting the corporate veil.

⁴This is the key authority on lifting the corporate veil and therefore it should be included in your answer.

At common law, the veil may be lifted when the corporate structure is a mere sham or façade concealing the true facts. In **Adams v Cape Industries plc** [1990] BCLC 479, the Court of Appeal held that the company was a façade where it has been used by a defendant to evade limitations imposed on his conduct by law or when the company structure was used to evade rights which third parties already possessed against him.⁴ As a director of Easyclean Ltd, Adrian secretly set up Pureclean Ltd and used it to steal the former's business opportunities. Although Adrian argues that Pureclean Ltd, instead of himself, should be liable to return the profits, it is very likely that the court will hold both Adrian and Pureclean Ltd liable because the corporate structure is used as a sham or façade.⁵ In **Jones v Lipman** [1962] 1 WLR 832, a vendor had agreed to sell a piece of land but subsequently changed his mind. He transferred the land to a company which he controlled. It was held that the company was set up by the defendant to avoid specific performance in relation to the transfer of land. Russell J held that the company was 'a device, a

⁵Remember to apply case law to the problem scenario instead of providing a descriptive account of the circumstances where the veil may be lifted.

[6]The facts of this case are similar to the problem question. The discussion of both the brief facts and judgment can further enhance your argument.

sham, a mask which he holds before his face in an attempt to avoid recognition by the eye of equity'. The veil was lifted and specific performance was ordered against both the vendor and the company.

Similarly, in **Gencor ACP Ltd v Dalby** [2000] 2 BCLC 734,[6] a director diverted to himself business opportunities which belonged to the company. The proceeds were paid directly to an offshore company which was wholly owned by him. The company had no staff or business and its only function was to receive profits. It was held that the company was no more than the director's offshore bank account; both the company and the director were held accountable for the profits. In **Trustor AB v Smallbone** [2001] 2 BCLC 436 the defendant was the former managing director of Trustor AB, where a large amount of money was missing. Some of it ended up in another company which was effectively controlled by the defendant. It was held that the defendant used the other company as a device or façade for the receipt of the money and therefore the corporate veil was lifted. Applying the above case law, it is highly likely[7] that the court will lift the corporate veil on the basis of fraud, sham or façade, so that both Adrian and Pureclean Ltd should be liable to return the secret profits.

[7]The phrase 'highly likely' shows that you appreciate the uncertainties of this area of law. It demonstrates better analytical skills than simply concluding that the court will definitely lift the corporate veil.

In relation to Adrian's agreement with the company, it can be argued that Adrian used the corporate form to avoid his contractual liabilities and therefore the veil should be lifted.[8] In **Gilford Motor Co v Horne** [1933] Ch 935, an employee entered into an agreement not to compete with his former employer after ceasing employment. In order to avoid this restriction he set up a company and acted through it. It was held that the company was formed as a device to mask the carrying on of business by the defendant in breach of his pre-existing legal duty. The corporate veil was therefore lifted and an injunction was issued against the company and the defendant.

[8]You should adopt a clear structure. This sentence demonstrates that your discussion has moved on to the second legal issues in relation to Adrian's agreement with the company.

[9]An agency relationship may be another valid ground for lifting the corporate veil. A consideration of whether an agency relationship exists between Adrian and Pureclean Ltd shows your sound understanding of this area of law.

In addition to the façade argument, it can also be argued that there is an agency relationship between Adrian and Pureclean Ltd.[9] If it can be proved that Adrian used Pureclean Ltd as his agent, Adrian as the principal should be liable for the company's debts according to the law of agency. There is no presumption of such an agency relationship between a company and its shareholders. In the absence of an express agency agreement it is very difficult to establish one. In **Smith, Stone & Knight Ltd v Birmingham Corp**

[10]This case provides some guidance on how an agency relationship can be established. It is also one of the very few cases where the veil was successfully lifted on the basis of an agency relationship. A clear discussion of this case makes your answer stand out.

[11]The judgments in *Salomon* v *Salomon* are very persuasive arguments against lifting the veil on the basis of an agency relationship. They are used here to illustrate the difficulties in establishing an agency relationship between a company and its shareholders.

[12]This phrase shows that you understand that this area of law is uncertain and lacks clear guidance.

[13]Your conclusion should directly refer back to the issues raised in the question and provide specific advice to the board of directors in Easyclean Ltd.

[1939] 4 All ER 116,[10] the parent company held almost all of the shares in the subsidiary and the profits of the subsidiary were treated as the profits of the parent company. The parent company was in effective control of the business and appointed the personnel who conducted the business. The veil was lifted on the ground of agency and it was held that whether there was an agency relationship was a question of fact in each case, such as who was really carrying on the business, who received the profits and who was in effective and constant control of the business. Following the above guidance, it appears that Adrian used Pureclean Ltd as his agent to receive the secret profits and to compete with Easyclean Ltd because he held all the shares in the company and was in effective control of the business. On the other hand, the court may be reluctant to lift the veil on this ground. In **Salomon *v* Salomon & Co Ltd**, both the court at first instance and the Court of Appeal held that Salomon used the company as his agent and therefore he should be liable for the company's debts. This argument, however, was rejected by the House of Lords.[11] An express agency relationship, such as a written agreement, is required for lifting the corporate veil on this ground.

It is concluded that the court is most likely[12] to lift the corporate veil on the basis of fraud, sham or façade. Adrian will most probably be liable for the return of profits to Easyclean Ltd and be liable for damages for breach of his agreement with the company.[13]

 Make your answer stand out

- Discuss whether Adrian has breached his fiduciary duties as a director of Easyclean Ltd, such as the duty to exercise his power for proper purposes (s 171), to act *bona fide* for the benefits of the company (s 172) and to avoid conflicts of interests (s 175).
- Consider whether the corporate veil could be lifted in the interest of justice by reference to *Wallesteiner* v *Moir* [1974] 3 All ER 217 and *Adams* v *Cape Industries plc* [1990] BCLC 479.

! Don't be tempted to...

■ Focus your answer solely on directors' duties. Although Adrian's breach of directors' duties is a relevant issue, your answer should focus on the law in relation to the lifting of corporate veil, which is the main issue in this question.

■ Ignore the agency argument. Some students do not apply the agency argument to the question or do not have a good understanding of the requirement of an *express* agency relationship.

? Question 4

Babycare Ltd is registered in England and has three wholly owned subsidiary companies in India, A Ltd, B Ltd and C Ltd. A Ltd purchases cotton from local stores, B Ltd manufactures baby clothes and C Ltd markets and sells them. All the profits flow back to Babycare Ltd.

A large number of babies in India recently suffered from severe skin infections because of the poor quality of the dyeing product which is used in the manufacturing process in B Ltd. The estimated amount of compensation is £20 million. B Ltd has a liability insurance cover of up to £5 million but has no other assets apart from its factories.

Discuss whether Babycare Ltd will be held liable for the claims against B Ltd.

Answer plan

→ Identify the key legal issues: lifting the corporate veil in a group structure.

→ Discuss whether the corporate veil can be lifted on the ground of mere façade so that the parent company Babycare Ltd will be held liable for the actions of its subsidiary B Ltd.

→ Examine whether the corporate veil can be lifted on the ground of an agency relationship between Babycare Ltd and B Ltd.

→ Evaluate whether the corporate veil can be lifted based on the single economic unit argument.

Diagram plan

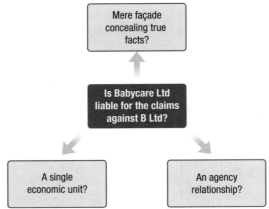

A printable version of this diagram plan is available from www.pearsoned.co.uk/lawexpressqa

Answer

[1]Rephrasing the question in your own words shows that you have understood the key legal issues raised.

This question requires an analysis of whether the parent company Babycare Ltd will be held liable for the claims against its subsidiary B Ltd; in other words, whether the corporate veil can be lifted in this group structure.[1] Both the parent company and its subsidiaries are incorporations which have been legally formed. A company, once incorporated, is a separate and distinct legal entity from the people who set it up: **Salomon *v* Salomon & Co Ltd** [1897] AC 22. In a company limited by shares, a shareholder is not liable for the company's debts. As Babycare Ltd holds shares in B Ltd, it enjoys the protection of limited liability in respect of debts of B Ltd. If the corporate veil could be lifted and the separate legal personality of B Ltd be ignored, Babycare Ltd would be liable for the claims against B Ltd.

[2]This is the leading case on lifting the corporate veil. You should show a good understanding of the judgments and summarise the facts of this case.

The court may lift the corporate veil if the corporate group structure is used as a mere façade concealing the true facts. In **Adams *v* Cape Industries plc** [1990] Ch 433[2] Cape Industries plc ('Cape') was an English mining company and its products were marketed through its subsidiary companies in the United States. A large number of factory workers who had suffered from inhaling asbestos dust obtained judgment in a Texas court against Cape. They argued unsuccessfully that Cape had been present in the United States and should be liable for the obligations of the subsidiary towards the tort victims. In particular, they contended that the use of the subsidiaries was a device or sham or cloak for grave impropriety on the part of the parent company, by removing their assets from the United States to avoid liability for asbestos claims.

The court considered whether the arrangements regarding the subsidiaries by the parent company constituted a façade so that the lifting of the corporate veil could be justified. It was held that: 'Whether or not this is desirable, the right to use a corporate structure in this manner is inherent in our corporate law ... Cape was in law entitled to organise the group's affairs in that manner and to expect that the court would apply the principle of **Salomon v Salomon & Co Ltd** [1897] AC 22 in the ordinary way.'[3] The company structure is a façade only when it has been used by a defendant to evade limitations imposed on his conduct by law (**Jones v Lipman** [1962] 1 WLR 832; **Gilford Motor Co Ltd v Horne** [1933] Ch 935) or when it is used to evade rights which third parties already possess against him (**Trustor AB v Smallbone** [2001] 2 BCLC 436). The Court of Appeal in **Adams** (above) held that each company was a separate legal entity from its shareholders and the presence of the US subsidiaries did not automatically amount to the presence of the English parent company. It can be argued, therefore, that the group structure of Babycare Ltd and its subsidiaries is legitimate and it is very unlikely that the court will hold the parent liable on the ground of fraud, sham or mere façade.[4]

The court may also consider whether there is an express agency relationship between Babycare Ltd and B Ltd.[5] If Babycare uses B Ltd as its agent, then Babycare as the principal should be liable for the claims against B Ltd. It was held in **Adams** (above) that there was no presumption that the subsidiary was acting as the agent of the parent company and the court refused to infer that there existed an agency agreement between them. A company was entitled to arrange the affairs of its group in such a way that the business carried on in a particular foreign country was the business of its subsidiary and not its own.

In the absence of an express agency agreement or the evidence of day-to-day control, it is very difficult to establish an agency relationship.[6] In **Smith, Stone & Knight Ltd v Birmingham Corp** [1939] 4 All ER 116 the parent company held almost all of the shares in the subsidiary and the profits of the subsidiary were treated

[3] A quotation of the important judgment demonstrates your detailed knowledge of this case and will add more credit to your answer.

[4] Apply the relevant law to the problem question whenever you can. It shows that you engage with the question throughout the answer.

[5] This sentence indicates that your discussion has progressed to the agency argument which may be another valid ground for lifting the veil.

[6] This sentence demonstrates that you understand the difficulties in proving an agency relationship. It will add credit to your answer by going beyond a simple narrative account of the agency theory.

[7]These sentences show your ability to analyse the problem scenario and apply the relevant law.

[8]The single economic unit argument should be discussed despite it has been rejected in later cases such as *Adams* v *Cape Industries* (1990). It demonstrates your sound knowledge of its background and the development at common law.

[9]This case and the name of the leading judge are worth learning.

[10]If you fail to show an accurate knowledge in relation to the single economic unit, your mark will be adversely affected.

[11]The examiners may be impressed by your discussion of a fairly recent case which shows your up-to-date knowledge.

[12]A concise conclusion directly addresses the question. It also enhances your arguments by summarising the courts' general approach towards lifting the corporate veil.

as the profits of the parent. The parent was in effective control of the business and also appointed the personnel who conducted the business. It was held that whether there was an agency relationship was a question of fact in each case, such as who was really carrying on the business, who received the profits and who was in effective and constant control of the business. The veil was lifted in this case on the ground of an agency relationship. Although Babycare Ltd holds all the shares in its subsidiaries and all the profits flow back to it, there is no evidence of the day-to-day control or an express agency agreement. It is therefore unlikely that the court would consider B Ltd as the agent of Babycare Ltd.[7]

It can also be argued that Babycare Ltd and its subsidiaries may be treated as one economic unit.[8] This theory was first put forward by Lord Denning[9] in **DHN Food Distributors Ltd *v* Tower Hamlets** [1976] 3 All ER 462, who argued that a group of companies was in reality a single economic entity and should be treated as one; the court was entitled to look at the realities of the situation to pierce the corporate veil. Slade J in **Adams** (above) rejected this argument by stating that there was no general principle that all companies in a group of companies were to be regarded as one.[10] The fundamental principle is that each company in a group of companies is a separate legal entity with separate legal rights and liabilities. The disapproval of the single economic unit theory was confirmed in **Ord *v* Belhaven Pubs Ltd** [1998] BCC 607,[11] where the court did not allow a plaintiff with a claim against one subsidiary company to substitute the parent company as defendant merely because the group might be a single economic unit. Given the judicial reluctance to ignore the **Salomon** principles, it is highly unlikely that the court will hold Babycare Ltd liable for the claims against B Ltd on the basis that the group structure is a mere façade, or there is an express agency relationship between them or that they should be treated as one economic unit.[12]

 Make your answer stand out

- Examine whether the court should lift the corporate veil in the interest of justice.
- Refer to academic debates on lifting the corporate veil in a group of companies, for instance Griffin, S., 'Holding companies and subsidiaries – the corporate veil' [1991] 12 *Company Lawyer* 16 and Rixon, F.G., 'Lifting the veil between holding and subsidiary companies' (1986) 102 LQR 415.

! **Don't be tempted to...**

- Have a vague understanding of the judgments in *Adams* v *Cape Industries plc* (1990). You must show a clear and detailed knowledge of this case in relation to the judgments on the lifting of the corporate veil.

- Treat it as an essay question on lifting the corporate veil. You should analyse the scenario of a group structure and focus on the issues with regard to façade, the agency relationship and the single economic unit argument.

Company constitution

3

How this topic may come up in exams

A company's constitution creates a statutory contract which binds the company and its members as well as its members *inter se* (s 33, Companies Act 2006). You are expected in an essay or problem question to show a good understanding of this statutory contract, in particular, with regard to its enforcement and the controversial principle established in *Hickman* v *Kent or Romney Marsh Sheepbreeders Association* [1915] 1 Ch 881. The alteration of a company's articles of association (s 21) and the restrictions on the exercise of this power are often examined. Your knowledge of shareholders' agreements may also be tested in an exam question.

■ Attack the question

📝 Question 1

'A member can compel the company not to depart from the contract with him under the articles, even if that means indirectly the enforcement of 'outsider' rights vested either in third parties or himself, as long as, but only so long as, he sues *qua* member and not *qua* outsider.' (Wedderburn, 'Shareholders' rights and the rule in *Foss* v *Harbottle*' [1957] CLJ 194 at 212–213)

Critically evaluate the above statement with regard to the enforcement of a company's articles of association.

Answer plan

➡ Consider the special features of the statutory contract under s 33, CA 2006.

➡ Examine the enforcement of a company's articles of association.

➡ Evaluate the principles established in *Hickman* v *Kent or Romney Marsh Sheepbreeders Association* [1915] 1 Ch 881.

Diagram plan

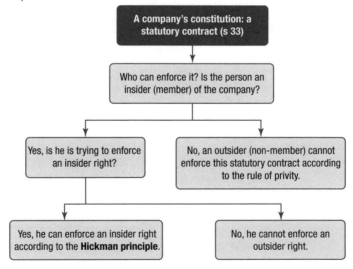

A printable version of this diagram plan is available from www.pearsoned.co.uk/lawexpressqa

Answer

This question requires an evaluation of Wedderburn's statement in relation to the enforcement of a company's articles of association by

[1]The reference to Wedderburn's statement in your introduction shows that you understand what the question is about and that you are able to engage with the question.

[2]This is a key provision that you should learn.

[3]You should discuss the special features of the articles of association by reference to case law. You will lose some marks if you go straight into the enforcement of the statutory contract without considering its special features.

[4]This sentence shows that you are aware of the current complicated state of this area of law. It also leads to the discussion of the different judicial approach in the next paragraph.

[5]You should demonstrate good knowledge of the judgment of this case, which was decided by the House of Lords.

a member.[1] Articles of association are the internal rule books for a company and are part of a company's constitution as defined in s 17 of the Companies Act 2006. They set out the rules for the running and regulation of the company's affairs.

Section 33 states that 'the provisions of a company's constitution bind the company and its members to the same extent as if there were covenants on the part of the company and of each member to observe those provisions'.[2] A company's articles of association therefore create a statutory contract between the company and its members, and between each individual member. The statutory contract has some features which are distinct from an ordinary contract, as the Court of Appeal explained in **Bratton Seymore Service Co Ltd v Oxborough** [1992] BCLC 693.[3] It originates from the statute instead of a bargain between parties; it will not be made invalid on the grounds of misrepresentation, mistake, undue influence or duress. This contract binds not only the present members but also future members who will join the company. Moreover, the contract can be amended by a special majority if three-quarters of the members vote in favour of the resolution (s 21), compared to the need to obtain the consent of all parties in an ordinary contract. More significantly, unlike an ordinary contract where the parties can enforce the rights contained therein, not every member can enforce a right contained in the articles of association against the company. The enforcement of this statutory contract has been subject to contradictory case law and constant academic debates.[4]

The following two cases illustrate the complexities when a member tries to enforce a company's articles. In **Eley v Positive Life Association** [1876] 1 EX D 88, the articles contained a clause which provided that a particular member would be appointed as a company's solicitor. He was not appointed as such and unsuccessfully sued the company for breach of that clause in the articles because there was no contractual relationship between a member as solicitor and the company. In some instances, however, the courts allowed a member to enforce a non-shareholder right conferred by the articles. In **Quin & Axtens Ltd v Salmon** [1909] AC 442[5] the company's articles contained a clause which stated that 'no resolution of directors on certain important matters would be valid if either of two named managing directors voted against the resolution'. The plaintiff, one of the managing directors, voted against such a resolution but the company tried to ratify it by a simple majority. The House of Lords enforced this clause and held the resolution invalid even though it indirectly enforced rights given to certain members in their capacity as directors.

There has been much discussion as to the capacity in which the articles are to be enforced and whether enforcement encompasses the entire articles or is limited to membership rights. Some guidance is provided in **Hickman v Kent or Romney Marsh Sheepbreeders Association** [1915] 1 Ch 881 in relation to which clauses can be enforced. In this case, the articles of association provided that disputes between the company and its members should be referred to arbitration. A member was in dispute with the company and commenced legal proceedings instead of arbitration. It was held that a company was entitled to enforce the articles against its own members; the member was bound by the articles and the dispute should be referred to arbitration. Astbury J held that: '... No article can constitute a contract between a company and a third person ... No right merely purporting to be given by an article to a person, whether a member or not, in a capacity other than as a member, as for instance, as solicitor, promoter, director, can be enforced against the company.'[6] Thus, a member can only enforce a membership right which is contained in the articles, such as the right to attend and vote at a general meeting (**Pender v Lushington** (1877) 6 Ch D 70) and the right to a declared dividend (**Wood v Odessa Waterworks Co** (1889) 42 Ch D 636). By contrast, a member cannot enforce his non-membership right (outsider right) such as the right to be the company's solicitor (**Eley** (above)) and the right to be a company director (**Beattie v E and F Beattie Ltd** [1938] Ch 708).[7]

The **Hickman** decision imposes *locus standi* restrictions on who can enforce the company's articles and prevents a floodgate of vexatious litigation against the company.[8] It reflects the courts' reluctance to get involved in the company's internal management according to the rule in **Foss v Harbottle** (1843) 67 ER 189.[9] This rule has two elements: first, the proper plaintiff in respect of an alleged wrong done to the company is *prima facie* the company; secondly, where the alleged wrong is a transaction which might be made binding on the company by a simple majority of the members, no individual member is allowed to bring a claim in respect of it. If a wrong is done

[6]It is worth stating the key judgment of this important case in relation to the enforcement of articles of association.

[7]Your discussion of the insider rights and outsider rights must be supported by the relevant case law authorities.

[8]The rationale behind the *Hickman* judgment demonstrates your sound understanding of this case and will gain you more marks.

[9]The reference to the rule in *Foss* v *Harbottle* will make your answer stand out because it shows your wider understanding of this area of law.

to a member personally and it is an infringement of his personal rights, then the rule in **Foss v Harbottle** does not apply and he can proceed with his personal claim. A distinction is drawn by the courts in order to reconcile the **Foss** rule and the enforcement of a s 33 statutory contract. A member can enforce provisions in the articles which create personal rights conferred on a member *qua* member. Breach of the provisions which relate to the matters of internal management of the company is a wrong done to the company; and therefore it cannot be challenged by individual shareholders. This distinction between membership rights and non-membership rights, however, is only an artificial line and is not clearly defined.[10]

[10]This sentence demonstrates that you are aware of the problems associated with the *Hickman* principle.

The **Hickman** decision appears to conflict with s 33.[11] The former states that only membership rights can be enforced whereas the latter does not make any distinction between membership and non-membership rights and simply states that 'those provisions' must be observed. The **Hickman** principle therefore has the effect of narrowing down the scope of rights which can be enforced under s 33. Moreover, it is difficult to reconcile the **Hickman** decision with an earlier and higher authority of the House of Lords in **Quin & Axtens Ltd v Salmon** (above). Wedderburn (1957) is of the opinion that every member has a personal right to see that the company is run according to the articles, except those already identified as concerning the internal procedures only. This view has been broadly shared by Gregory (1981), Goldberg (1985) and Drury (1986).[12] The current law on the enforcement of a company's articles is still complicated and confusing.[13] Further reforms are needed to clarify the distinction between insider and outsider rights and to achieve more consistency in this area of law.[14]

[11]This is one of the main reasons why the *Hickman* decision is often challenged.

[12]The discussion of the academic opinions shows your wider knowledge of the debates on this area of law. It will add more credit to your answer.

[13]Refer back to the question in your conclusion.

[14]This sentence, which expresses your opinion on the need for future reforms, will gain you more marks.

✓ Make your answer stand out

- Discuss the reform proposals put forward by the Company Law Review Steering Group, in particular, the catch-all solution whereby all the articles would be enforceable by the members against the company and each other unless the contrary was provided.

- Point out that it is preferable in practice to bring an unfair prejudice petition under s 994 of the Companies Act 2006 than to enforce a company's articles.

- Further reading on the enforcement of a company's articles of association: Drury, R. 'The relative nature of a shareholder's right to enforce the company contract' (1986) *Cambridge Law Journal* 219; Goldberg, R. 'The controversy on the section 20 contract revisited' (1985) 48 *Modern Law Review* 158; Gregory, R. 'The section 20 contract' (1981) 44 *Modern Law Review* 526.

! Don't be tempted to...

- Only focus on the case of *Hickman*. It is essential to discuss other cases which illustrate different judicial approach to the enforcement of a company's articles of association, for example, *Quin & Axtens* v *Salmon* (1909).
- Discuss insider rights and outsider rights without reference to the relevant case law.

? Question 2

Tom, Jerry and Fiona incorporated Quality Tyres Ltd in 2009. The company's share capital is divided into 1,000 ordinary shares. All three are directors and shareholders who hold 250, 350 and 400 shares respectively.

The standard Model Articles of Association for private companies limited by shares are adopted with the additional clauses which state that: 'Fiona shall be the company director for life. On any resolution to remove her as a director she is entitled to two votes per share on a poll.'

Tom and Jerry recently are unhappy with Fiona's performance at board meetings and want to remove her from the board of directors.

Advise Tom and Jerry.

Answer plan

- → Discuss the statutory requirements for the removal of a director (s 168, Companies Act 2006).
- → Consider how a member can enforce the company's articles of association.
- → Analyse whether Fiona can rely on the articles to remain as a director for life.
- → Examine whether Fiona can enforce the article in relation to two votes per share on any resolution to remove her.
- → Evaluate whether Tom and Jerry can alter the articles (s 21, Companies Act 2006).

Diagram plan

Can Fiona rely on the company's articles to remain as a director?

↓

No, she cannot enforce an outsider right according to the *Hickman* principle.

↓

Can Fiona rely on the clause which entitles her 'two votes per share'?

↓

Yes, she can according to *Bushell* v *Faith*.

↓

Can Tom and Jerry remove Fiona by an ordinary resolution at a general meeting (s 168)?

↓

No. Tom and Jerry have 600 votes but Fiona has 400 x 2 = 800 votes. An ordinary resolution for removing Fiona from the board cannot be passed.

↓

Can Tom and Jerry alter or delete the *Bushell* v *Faith* clause in the articles following s 21?

↓

No. Weighted voting rights are considered as class rights, which can only be varied according to s 630.

A printable version of this diagram plan is available from www.pearsoned.co.uk/lawexpressqa

[1]In your introduction, identify the key legal issues that need to be addressed.

[2]There are different ways of voting at a general meeting such as voting on a show of hands or on a poll; the methods of calculating the number of votes are different accordingly. On a show of hands, every member present in person has one vote. On a poll, every member has one vote in respect of each share. The poll vote is adopted in most companies and therefore used here as an example.

Answer

In answering this question, it is necessary to examine how a director can be legally removed from the board and whether Fiona can remain as a company director by relying on the company's articles of association.[1] Section 168 states that: 'A company may by ordinary resolution at a meeting remove a director before the expiration of his period of office, notwithstanding anything in any agreement between it and him.' An ordinary resolution can be passed by a simple majority (s 282). If a poll vote[2] is taken at a general meeting on a resolution to remove Fiona, every member has one vote in respect of each share (s 284). As Tom and Jerry hold 600 shares in total whilst Fiona has 400 shares; *prima facie*, an ordinary resolution can be passed to remove Fiona. Fiona,

[3]The case of *Bushell* v *Faith* and the weighted voting right are often examined in a problem question with regard to the enforcement of a company's articles. Make sure you understand how the weighted voting right is applied.

however, is entitled by the articles to two votes per share on any resolution to remove her as a director.

The validity of the weighted voting right is recognised in **Bushell v Faith** [1970] AC 1099,[3] where two sisters and a brother were equal shareholders of the company with 100 shares each. The two sisters proposed to remove their brother as a director by an ordinary resolution. The brother challenged the removal on the grounds that the company's articles of association provided that on a resolution to remove a director from office 'any shares held by that director shall on a poll in respect of such resolution carry the right to three votes per share'. As the sisters had 200 votes whilst the brother had 300 votes, an ordinary resolution could not be achieved. The House of Lords by a majority approved the use of this clause despite Lord Morris, who gave the dissenting judgment, criticised that such device made a mockery of the law.[4] On the resolution to remove her from the board, Fiona would have 800 votes (400 x 2) whilst Tom and Jerry have 600 votes in total; therefore an ordinary resolution could not be passed for this purpose.[5]

[4]The name of the dissenting judge and the key judgment show your sound knowledge of this case.

[5]Remember to apply the case law to this problem scenario.

Another issue is whether Fiona can rely on the articles to be a company director for life.[6] Articles of association, which are part of the company's constitution as defined in s 17, create a statutory contract between the members and the company (s 33). The enforcement of this statutory contract is different from an ordinary contract.[7] It has been established that an outsider right which is contained in this contract cannot be enforced. In **Hickman v Kent or Romney Marsh Sheepbreeders Association** [1915] 1 Ch 881, Astbury J made a clear distinction between insider and outsider rights; he held that: 'No right merely purporting to be given by an article to a person, whether a member or not, in a capacity other than as a member, as for instance, as solicitor, promoter, director, can be enforced against the company.'[8] The right to be a company director is considered as an outsider right in **Beattie v E and F Beattie Ltd** [1938] Ch 708, where the articles of association provided that all disputes between the company and a member must be referred to arbitration. The defendant director who was also a member was sued for breach of duty and sought to rely on this clause. It was held that he could not rely on the article because it did not constitute a contract between the company and the defendant in the capacity as a director. Similarly, the right to be a company solicitor is an outsider

[6]Move on to the next legal issue after addressing the weighted voting rights in full. This sentence shows that your answer focuses on the question asked.

[7]You can discuss the special features of the statutory contract in detail here; for instance, it is binding on future shareholders and a special resolution is required for its alteration.

[8]It is worth learning this important judgment by Astbury J which distinguished between insider rights and outsider rights.

9This is another example of an outsider right, which will gain you more marks.

10An examination of other options makes your answer stand out.

11Some students may forget to discuss the common law restrictions on the exercise of s 21.

12The analysis of class rights adds more credit to your answer. You will lose some marks if you fail to show a good understanding of the requirements in relation to the variation of class rights.

13This case is essential here because it establishes that weighted voting rights are class rights and therefore they attract the special protection under s 630.

right and cannot be enforced.9 In **Eley v Positive Government Securities Life Assurance Co Ltd** (1876) 1 ExD 88, the articles of association provided that Eley shall be the solicitor of the company. When the company started to instruct another solicitor, Eley who was also a member of the company unsuccessfully brought an action for breach of contract. Applying the common law to the problem scenario, Fiona cannot rely on the articles to remain as a director for life.

Tom and Jerry may consider other options to remove Fiona, for instance, by removing the clause which gives Fiona the weighted voting right.10 According to s 21, an alteration of articles requires a special resolution which must be passed by a majority of not less than 75% (s 283). The articles must also be altered in good faith for the benefits of the company as a whole: **Allen v Gold Reefs of West Africa Ltd** [1900] 1 Ch 656.11 The judgment, however, offers little guidance as to the scope and substance of the subjective test. Evershed MR in **Greenhalgh v Arderne Cinemas Ltd** [1950] 2 All ER 1120 held that 'the company as a whole' meant the shareholders as a body. As Tom and Jerry hold 600 shares which account for 60% of the company's share capital, a special resolution is unlikely to be passed for the alteration of articles.

Even if Tom and Jerry held more than 75% of the company's shares, the weighted voting right clause would be unlikely to be amended or deleted by s 21.12 In **Cumbrian Newspapers Group Ltd v Cumberland and Westmoreland Herald Newspaper and Printing Co Ltd** [1986] 2 All ER 816,13 the articles entitled a member to appoint a director so long as he held 10% of the shares. It was held that the rights or benefits that, although not attached to any particular shares, were conferred on the beneficiary in the capacity of member of the company and they created class rights. Scott J held that the articles which gave a director weighted voting rights as those in **Bushell v Faith** created class rights. Class rights can only be varied in accordance with the company's articles, or where the company's articles contain no such provision, the holders of three-quarter shares of that class must consent to the variation (s 630). As Fiona is the only person in the class of shares with weighted voting right, the right cannot be varied without her consent and it is unlikely that she will agree to such variation.

[14] The discussion of the issue of shares will make your answer stand out. Some students may not be able to associate the topic of shares with the removal of directors.

[15] A service contract between a director and the company is quite common in practice. The implications of such a contract should be discussed when a director is removed from office. It adds extra credit to your answer.

Tom and Jerry may also consider issuing more shares to themselves or people outside the company (s 551)[14] so that they can have sufficient votes to pass an ordinary resolution and remove Fiona. As directors of the company, they must exercise their power for proper purposes (s 171) and comply with shareholders' pre-emption rights (s 561). Fiona may bring an unfair prejudice petition against such issue of shares under s 994: **Re a Company (No 005134 of 1986), ex p Harries** [1989] BCLC 383. In addition, if Fiona has a separate service contract[15] with the company and she was removed in breach of the terms of this contract, the company may be liable for damages: **Southern Foundries (1926) Ltd *v* Shirlaw** [1940] 2 All ER 445.

✓ Make your answer stand out

- Discuss the possibility of increasing share capital in detail. According to s 551, directors may exercise the power to allot shares only if authorised to do so by the articles or by an ordinary resolution. As Tom and Jerry hold 60% of the company's shares, Fiona's shareholding may be diluted by the allotment of more shares and her weighted voting right may not be able to prevent her from being removed.

- Consider that Tom and Jerry may breach their fiduciary duties in s 172 if the increase of share capital is designed to dilute Fiona's shareholding.

- Analyse the dissenting judgment of Lord Morris in *Bushell* v *Faith* (1970) in more detail by making reference to Fang Ma, 'Removal of Directors: Lord Morris in *Bushell* v *Faith* [1970] AC 1099', in N. Geach and C. Monaghan (eds) *Dissenting Judgments*, with a Foreword by Lord Nicholls of Birkenhead (Wildy, Simmonds and Hill, 2011).

! Don't be tempted to...

- Give an incomplete answer by discussing only part of the additional clauses in the articles. You should analyse the clauses in relation to both Fiona's right to remain as a director and her weighted voting right.

- Forget to consider the class rights which are attached to the weighted voting rights. You should pay special attention to the requirements for a variation of class rights under s 630.

- Jump to the conclusion that Fiona cannot be removed from the board. You should analyse the legal issues one by one on the enforcement of the articles and consider other possible ways of removing Fiona.

📝 Question 3

'A company is free to alter its articles of association by a special resolution without any restriction.'

Evaluate the above statement.

Answer plan

→ Discuss the statutory requirements for an alteration of a company's articles of association under s 21, CA 2006.

→ Examine the common law restrictions on the company's power to alter its articles: *Allen v Gold Reefs of West Africa Ltd* [1900] 1 Ch 656.

→ Evaluate the statutory limitations on s 21 including the provisions for entrenchment articles (s 22), a variation of class rights (s 630) and some specific requirements (s 25).

Diagram plan

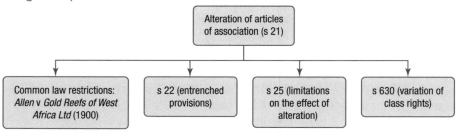

A printable version of this diagram plan is available from www.pearsoned.co.uk/lawexpressqa

Answer

The articles of association, as a part of a company's constitution, constitute a statutory contract between the company and its members and between its members *inter se* (s 33, Companies Act 2006). Unlike an ordinary contract where the consent of all parties is required for its amendment, the articles may be altered by a special resolution (s 21), which means a resolution passed by a majority of not less than 75% (s 283). It is argued that the power to alter the articles is not entirely unrestricted and some limitations are imposed both at common law and by statutory provisions such as s 22, s 25 and s 630.[1]

At common law, the power to alter the articles must be exercised *bona fide* for the benefit of the company as a whole: **Allen v Gold**

[1] This sentence states your arguments and sets out a clear structure for your answer.

[2]This is the common law
restriction on the alteration
of a company's articles and
therefore it is a key quote
which should be learnt by
heart.

[3]The reference to academic
opinion enhances your critical
analysis and adds more credit
to your answer.

[4]This sentence includes the
two key authorities on the
interpretations of the common
law test. It also leads to the
discussion which follows in
the next two paragraphs.

[5]This is an important
judgment and should be
stated accurately. Some
students know about this case
but cannot provide a precise
summary of the judgment.

[6]Try to learn the name of the
leading judge. It shows your
specific knowledge of this
case.

[7]The introduction of the
objective test makes this case
stand out.

Reefs of West Africa Ltd [1900] 1 Ch 656. Lindley MR held that the power 'must be exercised, not only in the manner required by law, but also *bona fide* for the benefit of the company as a whole'.[2] An alteration of articles therefore can be challenged for a lack of good faith or if it is not for the benefit of the company as a whole. This test of 'bona fide for the benefit of the company as a whole' is criticised by Rixon (1986) as 'almost meaningless' when adjusting shareholders' conflicting interests.[3] The judgment in **Allen** (above) offers little guidance as to the meaning and scope of the test, which is still unclear despite the interpretations of the test by the Court of Appeal in **Shuttleworth v Cox Bros & Co (Maidenhead) Ltd** [1927] 2 KB 9 and **Greenhalgh v Arderne Cinemas Ltd** [1950] 2 All ER 1120.[4]

In **Shuttleworth** (above), the company's articles provided that the plaintiff and four other directors would hold office unless they were disqualified on one of six specified grounds. The plaintiff failed to account for company money and property. The articles were altered to add a further ground for disqualification that any director should resign if requested in writing by all his co-directors. After the alteration, the plaintiff was asked to resign and unsuccessfully challenged the validity of the alteration. It was held that it was for the shareholders, and not for the court, to decide whether an alteration of articles was for the benefit of the company, provided that it was not of such a character as that no reasonable men could so regard it.[5] Scrutton LJ[6] stated that: '... provided there are grounds on which reasonable men could come to the same decision, it does not matter whether the court would or would not come to the same decision or a different decision. It is not the business of the court to manage the affairs of the company.' Both the subjective and objective tests were adopted in this judgment. The subjective test of *bona fide* was followed where the court looked at whether the shareholders honestly believed that they were acting in the best interests of the company as a whole in altering the articles. The objective test of 'reasonable men' was also considered so that an alteration would not stand if no reasonable men could consider it to be for the benefit of the company.[7]

In **Greenhalgh** (above), the company's articles stated that any shareholder who wished to sell their shares should offer them first to existing shareholders. A special resolution was passed for the alteration of the articles so that the shares could be sold directly to an outsider with the approval of an ordinary resolution. A minority shareholder challenged the validity of this alteration. The Court of Appeal rejected his claim and held that a voting shareholder should 'proceed on what, in his honest opinion, is for the benefit of the company as a whole'.[8] The alteration was merely a relaxation of the stringent restrictions on the transfer of shares and therefore it was *bona fide* for the benefit of the company as a whole.

[8]Pay attention to this judgment because it confirms the subjective test of the common law restriction.

It should be noted that the courts are very reluctant to challenge a shareholder resolution for a lack of *bona fide* because the passing of a shareholder resolution is generally viewed as upholding the majority rule as established in **Foss v Harbottle** (1843) 2 Hare 461. In **Citco Banking Corp NV v Pusser's Ltd** [2007] 2 BCLC 483,[9] the company's articles were altered to give the chairman a voting control of the company. The Privy Council followed **Shuttleworth** (above) and held the alteration valid. Lord Hoffmann confirmed that the test was whether reasonable shareholders could consider the alteration to be for the benefit of the company.

[9]A more recent case shows your up-to-date knowledge. This case also reaffirms the objective test established in *Shuttleworth* (1927).

In addition to the common law restrictions, some limitations are imposed by the Companies Act 2006.[10] A company's articles may contain provisions for entrenchment so that the specified provisions of the articles may not be amended by a special majority; instead they can only be amended if conditions are met or procedures are complied with, by agreement of all the members of the company or by a court order (s 22). Such provisions may only be made in the company's articles on formation or by an amendment of the company's articles agreed to by all the members of the company.

[10]This sentence indicates that your answer has moved on from a discussion of the common law to the statutory provisions.

Moreover, a member of a company is not bound by an alteration to its articles after the date on which he became a member in either of the following situations (s 25):[11] first, if it requires him to take or subscribe for more shares than the number held by him at the date on which the alteration is made; secondly, if it increases his liability as at that date to contribute to the company's share capital or otherwise to pay money to the company. These provisions do not apply where the member agrees in writing to be bound by the alteration, either before or after the alteration is made.[12]

[11]An evaluation of the conditions in s 25 is often missing in the exam answers.

[12]Try to provide a sound discussion of s 25 by evaluating the situations where it does not apply.

Where the alteration of the articles constitutes a variation or abrogation of class rights, the procedure in s 630 must be followed.

Class rights, which are rights attached to a class of a company's shares, can be altered in accordance with the provision in the company's articles; or where the company's articles contain no such provision, the holders of at least three-quarter shares of that class consent to the variation in writing or by a special resolution at a separate class meeting (s 630).

[13]Refer back to the question in your conclusion and briefly summarise your arguments. It shows that you are able to put forward a sound argument in a clear structure.

It is concluded that a company's articles of association can be altered subject to the common law test and the statutory provisions.[13] The interpretations of the common law test of 'bona fide for the benefit of the company as a whole', however, need to be further clarified in order to provide more guidance and achieve more certainty in this area of law.[14]

[14]This sentence shows your analysis of the common law and its need for reform. It will gain you more marks.

✓ Make your answer stand out

- Explain what is meant by a variation of class rights. The courts have drawn an artificial distinction between matters affecting the rights attaching to each share and matters affecting the enjoyment of those rights. Only variation which affects the rights attached to each share attracts the protection of the procedure in s 630.

- In relation to the test of 'bona fide for the benefit of the company as a whole', discuss *Sidebottom* v *Kershaw, Leese & Co Ltd* [1920] 1 Ch 154 and *Dafen Tinplate Co Ltd* v *Llanelly Steel Co Ltd* [1920] 2 Ch 124.

- Examine the circumstance where a shareholder enters into a shareholder agreement, for example, a voting agreement (*Russell* v *Northern Bank Development Corp Ltd* [1992] BCLC 1016).

! Don't be tempted to...

- Consider the common law restrictions on the power to alter the articles without reference to the cases of *Shuttleworth* (1927) and *Greenhalgh* (1950).

- Only focus on the common law restrictions imposed by *Allen* v *Gold Reefs of West Africa Ltd* [1900] 1 Ch 656. The statutory provisions must also be discussed in your answer.

❓ Question 4

Chris, Peter and Simon are all directors of Prime Coffee Ltd; each holds 80%, 15% and 5% of its issued shares. Its articles of association contain the following clauses: 'The company's director Peter shall be paid £50,000 per annum. As long as Peter holds 15 per cent of the company's shares, he is entitled to nominate a director.'

Peter has an agreement with the company that it will not alter its articles with regard to his right of nomination without his consent. He also has a service contract with the company which entitles him to £50,000 per annum as a director.

Chris recently finds out that Peter is secretly competing with Prime Coffee Ltd and he proposes to make the following changes to the articles:

1. All the directors should be appointed by the general meeting.
2. Peter's salary shall be reduced to £30,000 per annum.
3. A clause shall be added in the articles with the effect of allowing the directors to purchase any shareholder's shares at a fair price if that shareholder's conduct is detrimental to the company's interests.

Advise Peter.

Answer plan

→ Discuss whether Peter's right to nominate a director can be altered by a special resolution.

→ Examine whether Peter can enforce his right in the articles in relation to the annual salary £50,000.

→ Evaluate whether the clause which has the effect of compulsory purchase of a shareholder's shares can be added to the articles.

Diagram plan

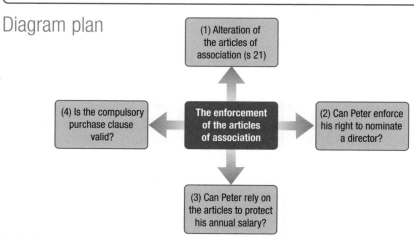

A printable version of this diagram plan is available from www.pearsoned.co.uk/lawexpressqa

Answer

Articles of association form part of a company's constitution which creates a statutory contract between the company and its members (s 33, Companies Act 2006). A company's articles may be altered by a special resolution at general meeting (s 21). As Chris holds more than 75% of the company's shares, *prima facie*[1], the articles can be altered; however, the power to alter the articles is subject to various restrictions.

[1]The phrase '*prima facie*' shows that you understand the complicated legal issues arising from this question.

1. Peter's right to nominate a director[2]

[2]Adopt a clear structure by using clear headings and address the legal issues one by one.

Chris proposes to alter the articles so that all the directors should be appointed by the general meeting. This will have the effect of depriving Peter of his right to nominate a director as long as he holds 15% of the company's shares. In **Cumbrian Newspaper Group Ltd *v* Cumberland & Westmoreland Herald Newspaper & Printing Co Ltd** [1986] 2 All ER 816, the claimant was given the right to nominate a director in the articles if he continued to hold a 10% shareholding in the defendant company. It was held that such right constituted a class right. A class right may only be varied under s 630 in accordance with provision in the company's articles, or if no such provision is contained in the articles, the holders of at least three-quarters in nominal value of the issued shares of that class must consent to the variation. As Peter is the only person in this class, his right of nomination cannot be varied without his consent.[3]

[3]Apply the relevant law to the problem question. It shows that you are engaging with the question rather than providing an essay-style answer.

2. Peter's salary

[4]Set out Peter's arguments against the proposed alteration of the articles. It shows that you are engaging with the question by analysing the problem scenario.

Chris proposes to alter the articles and reduce Peter's annual salary from £50,000 to £30,000. Peter may try to prevent the company from doing so by relying on the articles and his service contract.[4] In **Hickman *v* Kent or Romney Marsh Sheepbreeders Association** [1915] 1 Ch 881,[5] it was held that members could only enforce membership rights contained in the articles; outsider rights could not be enforced. Membership rights include the right to attend and vote at shareholder meetings (**Pender *v* Lushington** (1877) 6 Ch D 70) and to receive declared dividend (**Wood *v* Odessa Waterworks Co**

[5]This is an important case on the enforcement of a company's articles of association because it provides some guidance on the distinction between insider and outsider rights.

(1889) 42 Ch D 636). Outsider rights are non-membership rights, including the right to be a solicitor (**Eley v Positive Government Security Life Assurance Co** (1876) 1 Ex D 88) and the right to be a director (**Beattie v E & F Beattie Ltd** [1938] Ch 708).[6]

The key issue is whether the right to a certain amount of salary is an insider right or an outsider right. In **Re New British Iron Co, ex p Beckwith** [1898] 1 Ch 324,[7] the company's articles provided that the annual salary of the board of directors shall be £1,000. The directors sought unsuccessfully to claim the arrears of their salaries when the company was in liquidation. It was held that the articles did not constitute a contract between the company and the directors for the payment of directors' salary. Peter's right in relation to his salary as a director is therefore considered as an outsider right and cannot be enforced if it is contained in the articles.

Peter may argue that the company's right to alter its articles is restricted by the term of the service contract.[8] This argument is most likely to be invalid because it is established that the company's statutory power under s 21 to alter its articles cannot be restricted contractually. In **Punt v Symons & Co Ltd** [1903] 2 Ch 506, it was held that the company could not contract out of its statutory right to alter its articles either by way of a separate contract or by a provision in the articles. Chris therefore can alter the articles by a special resolution to reduce Peter's annual salary as long as the power is exercised *bona fide* for the benefit of the company as a whole: **Allen v Gold Reefs of West Africa Ltd** [1900] 1 Ch 656. Peter may, nevertheless, sue the company for damages if the alteration of the articles breaches his service contract: **Southern Foundries Ltd v Shirlaw** [1940] 2 All ER 445.[9]

3. Compulsory transfer clause

Chris proposes to add a clause in the articles so that directors can purchase any shareholder's shares if that shareholder's conduct is detrimental to the company's interests. Peter may argue that the proposed alteration of the articles is not in good faith for the benefit of the company. In **Allen** (above), it was held that the court could set aside a proposed alteration of the articles which was not *bona fide* for the benefit of the company as a whole. The test for '*bona fide* for the benefit of the company as a whole', however, is not clear. In **Sidebottom v Kershaw, Leese & Co Ltd** [1920] 1 Ch 154, the defendant company altered its articles by allowing the directors to buy out shareholders at a fair price who competed with the company's business. The Court of Appeal held that the alteration was valid as the resolution had been passed *bona fide* for the benefit of the company as a whole.[10]

By contrast, in **Dafen Tinplate Co Ltd v Llanelly Steel Co Ltd** [1920] 2 Ch 124,[11] the company was formed on the basis of an expectation that the shareholders would purchase supplies from the company. One shareholder began purchasing his supplies from another company in which he had an interest. The company altered the articles with the effect that the majority of shareholders could determine that the shares of any shareholders should be offered for sale by a director at a fair value to be fixed by the directors. The alteration was disallowed by the court, as it went beyond what was necessary to benefit the company. The alteration was for the benefit and advantage of the majority shareholders. Peterson J stated that: 'The question is whether in fact the alteration is genuinely for the benefit of the company.'[12]

As Peter is competing with Prime Coffee Ltd, it is very difficult for him to convince the court that this amendment of articles is not for the benefit of the company. The court is more likely to follow **Sidebottom** (1920) and allow the alteration when the shareholder's conduct is detrimental to the company's business.[13] Peter may bring an unfair prejudice petition under s 994 to challenge the alteration of the articles but it is unlikely to succeed because his own conduct may not render the alteration unfair.[14]

✓ Make your answer stand out

- Examine in detail the meaning of '*bona fide* for the benefit of the company as a whole' by reference to *Shuttleworth* v *Cox Bros & Co (Maidenhead) Ltd* [1927] 2 KB 9 and *Greenhalgh* v *Arderne Cinemas Ltd* [1950] 2 All ER 1120.
- Refer to the academic debates on the validity of a compulsory transfer clause in the articles such as: Hannigan, 'Altering the articles to allow for compulsory transfer – dragging minority shareholders to a reluctant exit' [2007] JBL 471.
- Consider whether Peter has breached his fiduciary duties in s 172 and s 175.

> ! **Don't be tempted to...**
>
> ■ Get confused with the right to be a director and the right to nominate a director. Some students may come to the wrong conclusion that Peter's right to nominate a director is an outsider right and therefore cannot be enforced.
>
> ■ Discuss the director's salary without reference to the case law authorities. Most students are able to recognise the outsider right but fail to analyse the relevant case law.
>
> ■ Omit the leading authorities of *Sidebottom* (1920) and *Dafen Tinplate Co Ltd* (1920) with regard to the compulsory transfer clause.

🔖 Question 5

'Shareholders' agreements are often favoured as being more flexible than the articles of association, more appropriate for temporary and personal obligations, both easier and more difficult to change than the articles of association and less public. These advantages are thought to outweigh the disadvantage that new shareholders are not automatically bound by the contract ...' (T. B. Little, 'How far does shareholder's freedom of contract extend? – *Russell* v *Northern Bank Corporation Limited* and other recent cases' (1992) ICCLR 351 at 355)

Undertake a critical evaluation of the above statement.

Answer plan

→ Examine the advantages and disadvantages of shareholders' agreements compared with a company's articles of association.

→ Discuss the distinctive features of the articles of association, in particular, the enforcement of a s 33 contract and the *Hickman* principle.

→ Focus on the enforcement of a shareholder's agreement, in particular, when a company is a party to the agreement.

Diagram plan

Articles of association | Shareholders' agreements

	Articles of association	Shareholders' agreements
Registration	Yes	No
Alteration	By a special resolution (s 21)	With the consent of all the parties
Automatically binding new members?	Yes	No
Enforcement	s 33 and *Hickman* v *Kent or Romney Marsh Sheepbreeders Association* [1915] 1 Ch 881	*Russell* v *Northern Bank Development Corporation Ltd* [1992] BCLC 1016

A printable version of this diagram plan is available from www.pearsoned.co.uk/lawexpressqa

Answer

¹This sentence demonstrates that you have identified the main legal issues raised in the question.

²The explanations of the articles of association and shareholders' agreements should be the starting point of your answer.

³Refer back to the question whenever you can. It shows the examiners that you are not simply providing a narrative answer.

This question requires a comparison of a shareholders' agreement and a company's articles of association.¹ The articles of association are internal rule books for the company and govern its internal running whilst a shareholders' agreement is a separate contract between some or all of the shareholders, or between the company and its shareholders.²

Articles of associations form a significant part of a company's constitution and must be filed with Companies House. By contrast, a shareholders' agreement is not normally treated as a company's constitution and usually addresses particular issues such as voting, the transfer of shares and the appointment of directors. A shareholders' agreement exists outside and separate from the articles; it is a private document and registration with Companies House is not required. A shareholders' agreement therefore offers the advantages of privacy and is 'more flexible and less public'.³

The articles of association are binding not only on the present members but also future members of the company. By contrast, a shareholders' agreement is an ordinary contract in the way that it is binding on the parties and is subject to all the usual contractual remedies. A new member of the company will not be bound by the agreement unless the person assents to it: **Greenhalgh v Mallard** [1943] 2 All ER 234. A shareholders' agreement is therefore 'more appropriate for temporary and personal obligations'.

[4]These sentences address the seemingly contradictory statement in the question that shareholders' agreements are 'both easier and more difficult to change than the articles of association'. They demonstrate your good analytical skills.

The articles of association may be amended by a special resolution at a general meeting if three-quarters of the members vote in favour of the resolution (s 21). By contrast, a shareholders' agreement can only be altered with the consent of all the parties to it; it is therefore 'more difficult to change than the articles of association'. An alteration of the articles must be registered with Companies House whilst the registration is not required for the amendment of a shareholders' agreement. In this sense, it is correctly argued that the agreement is 'easier to change than the articles'.[4]

[5]Point out the most important issue that you will discuss in detail. It also indicates where you are going with your answer.

The most significant differences between the articles and a shareholder agreement lie in their enforcement.[5] The articles constitute a statutory contract between the company and its members, and between members *inter se* (s 33). The enforcement of this statutory contract is governed by the decision in **Hickman v Kent or Romney Marsh Sheepbreeders Association** [1915] 1 Ch 881, where the articles provided that disputes between the company and a member should be referred to arbitration. A member in dispute with the company commenced legal proceedings. It was concluded that the member was bound by the articles and the dispute should be referred to arbitration. Astbury J held that: 'No right merely purporting to be given by an article to a person, whether a member or not, in a capacity other than as a member, as for instance, as solicitor, promoter, director, can be enforced against the company.'[6] Thus, a member can only enforce a membership right which is contained in the articles, such as the right to attend and vote at a general meeting (**Pender v Lushington** (1877) 6 Ch D 70) and the right to a declared dividend (**Wood v Odessa Waterworks Co** (1889) 42 Ch D 636). Non-membership rights cannot be enforced, such as the right to be a company solicitor (**Eley v Positive Government Security Life Assurance Co Ltd** (1876) 1 Ex D 88) or a director (**Beattie v E and F Beattie Ltd** [1938] Ch 708).

[6]This is a very important judgment that you should learn. The name of the leading judge shows your specific knowledge of this case.

[7]You should discuss the enforcement of a shareholders' agreement in two aspects: first, when it is merely between shareholders; and, secondly, when it is between shareholders and the company. Many students do not differentiate between these two aspects.

By comparison, it is easier to enforce a shareholders' agreement in the sense that it is not governed by the **Hickman** principle. The courts are willing to enforce the agreement if it is merely between shareholders.[7] Shareholders, for instance, may enter into agreements to determine the way in which they exercise their voting rights. In **Puddephatt v Leith** [1916] 1 Ch 200 the court compelled a shareholder to vote as was agreed in the shareholders' agreement.

In **Greenwell v Porter** [1902] 1 Ch 530 the defendant shareholders agreed to exercise their power to secure the election of two named persons as directors of a company and to vote for their re-election afterwards. When the defendants subsequently tried to oppose the re-election of one of the two named persons, the court granted an injunction restraining them from voting in any way inconsistent with the agreement.

If the company is a party to a shareholders' agreement which affects the statutory obligation of the company, it may not be enforceable. In **Punt v Symons & Co Ltd** [1903] 2 Ch 506 it was held that a company could not contract out of the right to alter its articles. The provision in the shareholders' agreement which binds the company not to alter its articles is therefore not enforceable. Similarly, in **Russell v Northern Bank Development Corporation Ltd** [1992] BCLC 1016,[8] an agreement was entered into between the company and its shareholders which provided, *inter alia*, that no further share capital would be created or issued without the consent of all the parties. The board of directors proposed to increase the company's share capital. One of the shareholders objected to this and was successful in obtaining a declaration that the agreement was binding on his fellow shareholders. The House of Lords held that the company's agreement not to increase its share capital was invalid because it was contrary to s 121 of the Companies Act 1985 which allowed a company to increase its share capital. This agreement was therefore not binding on the *company* itself; however, an agreement *outside* the articles between shareholders as to how they would exercise their voting rights on a particular resolution was valid. It emphasised that the shareholders' agreement was of a personal nature and was not embodied in the articles.

The case of **Russell** (above) confirms the principle that a company cannot contract out of its statutory power under s 21 to alter its articles by a shareholder agreement. A different judicial approach was taken when dealing with the issue as to whether the company can contract out of statutory provisions by its articles.[9] In **Bushell v Faith** [1970] AC 1099, a weighted voting right was included in the articles whereby in the event of a resolution to remove a director that director's shares would carry three votes per share. This has the effect of preventing that director from being removed by an ordinary resolution (now under s 168, Companies Act 2006). The House of

[8]This is a House of Lords authority on the validity of a shareholders' agreement. You should have a good understanding of the judgment of this case.

[9]A consideration of the different judicial approach shows your sound knowledge of this legal issue and will gain you more marks.

[10]Your conclusion should echo the legal issues that arise in the question. A succinct conclusion will enhance your arguments and complete your answer.

Lords held that the article in question was not inconsistent with the statutory power which was silent on the allocation of voting rights for an ordinary resolution.

In conclusion, shareholders' agreements are more flexible and private, more difficult to change and easier to enforce than the articles of association.[10]

✓ Make your answer stand out

- Point out that not all the clauses in the articles can be altered by a special resolution in accordance with s 21. You can discuss the common law restrictions and the different requirements for the variation of class rights (s 630) and the entrenchment articles (s 22).
- Refer to academic debates on the enforcement of a shareholders' agreement such as: Sealy, L. 'Shareholders' agreements – an endorsement and a warning from the House of Lords' [1992] CLJ 437; Davenport, B. J. 'What did *Russell* v *Northern Bank Development Corporation Ltd* decide?' (1993) 109 LQR 553; Riley, C. A. 'Vetoes and voting agreements: some problems of consent and knowledge' (1993) 44 NILQ 34; Ferran, E. 'The decision of the House of Lords in *Russell* v *Northern Bank Development Corporation Ltd*' [1994] CLJ 343.

! Don't be tempted to...

- Provide an answer without detailed analysis of *Russell* v *Northern Bank Development Corporation Ltd* (1992). This is a very important case in relation to shareholders' agreements and must not be omitted in your answer.
- Give a narrative list of a comparison between the articles of association and shareholders' agreements. You should focus on the main differences which lie in their enforcement.

Directors' duties

How this topic may come up in exams

Directors' general duties which existed in common law rules and in equitable principles are codified in the Companies Act 2006. The codified duties are very popular exam topics and therefore essential for your revision. Each of the general duties in ss 170–177 can be assessed in an essay or problem question, either on its own or with other duties. Section 172, in particular, has received considerable academic attention with regard to the enlightened shareholder value. You may also need to consider the law on shareholder remedies in problem questions in relation to directors' breach of duties.

■ Attack the question

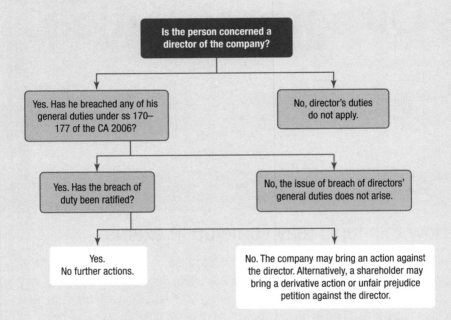

Is the person concerned a director of the company?

Yes. Has he breached any of his general duties under ss 170–177 of the CA 2006?

No, director's duties do not apply.

Yes. Has the breach of duty been ratified?

No, the issue of breach of directors' general duties does not arise.

Yes. No further actions.

No. The company may bring an action against the director. Alternatively, a shareholder may bring a derivative action or unfair prejudice petition against the director.

A printable version of this diagram plan is available from www.pearsoned.co.uk/lawexpressqa

🔖 Question 1

'The Company Law Review, in line with its objectives of maximising clarity and accessibility, recommended that the duties of directors should be codified by way of a statutory restatement ... the issue of restating directors' duties in statutory form caused considerable controversy and generated widespread debate.' (Dignam & Lowry, *Company Law*, 5th ed., (Oxford University Press 2009), p. 299)

Evaluate the above statements.

Answer plan

➡ Examine directors' general duties in ss 170–177 of the Companies Act 2006.

➡ Compare the codified duties with their equivalent common law duties.

➡ Discuss in detail the duty in s 172 which arguably has made one of the most significant changes in the CA 2006.

➡ Evaluate whether the codification of directors' duties has improved or clarified this area of law.

Diagram plan

Directors' duties at common law: fiduciary duties and the duty of care, skill and diligence

Compare and contrast

Directors' general duties: ss 170–177 of the Companies Act 2006

Assess the benefits and problems with regard to the codification of directors' duties

A printable version of this diagram plan is available from www.pearsoned.co.uk/lawexpressqa

Answer

[1]These opening sentences identify the key legal issues raised in the question and reassure the examiner that you clearly understand what is being asked in the question.

This question requires a discussion of the codification of directors' duties and an evaluation of whether it has clarified or improved this area of law. Although codification offers some advantages such as clarity and accessibility, it is argued that it has led to some uncertainties.[1]

A director is defined in s 250 as including 'any person occupying the position of a director, by whatever name called'. There are three categories of director: *de jure, de facto* and shadow directors (**Re Hydrodan (Corby) Ltd** [1994] BCC 161). All companies must have at least one director and public companies must have at least two (s 154). Directors owe their general duties to the company, not to its shareholders: s 170(1), **Percival v Wright** (1902) 2 Ch 421. They are considered as a company's trustees or agents and are in a fiduciary position in relation to the company: **Bristol and West Building Society v Mothew** [1998] Ch 1. Consequently, they must first and foremost act in good faith and in the best interests of the company. Directors also owe the duty of care and skill to the company at common law: **Re City Equitable Fire Insurance** [1925] Ch 407.[2]

[2]This shows your sound understanding of directors' fiduciary duties and common law duties prior to the CA 2006.

The Law Commission (Consultation Paper, 1998) considered that the complex law on directors' duties in equitable principles and at common law should be reformed and made simpler by a statutory form. It assessed the advantages of codification such as certainty and accessibility against its disadvantages such as loss of flexibility.[3] The duties are now codified in the CA 2006. Despite the codification, previous case law is still relevant to its application and interpretation because directors' general duties should be interpreted and applied in the same way as common law rules or equitable principles (s 170). The general duties in ss 170–177 are assessed by comparison with their corresponding common law rules.[4]

[3]The reference to the Law Commission Consultation Paper demonstrates your good understanding of the background of the codification of directors' duties. It will earn you more marks.

[4]This sentence sets a clear structure for the discussion of directors' duties in your answer.

Section 171 states that directors must act in accordance with the company's constitution and that they should only exercise their powers for the purposes for which they have been conferred. It codifies the common law duty to act for proper purposes as established in **Hogg v Cramphorn** [1967] Ch 254 and **Howard Smith Ltd v Ampol Petroleum** [1974] AC 821. Section 171 has made the law more accessible whilst maintaining the clarity of the common law.[5]

[5]This sentence goes beyond a descriptive account of s 171 and shows your critical analysis skills. It will add more credit to your answer.

Section 172 requires that a director act in the way he considers, in good faith, would be most likely to promote the success of the company for the benefit of its members as a whole. Directors must also have regard to the factors in the non-exhaustive list, such as the likely consequences of any decision in the long term, the interests of the company's employees, the company's business relationships with suppliers and customers, the impact on the community and environment, the reputation of the company and the need for the company to act fairly as between members. This duty is based on the common law duty to act *bona fide* in the interests of the company: **Re Smith & Fawcett** [1942] 1 All ER 542. It is subjective in nature in the sense that it is what a director considers, not what a court considers, would be most likely to promote the success of the company: **Bristol & West Building Society v Mothew** (above). Section 172 is much wider in scope than the previous case law; it introduces the enlightened shareholder value whereby the company should be run to generate maximum wealth for shareholders but also to take a properly balanced view of the wider implications of decisions over time.[6] Keay (2007) argues that s 172 is pivotal in providing guidance for directors in their activities and what a director should be aiming towards. The Law Society, however, criticises the fact that there is no indication in s 172 as to the meaning of the success of the company. This may lead to increased uncertainty because directors may have different interpretations. Moreover, the liabilities of directors seem to have been increased, which may deter people from taking up directorship.[7]

[6]This sentence compares s 172 with the common law rules. A discussion of the enlightened shareholder value is essential for an excellent understanding of s 172.

[7]The discussion of the problems of s 172 by reference to academic opinions makes your answer stand out.

A director is required under s 173 to exercise independent judgement. It clearly restates the principle that a director should not fetter his discretion as established in **Fulham Football Club and Others v Cabra Estates plc** [1994] 1 BCLC 363. Section 174 states that a director has a duty to exercise reasonable care, skill and diligence. It replaces the previous common law duties as established in **Dorchester Finance Co Ltd v Stebbing** [1989] BCLC 498 and **Re Barings plc** [2002] 1 BCLC 401. The subjective and objective tests at common law are also adopted.[8]

[8]If time permits, the dual tests for the levels of care, skill and diligence required in s 174 should be discussed in more detail.

Section 175 codifies the no-conflict and no secret profit rules at common law: **Cook v Deeks** [1916] 1 AC 554 and **Regal (Hastings) Ltd v Gulliver** [1942] 1 All ER 378. A director must avoid a situation in which he has, or can have, a direct or indirect interest that conflicts, or possibly may conflict, with the interests of the company. It applies in particular to the exploitation of any property, information or opportunity. This duty is not infringed if the matter has been effectively authorised by disinterested directors (s 175(4)).[9] A director must not accept a benefit from a third party conferred by reason of him being a director (s 176). He must also

[9]The authorisation is an essential part of s 175 and should not be omitted in your answer.

declare the nature and extent of any interest to other directors, if he is in any way interested in a proposed transaction or arrangement with the company (s 177). It codifies the self-dealing rules as established in **Bentinck v Fenn** (1887) 12 App Cas 652 and **Aberdeen Railway Ltd v Blaikie** (1854) 1 Macq 461.

The codification of directors' duties has clarified the complex rules at common law and made it easier for shareholders to detect and redress directors' breach of these duties. Significant problems, however, still exist. The duty to promote the success of the company, for example, is drafted in vague and ill-defined language. Moreover, a link to directors' duties at common law remains (s 170(4)) and there is likely to be a period of uncertainty for the courts during which they will need to decide how to apply and interpret the new law. The Law Society has expressed concerns that it may result in new uncertainty, increased costs and legal bureaucracy. Despite all these initial concerns, it is argued that the codification, in overall terms, does not change the essential nature of directors' general duties and it is most likely to prove beneficial in the long run because of its improved clarity and accessibility.[10]

[10]The conclusion should directly address the question which requires a critical evaluation of a codification of directors' duties. It should also clearly summarise your main arguments on the concerns and benefits of the codification.

 Make your answer stand out

- Consider in more detail the changes introduced by s 172.
- Discuss the duty in s 182 in respect of an existing transaction with the company.
- Evaluate whether the duty of disclosure under s 177 is more onerous than before.
- Discuss the rules in relation to ratification in s 239 and compare them with those at common law.
- Further reading on the codification of directors' duties: Law Commission Consultation Paper (No. 153), *Company Directors: Regulating Conflicts of Interests and Formulating a Statement of Duties*; Attenborough, D. 'The Company Law Reform Bill: an analysis of directors' duties and the objective of the company' (2006) 27 *Company Lawyer* 162.

> **!** **Don't be tempted to...**
>
> ■ Simply describe directors' duties at common law and then the codified duties. You
> should discuss each of the codified duties by comparing with its correspondence at
> common law.
>
> ■ Provide an answer without reference to case law. You should be aware that the case
> law is still relevant in the interpretation and application of the codified duties.
>
> ■ Simply describe the duties without any critical analysis. You must evaluate the strength
> of the codified duties and the problems of codification.

? Question 2

Ben, Harry and Samuel are all directors of Summer T-shirts Ltd, which designs and sells
T-shirts. They hold 55%, 15% and 30% of the company's shares respectively. The company's
share capital consists of 1,000 ordinary shares.

The articles of association, which otherwise follow the Model Articles for private companies
limited by shares, contain the provision that: 'The directors have unrestricted power to
allot shares.' Ben and Harry did not get along well with Samuel and they intended to
dilute Samuel's shareholding so that Samuel would not have the power to block a special
resolution at shareholder meetings. Ben and Harry only allotted to their friend Emily 500
ordinary shares, which Samuel was also interested in purchasing.

Ben and Harry recently have signed a contract with Hien Ltd, a Vietnamese company
which supplies cotton T-shirts. They know that Hien Ltd has a reputation for poor industrial
relations and suspect that the clothes are made of materials which are not environmentally
friendly. Samuel is unhappy about this but Ben and Harry insist that the T-shirts are cheap
and their only concern is to maximise the company's profits.

Advise Samuel as to whether Ben and Harry have breached any of their general duties as
directors in the Companies Act 2006.

Answer plan

→ Assess whether Ben and Harry breached their duties in s 171 in relation to the
allotment of shares.

→ Discuss whether Ben and Harry breached their duties in s 172 in relation to the
contract with Hien Ltd.

Diagram plan

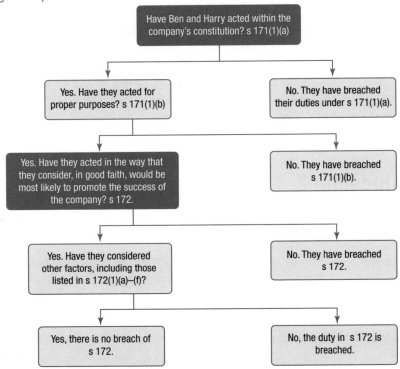

A printable version of this diagram plan is available from www.pearsoned.co.uk/lawexpressqa

Answer

[1]You should identify the key legal issues in the introduction so that your examiners know that you are able to understand the context of the subject and engage with the question.

The key legal issues here are whether Ben and Harry breached their general duties as directors of Summer T-shirts Ltd when they allotted shares only to Emily and when they signed the contract with Hien Ltd.[1] Directors' duties at common law and in equitable principles are now codified in ss 170–177, Companies Act 2006. Despite the codification, previous case law is still relevant to its application and interpretation (s 170). Directors owe their general duties to the company, not to its shareholders: **Percival v Wright** [1902] 2 Ch 421.

[2]Adopt a clear structure by using headings in your answer.

Allotment of shares[2]

Where a private company has only one class of shares, the directors may exercise any power of the company to allot shares of that

³Section 550 is the
fundamental basis of your
discussion in relation to the
allotment of shares. These
sentences demonstrate
your good knowledge on the
subject of share capital.

class (s 550). Directors in a private company have authority to allot shares if they are authorised to do so by the articles of association or an ordinary resolution.³ Summer T-shirts Ltd has only one class of shares and its articles grant directors unrestricted power to allot shares. As Ben and Harry hold 70% of the company's shares, either a board decision which requires a majority voting or an ordinary resolution at a shareholder meeting which requires a simple majority (s 282) can be passed.

It should be noted, however, that Samuel may have pre-emption rights. Unless such rights are excluded or disapplied, the existing shareholders must be offered new shares before they are offered to people outside the company (s 561). In this way, a shareholder can protect his proportion of the total equity of a company. If they are not excluded or disapplied in the company's articles, Samuel's pre-emption rights have been infringed and he may bring an unfair prejudice petition under s 994 against the company's failure to allot shares on a rights basis: **Re a Company (No. 005134 of 1986), ex p Harries** [1989] BCLC 383.⁴

⁴This paragraph examines
the pre-emption rights and
the possible remedies for
an infringement of such
rights. It shows your wider
understanding of company
law beyond directors'
duties and will impress your
examiners.

It is essential to discuss whether Ben and Harry have breached their duties in relation to the allotment of shares. A director must act in accordance with the company's constitution and only exercise powers for the purposes for which they are conferred (s 171). Section 171 restates the proper purposes rule at common law that directors should only exercise their powers for a proper purpose and not for any collateral purpose: **Hogg v Cramphorn** [1967] Ch 254.⁵

⁵The reference to previous
case law is essential for
the discussion of s 171
because it still applies in the
interpretation and application
of the codified duty.

Ben and Harry acted in accordance with the company's constitution in relation to the allotment of shares; however, it is important to examine whether they exercised this power for an improper purpose. In **Howard Smith Ltd v Ampol Petroleum** [1974] AC 821 directors abused their fiduciary powers by authorising the issue of shares for the purpose of altering the voting power in the company and such issue was held invalid. Lord Wilberforce established the four-step test in order to decide whether the actual exercise was proper. First, construe the article conferring the power in order to ascertain the nature of the power and its limits. Here it refers to the interpretation of the provision in the articles which grants directors unrestricted power to allot shares. Secondly, determine the substantial purpose(s) for which this power should be exercised. The substantial purpose for allotting shares in Summer T-Shirts Ltd should be to increase the company's share capital and promote the company's commercial interests. Thirdly, identify the substantial purpose(s) for which the power was actually excised. Ben and Harry exercised the power to manipulate share capital and dilute Samuel's shareholding. Finally, compare the actual purpose with the permissible purposes for the exercise of that power. By diluting Samuel's shareholding instead of promoting the company's interests, Ben and Harry did not exercise the power for proper purposes and therefore the allotment was invalid.[6] Samuel could also argue that Ben and Harry breached their duties in s 172 because they did not act in good faith or for the best interests of the company with regard to the allotment of shares.[7]

[6]The application of the four-step test demonstrates your ability to apply the relevant law to the problem question.

[7]The reference to s 172 will earn you more marks as it shows your excellent understanding of directors' duties.

The contract with Hien Ltd

Section 172 requires that a director act in the way he considers, in good faith, would be most likely to promote the success of the company for the benefit of its members as a whole. In doing so, directors must have regard to a number of factors, such as the likely consequences of any decision in the long term, the company's business relationships with suppliers and customers, the impact on the community and environment and the reputation of the company. This duty is based on the pre-existing duty to act *bona fide* in the interests of the company (**Re Smith & Fawcett** [1942] 1 All ER 542). It is very difficult to prove a breach of this duty because the test for this duty is subjective: **Regentcrest plc v Cohen** [2001] 2 BCLC 80. A director must act in the way he considers, not what a court may consider, would be most likely to promote the success of the company. This reflects the traditional concern that the courts must not get involved in reviewing the exercise of business judgement by directors: **Carlen v Drury** (1812) 1 Ves & B 154. Ben and Harry could argue that they acted in the way they believed would promote the success of the company by dealing with Hien Ltd. There are, however, some limits to this subjective test at common law. In **Charterbridge Corp Ltd v Lloyds Bank Ltd** [1970] Ch 62, an objective test was introduced where the court considered whether an intelligent and honest director could in the whole of the circumstances reasonably believe the transaction to be for the benefit of the company. This objective test is not codified in s 172 and it is unclear whether the courts, in interpreting s 172, will consider whether an

[8]This sentences shows that you are aware of the objective element at common law and more importantly, the uncertainties in its application in s 172. The latter will gain you more marks.

[9]This paragraph discusses the list of factors in s 172 and applies it to the problem question. Some students only focus on the requirements of 'good faith' and 'for the success of the company' in s 172. A consideration of the list of factors is often omitted.

intelligent and honest director would believe the transaction is for the benefit of the company.[8]

Directors must also have regard to the non-exhaustive list of factors in s 172(1)(a)–(f), which reflects the enlightened shareholder value as opposed to the traditional theory of shareholder primacy. Although Ben and Harry may honestly believe that the contract is in the financial interests of the company, it appears that they have not considered the factors listed in s 172, in particular, the impact on the community and environment as well as the reputation of the company. It is therefore argued that they breached their duties in s 172, unless they can prove otherwise that they have considered these factors in reaching their decisions.[9]

✓ Make your answer stand out

- Briefly discuss the controversial debates surrounding s 172 in relation to the enlightened shareholder value and those factors listed in s 172(1). As this is a problem question, a detailed discussion of these issues, however, is not appropriate.

- Assess whether the breach of duties can be ratified at general meeting (s 239).

- Evaluate the legal actions which Samuel can bring against the breach of duties by Ben and Harry, such as the derivative action (ss 260–264) and unfair prejudice petition (s 994).

! Don't be tempted to...

- Describe all of the directors' duties. You should only discuss those duties which are relevant to this problem question.

- Ignore the common law on directors' duties. Despite codification, the common law is still relevant in the application and interpretation of the statutory duties.

- Discuss s 172 without reference to *Charterbridge Corp Ltd* v *Lloyds Bank Ltd* [1970] Ch 62. This is an important case as it may place some restrictions on the subjective test in s 172.

- Discuss s 171 without reference to the four-step test established in *Howard Smith Ltd* v *Ampol Petroleum* [1974] AC 821.

Question 3

'Section 172 of the Companies Act 2006 has introduced into English company law the concept of enlightened shareholder value. It appears to be a dramatic shift from the common law position.'

Critically discuss the above statement. Has the English company law adopted the stakeholder theory?

Answer plan

→ Discuss directors' duty in s 172 by making a comparison with the previous common law duty.

→ Analyse the corporate governance issues, in particular, the shareholder primacy and stakeholder theories.

→ Evaluate the enlightened shareholder value which is introduced by s 172.

→ Conclude whether the stakeholder theory has been adopted in English company law.

Diagram plan

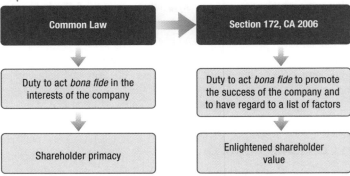

A printable version of this diagram plan is available from www.pearsoned.co.uk/lawexpressqa

Answer

A director must act in a way he considers, in good faith, would be most likely to promote the success of the company for the benefit of its members as a whole (s 172). In doing so, he is obliged to have specific regard, among other matters, to the interests of company's employees, the impact of the company's operations on the community and the environment, and the need to act fairly between members of the company. Section 172 not only codifies the

[1]These two sentences outline
the main arguments and
reassure the examiner that
you know exactly what the
question is about in terms of
its subject content.

common law duty to act *bona fide* in what the director considers –
not what a court may consider – is in the interests of the company
(**Re Smith & Fawcett Ltd** [1942] 1 All ER 542) but also introduces
the new concept of enlightened shareholder value. It is argued that
the English company law has moved closer to, but has not firmly
adopted, the stakeholder theory.[1]

The test in s 172 remains subjective because what constitutes
the success of the company depends on the director's good faith
judgement. It appears that there are no objective criteria in s 172
against which the actions of directors can be assessed and therefore,
it is very difficult to prove a breach of this duty. At common law,
nevertheless, objective considerations were introduced by the courts
to supplement the subjective test.[2] In **Charterbridge Corp Ltd v
Lloyds Bank Ltd** [1970] Ch 62, the courts considered whether
an intelligent and honest director could in the whole of the circumstances reasonably believe the transaction to be for the benefit of the
company. Section 172 makes no reference to this objective consideration; however, given the significant role of common law rules in
the interpretation and application of the codified duties (s 170(3) and
(4)), Keay (2007) incisively argues that it is most likely that the courts
would consider the objective test in assessing directors' actions.[3]

There are many theories as to in whose interests the company should
be run. The traditional approach in the United Kingdom is the shareholder value principle (or shareholder primacy), whereby a company
should be run for the wealth maximisation of its shareholders above
those of other parties such as customers and suppliers. Directors
are under a duty to act in the interests of the company (**Percival v
Wright** [1902] 2 Ch 421), which are interpreted as the best interests
of present and future shareholders (**Hutton v West Cork Railway
Company** (1883) LR 23 Ch D 654). The shareholder value theory
reflects the view that shareholders are the owners of the company
and bear the residual risks.[4]

The stakeholder theory (or the pluralist approach), by contrast,
emphasises the interests of stakeholders, who can affect or be
affected by a company's activities. It requires that directors manage
the company for the benefit of all the stakeholders. The stakeholder
theory was considered in the Company Law Review Steering Group
(*The Strategic Framework*, 1999) but is not adopted in the CA 2006,

[2]The objective test at
common law is often ignored
by students. A discussion
of this test by reference to
case law shows your sound
understanding and will make
your answer stand out.

[3]The reference to academic
opinion on the uncertainties of
the objective test will gain you
more marks because it goes
beyond a pure description of
s 172 and the relevant case
law.

[4]The traditional shareholder
value approach is an essential
part of your answer because,
without it, you cannot
demonstrate how s 172 is
different from the traditional
approach.

[5] The reference to the CLRSG report shows your excellent knowledge of this topic. It adds more credit to your answer.

[6] You should explain clearly what is meant by the enlightened shareholder value approach.

[7] The differences between this new approach and the shareholder/stakeholder value are very important here because they directly address the issues raised in the essay question.

[8] These sentences examine the ambiguities in the application of s 172 and the difficulties in balancing the various interests of stakeholders. They refer back to the question in relation to the enlightened shareholder value.

mainly due to the difficulties faced by directors in balancing the interests of different groups and the concerns in enforcing these duties.[5]

The enlightened shareholder value is adopted as an alternative approach, as it is perceived to be able to better achieve wealth generation and competitiveness for the benefit of all. The non-exhaustive list in s 172(1) which a director has to consider in making decisions seeks to capture this new approach. A company should be run to generate maximum wealth for shareholders and at the same time directors should take a properly balanced view of the implications of decisions over time and foster effective relationships with employees, customers and suppliers, and in the wider community.[6] Despite the introduction of the non-exhaustive list, it is clear that shareholder primacy is still dominant in the United Kingdom because a director must act to promote the success of the company for the interests of members as a whole. Kiarie (2006) is of the similar view that the enlightened shareholder value appears a compromise between the shareholder primacy and stakeholder theory by maintaining the primacy of shareholders' interests whilst considering other stakeholders' interests.[7]

Section 172 provides, for the first time, some guidance on directors' objectives in conducting the company's affairs. It is beneficial in the wider context and in the long term; however, there are two inherent problems. First, the long list of factors may extend the administrative process and lengthen the time the board takes to make decisions because directors must do all they reasonably can to have regard to these factors. It is unclear which criteria should be used to assess objectively whether the action of the directors has led to the success of the company.[8] Attenborough (2006) suggests that s 172 grants directors discretion to give their own interpretations of success. This may lead to increased uncertainty because directors may have different interpretations of the meaning of success. Moreover, the factors listed in s 172 are not exhaustive and other relevant factors should also be taken into account. It is unclear whether a director would be in breach of this duty if he considered all the factors, except the one relating to the environment. It is also problematic when there is a conflict between two or more of the factors, for example, if a decision benefits the employees but is detrimental to the community or the environment.

[9]The lack of enforcement by stakeholders further strengthens the argument that the stakeholder theory is not adopted in English company law. This is often omitted in students' answers.

Secondly, while shareholders may bring a derivative action against directors for breach of duties (ss 260–264), there is a lack of procedure for other stakeholders such as employees or the community to hold directors accountable if the directors fail to have regard to their interests set out in s 172(1).[9] As derivative actions are only available to *members* of the company (s 260), it is most likely that directors will continue to exercise their power to promote the success of the company for the benefit of its members. As rightly observed in Boyle & Birds (2007, p. 618), the effect of s 172 is more likely to be 'educational rather than in any sense restrictive'.

[10]The conclusion relates back to the question on the enlightened shareholder value and reinforces your argument that the stakeholder theory is not firmly adopted in the United Kingdom.

It can be concluded that s 172 aims to strike a delicate balance between the traditional shareholder value and the stakeholder approach. Although directors are required to consider various stakeholder interests in the light of enlightened shareholder value, it is argued that the stakeholder theory has not been adopted in English company law as shareholders' interests are still paramount in directors' decision-making.[10]

 Make your answer stand out

- Point out that shareholders may challenge directors' breach of duties by bringing an unfair prejudice petition according to s 994, CA 2006.

- In relation to the test for the duty to act in good faith in s 172, consider *Fulham Football Club* v *Cabra Estates plc* [1992] BCLC 863 and *Re Southern Counties Fresh Foods Ltd* [2008] All ER (D) 195 (Nov).

- Discuss the shareholder theory, stakeholder theory and enlightened shareholder value by reference to more academic opinions, in particular Keay, A. R. 'Enlightened shareholder value, the reform of the duties of company directors and the corporate objective' [2006] LMCLQ 335 and Yap, J. L. 'Considering the Enlightened Shareholder Value Principle' (2010) 31 *Company Lawyer* 35.

> ## ❗ Don't be tempted to...
>
> ■ Give a narrative account of s 172 and the previous duty at common law. Although this shows some understanding of the relevant law, it is far from sufficient. You need to analyse the changes introduced in s 172 in relation to the enlightened shareholder value.
>
> ■ Provide an answer without reference to academic opinions. As there is very little case law on s 172, it is essential to engage in a wide range of academic debates in your answer.
>
> ■ Describe the seven main duties of directors in ss 170–177, CA 2006. This is greatly discouraged; your answer should focus on the key issues with regard to s 172 and the enlightened shareholder value.

📰 Question 4

'Though the standard expected is now clearly identified [in s 174, Companies Act 2006], the content of this duty [of care and skill] is still under development by the courts and it is not always easy to draw from the cases a comprehensive and coherent statement of what is required of directors.' (Hannigan, *Company Law*, 2nd ed., (Oxford University Press, 2009), p. 224)

In the light of the above statement, analyse the development of director's duty of care, skill and diligence.

Answer plan

→ Examine the development of the duty of care and skill at common law in three main aspects:

– the required standards;

– directors' continuous attention of the company's affairs; and

– the delegation of power.

→ Discuss the duty of care, skill and diligence in s 174 and the dual objective and subjective standards.

→ Evaluate the problems associated with the duty in s 174.

Diagram plan

The common law duty of care, skill and diligence $\Rightarrow$ The codified duty in s 174, CA 2006 $\Rightarrow$ The problems associated with s 174 and its future reforms

A printable version of this diagram plan is available from www.pearsoned.co.uk/lawexpressqa

Answer

The duty of care, skill and diligence has evolved at common law over a long period of time and it is now stated in s 174, Companies Act 2006. Despite the codification, it is correctly argued that there is little guidance as to the content of this duty in terms of what is expected of a reasonably diligent director in his participation in the conduct of the company's affairs.[1]

[1]You should identify the key legal issues in the introduction so that the examiner knows where you are going with your answer.

Directors are often granted wide power to manage the company's business according to the general management clause[2] in the Model Articles of Association (Art 3). Various duties are therefore imposed on directors to curb their potential abuse of power. Before the codification of directors' duties, directors owed to the company fiduciary duties and the duty of care and skill at common law: **Percival v Wright** [1902] 2 Ch 421. The distinction between these two types of duties is explained by Millett LJ in **Bristol & West Building Society v Mothew** [1996] 4 All ER 698. The essence of fiduciary duties is loyalty and a breach of them attracts equitable remedies; whilst the duty of care and skill is related to competence and the remedy is compensation to the company for the harm caused.[3]

[2]The general management clause in the Model Articles shows your good understanding of directors' wide-ranging power.

[3]These two sentences explore the differences between the two types of duties. They demonstrate your sound understanding of the wider context of directors' duties and will gain you more marks.

A director must exercise reasonable care, skill and diligence (s 174). This means the care, skill and diligence that would be exercised by a reasonably diligent person with the general knowledge, skill and experience that may reasonably be expected of a person carrying out the functions carried out by the director in relation to the company (s 174(2)(a)), and the general knowledge, skill and experience that the director has (s 174(2)(b)).[4] Section 174(2)(a) sets an objective minimum standard of a reasonably diligent person who has taken on the office of director, taking into account of the functions undertaken. Section 174(2)(b) sets a subjective standard in relation to the personal attributes of the director, which may raise the objective minimum standard. Section

[4]If you cannot remember this long provision during an exam, try to summarise it, for example, by stating that 'the standards required are the general knowledge, skill and experience that may reasonably be expected of a person and that the director actually has'.

[5] The reference to the Insolvency Act 1986 demonstrates your good knowledge of the duty of care, skill and diligence. It will help you gain more marks.

[6] This sentence ties your answer back to the question with regard to the development of the duty at common law.

[7] The reference to an early case shows the low standard required of directors and forms the starting point of your discussion of the development of this duty.

[8] This sentence sets a clear structure for the analysis that follows.

[9] These sentences demonstrate your analytical skills by assessing the subjective approach. It will make your answer stand out.

174 is closely modelled on s 214(4) of the Insolvency Act 1986, which defines negligent conduct for the purposes of wrongful trading.[5] The current standards of care, skill and diligence adopted in s 174 are the results of its continual development at common law over 100 years.[6]

Some early decisions in the nineteenth century indicated that the courts generally had low expectations of the standard of care to be expected of directors. In **Re Cardiff Savings Bank, Marquis of Bute's case** [1892] 2 Ch 100, the director of a bank attended only one board meeting in 38 years. It was held that he did not share responsibility for the bank's heavy loss caused by the irregular conduct of its trustees and managers. Stirling J formulated the intermittent theory of directors' duties where a director must exercise care at the meetings at which he was actually present, but owed no duty to attend any specific meeting.[7]

In **Re City Equitable Fire Insurance Co Ltd** [1925] Ch 407 Romer J reviewed earlier authorities and summarised the principles for the director's duty of care in three aspects: the required standards, directors' continuous attention of the company's affairs and the delegation of power.[8] First, a director need not exhibit in the performance of his duties a greater degree of skill than might reasonably be expected of a person of his knowledge and experience. Second, a director was not bound to give continuous attention to the affairs of his company. His duties were of an intermittent nature and he was not bound to attend all meetings. Third, all duties, with regard to the exigencies of business and the articles of association, might properly be left to some other official. A director was, in the absence of grounds for suspicion, justified in trusting that official to perform such duties honestly. This judgment therefore set a pure subjective standard test and no minimal standard of competence was required. This highly subjective approach caused many problems because the law required very little from a director who had no experience or knew nothing. This judicial lenience might have contributed to the corporate governance scandals of the 1980s.[9]

The dual objective and subjective tests in s 214(4) of the Insolvency Act 1986 were accepted and applied in **Norman v Theodore Goddard** [1991] BCLC 1028 and **Re D'Jan of London Ltd** [1994] 1 BCLC 561. In **Re D'Jan**, it was held that a director was negligent for signing an insurance proposal without checking it. The information provided in the form was incorrect and the insurance company refused to pay when the company's premises were burnt down. These tests are far more rigorous than the initial subjective test and they are effectively enacted in s 174.[10]

With regard to director's continuous attention and the delegation of power, the modern authority has moved away from the judgments in **Re City Equitable Fire Insurance Co Ltd**. In **Re Barings plc (No. 5)** [2000] 1 BCLC 523 a number of senior directors failed to supervise a rogue trader within the bank, which resulted in a loss of £827 million and the collapse of the bank. The directors were found to be unfit and disqualified. It was held that directors, both collectively and individually, had a continuing duty to acquire and maintain a sufficient knowledge of the company's business to enable them to discharge their duties. Whilst directors, subject to the articles of association, are entitled to delegate particular functions to those below them in the management chain and to trust their competence and integrity to a reasonable extent, the delegation of power does not absolve a director from the duty to supervise the discharge of the delegated functions.[11]

Although little was expected of directors in terms of care and skill in the past, more recent cases suggest a movement towards an objective standard of care and the application of the tests in s 214 of the Insolvency Act 1986. Section 174 consolidates the previous development of this duty at common law and introduces an objective standard of care which could be enhanced by the actual knowledge, skill and experience of a particular director. As Gower & Davies (2008, p. 494) incisively argue, the move from a subjective to an objective test will give the courts a greater role in defining the functions of the board while trying to avoid the use of hindsight.[12] Further development of case law may help clarify the exact content of the duty of care, skill and diligence.[13]

✓ **Make your answer stand out**

- Discuss the enforcement of a breach of duty of care and skill. The higher standard of the duty of care and the broader scope of derivative actions may open the litigation floodgates against directors.

- Consider the influence of ss 6–9 of the Company Directors Disqualification Act 1986 on the standards of directors' conduct by reference to *Bishopsgate Investment Management Ltd* v *Maxwell (No. 2)* [1994] 1 All ER 261.

- Evaluate the problems of the current standards required for directors in s 174 by reference to academic opinions, in particular, Finch, V. 'Company directors: who cares about skill and care?' (1992) 55 MLR 179 and Riley, C. A. 'The company director's duty of care and skill: the case for an onerous but subjective standard' (1999) 62 MLR 697.

! **Don't be tempted to...**

- Get confused with the objective test and the subjective one in s 174(1). Make sure you clearly understand what each test means.

- List all directors' duties in ss 170–177 of the Companies Act 2006. Some students tend to have a slow and lengthy introduction by describing all the codified duties. Although they show your general knowledge of directors' duties, they add very little to your answer.

- Simply provide the names of particular cases without explaining the key legal principles. In order to show your accurate understanding, you must discuss the relevant judgments in detail.

- Rely solely or heavily on the old authority – *Re City Equitable Life Insurance Co Ltd* [1925] Ch 407 – which no longer represents good law. It is important to discuss the modern rules such as those laid down in *Re Barings plc (No. 5)* [2000] 1 BCLC 523.

? **Question 5**

Allen, Grant and Jordan are all shareholders and directors of Spring Garden Ltd. It recently rejected a supply contract when Jordan, who was in charge of purchasing, convinced the board that the product was not suitable for the company's current market. A week later, Jordan secretly took up the contract in his personal capacity without informing the company and made a huge profit from it. When challenged by Allen and Grant, Jordan argued that the company had not lost out because it would not have been able to fulfil the contract anyway.

Advise Allen and Grant as to whether Jordan breached any of his duties as a director in Spring Garden Ltd.

Answer plan

→ Examine whether Jordan has breached his duty in s 175 by secretly taking up the contract.

→ Discuss the possibility of authorisation of the conflict of interests (s 175).

→ Evaluate whether Jordan breached his duty in s 172.

→ Analyse the possibility of ratification of Jordan's breach of duties (s 239).

Diagram plan

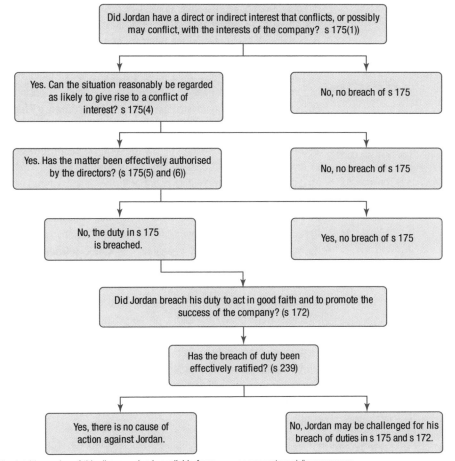

A printable version of this diagram plan is available from www.pearsoned.co.uk/lawexpressqa

Answer

[1] The introduction identifies the key legal issues and it shows where you are going with the answer.

The legal issue here is whether Jordan, as a director, has breached his duties when he secretly took up a contract which had been rejected by the company.[1] Directors' general duties are codified in ss 170–177 of the Companies Act 2006; nevertheless, the previous case law and equitable principles are still relevant in their application and interpretation (s 170(4)).[2] As established in **Percival v Wright** [1902] 2 Ch 421, directors owe their general duties to the company (s 170(1)).

[2] This sentence highlights your clear knowledge of the codification of directors' duties and the relevance of previous case law.

A director must 'avoid a situation in which he has, or can have, a direct or indirect interest that conflicts, or possibly may conflict with the interests of the company' (s 175). It covers both actual and potential conflicts[3] between the interests of a director and those of the company. The phrase 'possible' is interpreted by Lord Upjohn as 'whether a reasonable man looking at the relevant factors and circumstances would think that there is a real sensible possibility of conflict' with the interests of the company (**Boardman v Phipps** [1966] 3 All ER 721).

[3] Note here that the potential conflicts of interests are also covered in s 175. Some students are not aware of this specific point.

Section 175 codifies the no-conflict rule and no secret profit rule at common law. In **Aberdeen Rly Co v Blaikie Bros** (1854) 1 Macq 461,[4] the chairman of its board of the company entered into a contract for the purchase of equipment with a partnership of which he was the managing partner. The company was entitled to set aside the contract and the director was held to account for any profit which he made on the conflicted transaction. In **Cook v Deeks** [1916] 1 AC 554 two directors diverted a contract in which the company was interested to another company which they had formed. It was held that the contract in equity belonged to the company and the directors were bound to hold it on behalf of the company. There was a clear conflict between their personal interests in securing the contract and their duty to secure it for the company. It appears that Jordan breached his duty under s 175, as it was very likely that his personal interests conflicted with the interests of the company when he convinced the board of the unsuitable product but took up the contract a few days later.[5]

[4] The case law here supports your discussion of the no-conflict rule at common law and will gain you more marks.

[5] Apply the relevant case law to the question scenario.

[6] This sentence refers back to the question and helps to move your answer to the next legal issue.

Jordan argued that the company had rejected the contract and therefore had not lost out.[6] This would not relieve him from the breach of s 175 which applies to 'the exploitation of any property, information or opportunity' and 'it is immaterial whether the company could take advantage of the property, information or opportunity' (s 175(2)). In **Regal (Hastings) Ltd v Gulliver** [1942] 1 All ER 378[7] the company could not finance the purchase of additional cinemas. Directors put up some capital for the purchase and later profited personally on the sale of the shares. The House of Lords held that these directors should return the profits to the company as they obtained their profits by reason and in the course of the execution of their office as directors. It made no difference whether the company could have taken up the opportunity or not. Similarly, a strict approach was taken in **Industrial Development Consultants Ltd v Cooley** [1972] 2 All ER 162.[8] Cooley was a managing director of IDC and was actively involved in negotiations with the Eastern Gas Board (EGB) to secure certain construction contracts for IDC. It became clear that EGB was not prepared to contract with IDC. One year later, Cooley resigned from IDC and took the same contracts offered by EGB. It was held that Cooley breached the no secret profit rule and was liable to account as information came to him while he was a managing director of the company. It is therefore reasonable to conclude that Jordan should be held accountable for the profits he made by taking advantage of the information he obtained in the course of being a director of Spring Garden Ltd.

The duty to avoid conflicts of interest is not infringed in either of the following two situations (s 175(4)).[9] First, if the situation cannot reasonably be regarded as likely to give rise to a conflict of interest (s 175(4)(a)).[10] Jordan's situation has clearly given rise to a conflict of interest because he made a personal profit out of the contract. Secondly, this duty is not infringed if it has been effectively authorised by disinterested directors (s 175(4)(b)). In a private company, authorisation may be given by the directors if nothing in the company's constitution invalidates such authorisation (s 175(5)). Authorisation is only effective when the following two conditions are met (s 175(6)): first, the quorum requirement at the meeting is met without counting the director in question or any other interested director; secondly, the matter was agreed to without the votes of these directors or would have been agreed to if their votes had not been counted. It appears that Jordan's conflict of interest was not authorised by the board. Even if Jordan intended to do so at a board

[7]This case adds more credit to your answer because it was decided by the House of Lords.

[8]This sentence links the discussion of these two cases together. The phrase 'strict approach' shows your analytical skills and gains you more marks.

[9]The law on effective authorisation is a significant aspect of s 175 and should be discussed in detail.

[10]Students often forget to discuss this exception in s 175(4)(a). Although it is straightforward and simple, you will lose some marks if it is not included in your answer.

meeting, authorisation would not be effective because he could not be counted towards the quorum and his votes would not be valid. It also seems unlikely that Allen and Grant would agree to authorise it.

Moreover, Allen and Grant may claim that Jordan breached his duty in s 172 to promote the success of the company; however, Jordan may argue that he acted in good faith and in the way he considered would be most likely to promote the success of the company for the benefit of its members as a whole. It is therefore very difficult for Allen and Grant to prove Jordan's breach of s 172 because of the subjective nature of this duty.[11]

[11]The discussion of its subjective nature adds more credit to your answer because it extends beyond a descriptive account of the duty in s 172.

Jordan, who is also a shareholder, might try to vote to ratify his breach of duty at a general meeting. The resolution for ratification can only be passed if the necessary majority is obtained disregarding votes in favour of the resolution by the director and any member connected with him (s 239). It is unclear whether Jordan holds a majority of the company's shares. Even if he does, an effective resolution to ratify his misconduct is unlikely to pass as his votes would have been disregarded.[12] The consequences of breach of general duties are the same as would apply if the corresponding common law rule or equitable principle applied (s 178). As he has breached his duty under s 175 and the chance of ratifying this misconduct appears very slim, Jordan will be held liable to return all the profits he made from the contract to the company.[13]

[12]The evaluation of the possibility of ratification goes beyond a simple description of directors' duties. It will make your answer stand out.

[13]Your conclusion should provide specific advice to Allen and Grant in relation to Jordan's breach of duties.

 Make your answer stand out

- Discuss other important cases on directors' duties in s 175, in particular, *Bhullar* v *Bhullar* [2003] 2 BCLC 241; *Item Software (UK) Ltd* v *Fassihi* [2005] 2 BCLC 91; *Gencor ACP Ltd* v *Dalby* [2000] 2 BCLC 734.

- Make reference to academic opinions on the director's duty to avoid conflicts of interest, such as Prentice D. and Payne, J. 'The corporate opportunity doctrine' (2004) 120 LQR 198 and Lowry, J. 'Judicial pragmatism: directors' duties and post-resignation conflicts of duty' [2008] JBL 83.

- Provide a list of directors' duties without applying them to the question. You should focus on the relevant duties and discuss them by reference to case law.

- Jump to conclusions. You need to examine the situations and analyse each of the legal issues in full.

- Fail to discuss authorisation and ratification. It is important to note that there would be no cause of action against a director if his breach of duties has been authorised or ratified.

Question 6

'Traditionally the courts have taken a strict approach to the no-conflict and no-profit rules at common law. These rules are relaxed in the Companies Act 2006 with respect to the authorisation and ratification of a director's conflicts of interest.'

Evaluate the above statements.

Answer plan

→ Analyse the no-conflict and no-profit rules at common law and the strict judicial approach.

→ Examine the duty to avoid conflicts of interest in s 175 and the requirements for authorisation.

→ Discuss the issue in relation to ratification of directors' breach of duties in s 239.

→ Conclude whether these duties have been relaxed and if so, what potential problems will arise.

Diagram plan

The no-conflict and no-profit rules at common law → s 175, Companies Act 2006 → Authorisation → Ratification

A printable version of this diagram plan is available from www.pearsoned.co.uk/lawexpressqa

Answer

Directors were under the duties to avoid conflicts of interests (no-conflict rule) and not to make secret profits from their positions (no secret profit rule) at common law. The courts traditionally have taken a strict approach in applying these rules. In **Bray v Ford**

[1896] AC 44, Lord Herschell held that 'a person in a fiduciary position ... is not ... entitled to make a profit; he is not allowed to put himself in a position where his interest and duty conflict'. This approach aims to prevent directors from pursuing their own interests at the expense of their company. It also helps reduce the company's agency costs in monitoring the conduct of its directors (Grantham, 2003). Business activities, however, may be stifled if onerous requirements are imposed on directors. A flexible approach needs to be developed to suit the needs of modern businesses.[1]

[1] These sentences outline the main arguments. They also demonstrate your critical analysis of the statement by exploring the reasons behind the different approaches.

The no-conflict and no-profit rules are now codified in the Companies Act 2006. Section 175(1) provides that a director must 'avoid a situation in which he has, or can have, a direct or indirect interest that conflicts, or possibly may conflict with the interests of the company'. This provision replaced the no-conflict rule where a director is liable to account for any profits made personally if his interests conflict with those of the companies. Its scope is broad in the sense that it covers not only actual conflict but also the possibility of conflict between the interests of a director and the interests of the company: **Boardman v Phipps** [1966] 3 All ER 721.[2] Section 175 also applies to the exploitation of any property, information or opportunity and it is immaterial whether the company could take advantage of the property, information or opportunity. This reflects the no-profit rule and mirrors the House of Lords' judgment in **Regal (Hastings) Ltd v Gulliver** [1942] 1 All ER 378 that the directors should return the profits to the company because they had obtained their profits by reason and in the course of the execution of their office as directors.[3] It made no difference whether the company itself was incapable of taking up the opportunity.[4] Similarly, in **Cook v Deeks** [1916] 1 AC 554, a corporate opportunity was regarded as a company's asset which might not be misappropriated by the directors. This rule equally applies to the situations where a director came across an opportunity personally instead of in his capacity as director: **Industrial Development Consultants Ltd v Cooley** [1972] 2 All ER 162. This strict approach could deter directors from pursuing their own interests at the expense of the company; nevertheless, it has been strongly criticised by Lowry and Edmunds (2000) as being too harsh on directors and unduly curbing entrepreneurial freedom to compete with companies.[5]

[2] You are analysing the scope of s 175 here instead of merely describing it. It will gain you more marks.

[3] This House of Lords case should be included in your answer because of its significance.

[4] Some students have the wrong understanding that the no-conflict rule does not apply if the company was unable to take up the opportunity.

[5] This sentence shows your wider understanding of the legal issue by engaging your discussion with academic literature. It will make your answer stand out.

A few court decisions have shown support for a flexible approach. In **Island Export Finance Ltd *v* Umunna** [1986] BCLC 460, Hutchinson J held that it was plainly in the public interest that directors should be free to exploit an opportunity in a new position. In **Balston Ltd *v* Headline Filters Ltd** [1990] FSR 385, it was held that a director did not breach his fiduciary duty by setting up a business in competition with his former company after his resignation, even where the intention to commence business was formed prior to the resignation. This more relaxed approach may promote the business activities but at the same time, there is a greater risk of the company being exploited by its own directors.[6]

The Company Law Review (*Completing the Structure*, 2000) expressed concerns that the common law on the no-conflict rule might fetter entrepreneurial and business activities. It recommended that the statutory statement of duties should only prevent the exploitation of business opportunities where there was a clear case for doing so. These concerns were echoed by the White Paper (2005, para 3.26) which emphasised that directors' duties should not impose impractical and onerous requirements which would stifle entrepreneurial activities.[7] These recommendations were carried out in the CA 2006 and the common law rules have been significantly altered by s 175(4) and (5) with regard to the board authorisation.[8]

The duty to avoid conflicts of interest is not infringed if the matter has been authorised by disinterested directors (s 175(4)). There is no need to gain shareholders' approval prior to entering into transactions with third parties where the interests of directors conflict with those of the company. This can be regarded as one step towards taking a more relaxed view of the no-conflict and no-profit rules. Authorisation is effective only if the following two conditions in s 175(6) are met. First, the director in question or any other interested director is not counted towards the quorum and any requirement as to the quorum at the meeting at which the matter is considered is met. Second, the matter was agreed to without counting the votes by the director in question or any other interested director.

A director, who breached his duty under s 175, will not be liable to return the profits if the breach has been ratified by a company's resolution (s 239(2)).[9] Where the resolution is proposed at a meeting, it is passed only if the necessary majority is obtained disregarding

[6]An analysis of the recent flexible approach goes beyond a description of case law. It also demonstrates your analytical skills and adds more credit to your answer.

[7]The reference to the Company Law Review and the White Paper shows your excellent knowledge of this subject and will impress your examiners.

[8]This sentence ties your answer back to the question in relation to the issue of authorisation.

[9]Try to use a new paragraph when you are moving on to the next issue. It makes it easier for your examiners to follow your answer and allocate marks.

votes in favour of the resolution by the director (if he is a member of the company) and any member connected with him (s 239(4)). The director or any such member is not prevented from attending, being counted towards the quorum and taking part in the meeting where the decision is considered. This approach helps to clarify the question as to whether directors can use their own votes for ratification. Section 252 defines what is meant by a person being connected with a director such as a director's family. Despite the company law reform, some problems still exist; for instance, shareholders may not make the right choice in exercising their votes for ratification at general meetings because of a lack of crucial information. Moreover, the distinction between wrongs which can or cannot be ratified has not been clarified in the Companies Act 2006.[10]

[10]The analysis of the problems of the current law on ratification demonstrates your excellent understanding.

[11]The conclusion refers back to the question and summarises your main arguments. A succinct conclusion helps complete and strengthen your answer and will gain you more marks.

In conclusion, it appears that the courts still take a strict approach towards the no-conflict and no-profit rules; nevertheless, such a rigorous approach is moderated by the potential authorisation and ratification of a breach of such duties. It is essential to strike a fine balance between imposing strict duties on directors and allowing some degree of entrepreneurial freedom.[11]

 Make your answer stand out

- Discuss the duty not to accept benefits from third parties in s 176 which forms part of the wider no-conflict duty.

- Analyse the self-dealing rules in s 177 and s 182. A director who is interested in a proposed or existing transaction with the company is required to declare the nature and extent of that interest to the other directors.

- Examine the different requirements for private companies (s 175(5)(a)) and public companies (s 175(5)(b)) in relation to authorisation.

- Compare the strict English approach to the corporate opportunity doctrine with the more relaxed and flexible approach in other common law jurisdictions such as Canada and Australia. The courts would consider the line of business of the particular company and the good faith of the director in question when determining whether or not a director has misappropriated a corporate opportunity: *Peso Silver Mines* v *Cropper* (1966) 58 DLR (2d) 1 and *Queensland Mines Ltd* v *Hudson* (1978) 52 ALJR 399.

- Make reference to academic opinions on the strict approach of the common law, such as Prentice, D. 'The corporate opportunity doctrine' [1974] MLR 464 and Worthington, S. 'Corporate governance: remedying and ratifying directors' breaches' [2000] LQR 638.

! **Don't be tempted to...**

- Examine other duties of directors. This is an essay question on the no-conflict and no-profit rules and therefore the discussion should focus on this area of law.

- Forget to discuss the law on authorisation and ratification, which are important parts of this question.

- Write everything you know about s 175 and the issue of ratification. You should refer your discussion to the question throughout your answer, in particular, with regard to the traditional strict judicial approach and the move towards a more flexible approach.

? Question 7

Ethan, Joshua and Daniel are all directors of Quality Sofa & Bed Ltd. The company desperately needed to purchase a warehouse. At a board meeting, Daniel successfully persuaded Ethan and Joshua that one particular warehouse was perfect for the company and that it was worth £140,000. Ethan and Joshua later discovered that Daniel was the owner of the warehouse and it was only worth £120,000.

Daniel, who is a chartered accountant, is in charge of insuring the company's warehouse against burglary and fire. He signed an insurance form without checking the content of the policy. The warehouse was burgled and the company suffered a loss of £30,000. The insurance company claimed that the insurance policy did not cover burglary and therefore refused to pay.

Ethan and Joshua recently found out that Daniel offered a cheaper price to a company's client, Paul Ltd, from which he obtained a personal benefit of £3,000.

Advise Ethan and Joshua as to whether Daniel breached any of his duties as a director of Quality Sofa & Bed Ltd.

Answer plan

→ Analyse whether Daniel breached the duties in s 177 and s 182 in relation to the warehouse transaction.

→ Discuss whether Daniel breached the duty of care, skill and diligence in s 174 in relation to the insurance policy.

→ Examine whether Daniel breached the duty not to accept a bribe from a third party in s 176 in relation to the personal benefit of £3,000.

Diagram plan

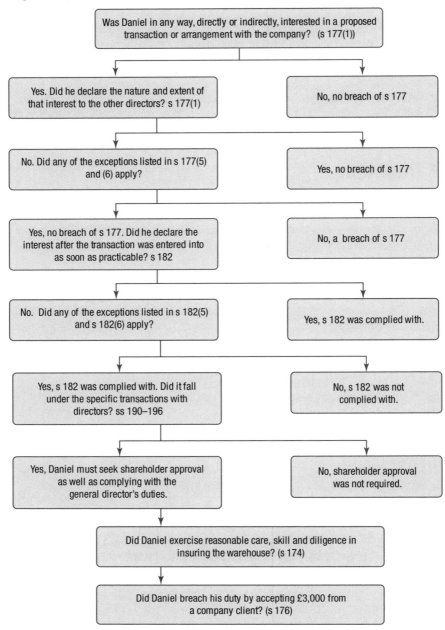

A printable version of this diagram plan is available from www.pearsoned.co.uk/lawexpressqa

Answer

[1]Your introduction should identify the main legal issues that arise from the question. It should also show careful planning and a clear structure for the answer.

The legal issues here are whether Daniel, as a director, has breached any of his duties in the Companies Act 2006 in relation to the sale of warehouse, the insurance form and the acceptance of £3,000 from a company client.[1]

The warehouse transaction[2]

[2]The use of headings is useful in clearly distinguishing each part of the answer.

[3]Pay attention to the 'proposed' transaction. An existing transaction with the company is covered by s 182, instead of s 177.

[4]The reference to case law is essential as the general duties are interpreted and applied in the same way as common law rules (s 170(4)).

If a director is in any way, directly or indirectly, interested in a *proposed* transaction[3] with the company, he must declare the nature and extent of that interest to the other directors before the transaction is entered into (s 177). It reflects the self-dealing rules at common law. In **Aberdeen Rly Co v Blaikie Bros** (1854) 1 Macq 461, the chairman of its board of directors of the company entered into a contract for the purchase of equipment with a partnership of which he was also the managing partner. The company was entitled to set aside the contract and the director was held to account for any profit which he made on the conflicted transaction. In **Gwembe Valley Development Co Ltd v Koshy** [2004] 1 BCLC 131,[4] the company's managing director sold foreign currency to the company from another business which he controlled. There was a conflict between the director's personal interest and the interests of the company as he acted on behalf of himself and the company at the same time in the transaction.

It appears that Daniel was directly interested in the transaction before it was entered into but he did not declare it to other directors. He was therefore in breach of s 177 unless one of the following exceptions applied. First, a declaration is not needed if the director in question is not aware of the interest or where the director is not aware of the transaction in question (s 177(5)). Secondly, a director need not declare an interest if it cannot reasonably be regarded as likely to give rise to a conflict of interest (s 177(6)(a)), or the other directors are already aware of it (s 177(6)(b)), or if it concerns terms of his service contract that have been or are to be considered by a meeting of the directors (s 177(6)(c)).[5] It is evident that Daniel was aware of the warehouse transaction and the situation can reasonably be regarded as likely to give rise to a conflict of interest. Moreover, neither Ethan nor Joshua was aware of the conflict of interest at

[5]The discussion of the situations where a declaration is not required demonstrates your excellent understanding of s 177. It will make your answer stand out.

[6]It is important to apply the relevant law to the problem scenario because it shows that you have a good grasp of the previous case law which still applies now.

[7]The consequences for directors' breach of duties are often omitted in students' answers. You should point out that, despite the codification of directors' duties, the consequences for breach of duties are the same as the corresponding common law.

[8]Note that a brief declaration of an interest in the transaction is insufficient for the purpose of s 182. Both the nature and the extent of the interest must be declared.

[9]Section 182 is often ignored by students. Your sound knowledge of s 182 will impress your examiners.

[10]The discussion of the requirement of shareholder approval in the substantial property transactions will gain you more marks because it demonstrates your excellent understanding of directors' duties.

[11]The test for a substantial property transaction which is laid out in s 191 is often missing in students' answers.

the time of entering into the transaction; the transaction was not related to terms of Daniel's service contract. It is therefore argued that neither of the exceptions applied to this transaction and Daniel breached his duty in s 177.[6]

The consequences for non-disclosure under s 177 are the same as would apply if the corresponding common law rules applied (s 178).[7] The contract with the company should be voidable and may be set aside by the company: **Movitex Ltd v Bulfield** [1988] BCLC 104. The company can hold the director to account for any profit which he has made from the transaction or to indemnify the company against any loss incurred.

Moreover, a director is also under the duty to disclose his interest in an existing transaction. Section 182 provides that a director who is in any way, directly or indirectly, interested in a transaction that has been entered into by the company, must declare the nature and extent of that interest[8] to the other directors as soon as is reasonably practicable. After the transaction was entered into, Daniel did not disclose his interest in the transaction; thus, he breached his duty in s 182.[9]

It is argued that Daniel also breached the specific duties in relation to the substantial property transactions which are governed by ss 190–196.[10] A company may not enter into an arrangement to acquire a substantial non-cash asset from a director, unless it has been approved by a resolution of the members of the company (s 190). The requirement of shareholder approval aims to provide shareholders with an opportunity to curb the potential abuse of power by directors. Shareholder approval is required only if, at the time the arrangement is entered into, the value of the asset exceeds 10% of the company's asset value and is more than £5,000, or exceeds £100,000 (s 191).[11] As the purchase price of the warehouse was £140,000, which exceeds £100,000, the warehouse transaction between Daniel and the company should be subject to shareholder approval. If shareholder approval was not obtained, the company should not be subject to any liability (s 190(3)).

The insurance form

A director must exercise reasonable care, skill and diligence that would be exercised by a reasonably diligent person with (a) the general knowledge, skill and experience that may reasonably be expected of a person carrying out the functions in question and (b) the general knowledge, skill and experience that the director has (s 174). The former sets an objective minimum standard whilst the latter raises the objective minimum standard in the light of the particular attributes of the director in question. In **Dorchester and Finance Co Ltd v Stebbing** [1989] BCLC 498, the non-executive directors, who were qualified accountants, had been negligent in signing blank cheques. Similarly, in **Re D'Jan of London Ltd** [1994] 1 BCLC 561, it was held that the director was negligent for signing an insurance proposal without checking its accuracy. The information provided in the form was incorrect and therefore the insurance company refused to pay when the company's premises burned down. Daniel, as an accountant with special knowledge in accounting, failed to exercise reasonable care, skill and diligence in checking the insurance policy carefully before signing; it can be argued therefore that he breached his duty in s 174.[12]

[12]This sentence refers back to the question in relation to the insurance form.

Acceptance of £3,000 from a third party

A director must not accept a benefit from a third party conferred by reason of his being a director or his doing anything as director (s 176). This duty is not infringed if the acceptance of the benefit cannot reasonably be regarded as likely to give rise to a conflict of interest (s 176(4)).[13] In the current scenario, Daniel accepted a bribe from a company's client, which could reasonably be regarded to give rise to a conflict of interest. He breached the duty in s 176 by accepting the benefit and exercising his powers in the interests of the third party rather than the company. It is concluded from the discussion of the above three circumstances that Daniel breached his duties under ss 177, 182, 190, 174 and 176 of the Companies Act 2006.[14]

[13]The discussion of s 176 is essential in your answer with regard to the acceptance of a bribe from a company client.

[14]The conclusion addresses the specific issues on directors' duties in relation to the warehouse transaction, the insurance form and the acceptance of a bribe.

Make your answer stand out

- Examine the consequences of the non-compliance with s 182. A director who has failed to comply with the statutory duty of disclosure under s 182 has committed an offence and, on conviction on indictment, is liable to a fine (s 183). The company, however, does not have a separate claim for damages against this director for non-compliance with s 182: *Coleman Taymar Ltd* v *Oakes* [2001] 2 BCLC 749.
- Discuss Daniel's breach of the duty to avoid conflicts of interest (s 175) in relation to the acceptance of a bribe from a third party.
- Consider Daniel's breach of duty in s 172 to promote the success of the company in relation to all of the three circumstances.

 Don't be tempted to...

- Get confused with the duty to avoid conflicts of interest (s 175) and the duty to declare interests with the transactions with the company (s 177). They are separate duties in the Companies Act 2006. The distinct situation where a director is interested in a proposed transaction with the company is governed by s 177, not s 175.
- Discuss all the legal issues at the same time. You should clearly structure your answer and address one legal issue in full before moving on to the next one.

🖎 Question 8

Steve and Mr and Mrs Walker were directors in London Hairdressing Ltd. In May 2009, the Walkers secretly sold two of the company's cars which were worth £50,000 to their son, Jason, for £6,000. The company went into insolvent liquidation in October 2010.

Advise Mr and Mrs Walker as to whether this transaction was valid and whether they breached any of their fiduciary duties.

Answer plan

→ Analyse whether the Walkers breached their fiduciary duties under ss 172, 177 and 182 of the CA 2006.

→ Discuss whether the sale of cars was considered as substantial property transaction: ss 190–196, CA 2006.

→ Examine whether the sale of cars to Jason was a transaction at an undervalue: s 238, IA 1986.

→ Consider that the court may make an order in s 423 of the IA 1986 in relation to the transaction at an undervalue.

→ Evaluate the summary remedy against delinquent directors according to s 212 of the IA 1986.

Diagram plan

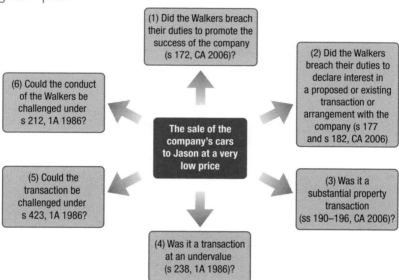

(1) Did the Walkers breach their duties to promote the success of the company (s 172, CA 2006)?

(2) Did the Walkers breach their duties to declare interest in a proposed or existing transaction or arrangement with the company (s 177 and s 182, CA 2006)

(6) Could the conduct of the Walkers be challenged under s 212, 1A 1986?

The sale of the company's cars to Jason at a very low price

(5) Could the transaction be challenged under s 423, 1A 1986?

(3) Was it a substantial property transaction (ss 190–196, CA 2006)?

(4) Was it a transaction at an undervalue (s 238, 1A 1986)?

A printable version of this diagram plan is available from www.pearsoned.co.uk/lawexpressqa

[1]This sentence shows that you are engaging with the problem question.

[2]The subjective nature of this duty is the key feature of s 172 and therefore it should be discussed and applied to the problem scenario. You can also make reference to the objective test for the duty to act *bona fide* at common law: *Charterbridge Corp Ltd v Lloyds Bank Ltd* [1970] Ch 62.

Answer

In relation to the sale of the company's assets at an unreasonably low price, it can be argued that the Walkers, as directors of the company, breached their fiduciary duties in ss 172, 177 and 182 of the Companies Act 2006.[1] Section 172 requires that a director act in the way he considers, in good faith, would be most likely to promote the success of the company for the benefit of its members as a whole. In particular, a director is required to consider or act in the interests of creditors of the company in certain circumstances (s 172(3)). It is very difficult, however, to prove that the Walkers breached this duty because of its subjective nature: **Regentcrest plc v Cohen** [2001] 2 BCLC 80).[2]

[3]You should distinguish between the duties under s 177 and s 182. Section 177 applies to the proposed transaction whilst s 182 applies to an existing transaction which has already been entered into by the company. Students are often not aware of this distinction.

[4]The reference to case law is essential as the general duties are interpreted and applied in the same way as the common law rules (s 170(4)).

[5]You should clearly state the test for substantial property transaction, which is important for an application of s 190. You will lose some marks if this test is not included in your answer.

[6]It should be noted that this legal issue in relation to the transaction at an undervalue arises because London Hairdressing Ltd went into liquidation; otherwise, s 238 would not apply.

[7]This is one of the key requirements in s 238. If the transaction was entered into outside the two year limit, it cannot be challenged as a transaction at undervalue under this section. You should also pay attention to the different time requirements for connected and unconnected persons.

Moreover, it can be argued that the Walkers breached their duties under s 177 and s 182 because of the failure to disclose their interest in the transaction to the other director, Steve. A director must declare the nature and extent of that interest to the other directors before the transaction is entered into, if he is in any way, directly or indirectly, interested in a *proposed* transaction[3] with the company (s 177) or in an existing transaction with the company (s 182). These duties reflect the self-dealing rules at common law. In **Aberdeen Rly Co v Blaikie Bros** (1854) 1 Macq 461,[4] the chairman of its board of directors of the company entered into a contract for the purchase of equipment with a partnership of which he was also the managing partner. The company was entitled to set aside the contract and the director was held to account for any profit which he made on the conflicted transaction.

A company may not enter into an arrangement under which a director of the company, or a person connected with him, acquires from the company (directly or indirectly) a substantial non-cash asset unless it has been approved by a resolution of the members of the company (s 190, CA 2006). Shareholder approval is required only if, at the time the arrangement is entered into, the value of the asset exceeds 10% of the company's asset value and is more than £5,000, or exceeds £100,000 (s 191).[5] Jason was connected with the Walkers and the value of cars exceeded £5,000, the car transaction therefore should be subject to shareholder approval if the value was more than 10% of the company's asset value in May 2009.

As the company went into insolvent liquidation, the transaction can be challenged by a liquidator if it was previously entered into by the company at an undervalue (s 238, Insolvency Act 1986).[6] A transaction at an undervalue arises if the company enters into a transaction with that person on terms that provide no consideration for the company, or for a consideration which is significantly less than that provided by the company (s 238(4), IA 1986). The court may make an order if the company has entered into a transaction with a connected person at an undervalue within two years (six months for unconnected persons) ending with the onset of insolvency.[7] Moreover, the transaction must have been entered into when the company was unable to pay its debts or it becomes unable to pay its debts in consequence of the transaction (s 240(2), IA 1986). This requirement is presumed to be satisfied when the transaction was entered into by a company with a connected person such as family members of directors. The court shall make such order as it thinks fit for restoring the position to what it would have been if the company had not entered into that transaction (s 238(3)). Such order shall not be made if the court is satisfied both that the company entered into the transaction in good faith and for the purpose of carrying on its business, and that there were reasonable grounds for believing that the transaction would benefit the company (s 238(5)).[8]

[8]An analysis of the specific circumstances where a transaction is not caught by s 238 will gain you more marks.

The company's cars were sold to Jason, who was considered as a connected person within two years ending with the onset of insolvency. It can be presumed, therefore, that the transaction was entered into when the company was unable to pay its debts or it became unable to pay its debts as a consequence of this transaction. Moreover, the transaction was made for a consideration which was significantly less than the value of the cars. It is unlikely that the directors could convince the court that the transaction was entered into in good faith or that the transaction would benefit the company. The court will order Jason to make payment to the liquidator in respect of benefits received by him from the company: **Re Paramount Airways Ltd** [1992] 3 All ER 1.[9]

[9]This sentence adds more credit to your answer because it applies the law to the question rather than simply stating the law.

The court may also make an order under s 423, IA 1986 in relation to the transaction at an undervalue.[10] If the court is satisfied that the transaction was entered into with the purpose of putting assets beyond the reach of the creditors or of prejudicing the interests of the creditors, the court may make such order as it thinks fit for restoring the position to what it would have been if the transaction had not been entered into, and protecting the interests of persons who are victims of the transaction. Section 423 covers a broader range of circumstances than s 238; for instance, it applies even when the company is not in liquidation or administration; there is no time limit in relation to the transaction in s 423, unlike the two-year limit in s 238.[11]

[10]Some students are not aware of the provision in s 423. As the problem question is essentially concerned with a transaction at an undervalue, your mark will be adversely affected if the discussion of s 423 is omitted in your answer.

[11]The comparison between s 238 and s 423 shows your excellent understanding with regard to transactions at an undervalue. It will make your answer stand out from those which only describe these two provisions.

The liquidator may also apply to the court according to s 212 of the IA 1986, which provides a summary remedy against delinquent directors.[12] The court may examine the conduct of the Walkers, if, in the course of the winding up of a company, it appears that they have misapplied or retained, or become accountable for, any money or other property of the company, or been guilty of any misfeasance

[12]The misfeasance procedure in s 212 is another power that the liquidator may exercise against directors. It is another ground on which the conduct of the Walkers may be challenged and therefore it should be included in a sound answer.

or breach of any fiduciary or other duty in relation to the company. As such, the court may compel the Walkers to repay the money or restore property or to make contribution to the company's assets as the court thinks just.

✓ Make your answer stand out

- Discuss that the Walkers may be liable for fraudulent trading under s 213 of the IA 1986. If, in the course of the winding up of a company, it appears that the business of the company has been carried on with intent to defraud creditors or for any fraudulent purpose, the court may declare that any persons who were knowingly parties to the carrying on of the business are to be liable to make such contributions (if any) to the company's assets as the court thinks proper.

- Consider that the Walkers may be held liable for wrongful trading under s 214 of the IA 1986. If at some time before the company was wound up, they knew or ought to have concluded that there was no reasonable prospect that the company would avoid going into insolvent liquidation. The court, on the application of the liquidator, may declare that the directors are liable to make such contribution (if any) to the company's assets as the court thinks proper. It shall not make a declaration if it is satisfied that the director took every step to minimise the potential loss to the company's creditors as he ought to have taken (s 214(3)): *Re Brian D Pierson Ltd* [2001] 1 BCLC 275.

- Point out that the Walkers may be disqualified under s 6 of the Company Directors Disqualification Act 1986 if the court is satisfied that their conduct as directors make them unfit to be concerned in the management of a company.

! Don't be tempted to...

- Describe directors' general duties in ss 170–177 of the CA 2006. You should only discuss the duties which are relevant to this question.

- Forget to apply the provisions in relation to the transaction at an undervalue in s 238, IA 1986. You should show your understanding of the implications which arise from the winding up of London Hairdressing Ltd.

- Apply the director's duty to avoid conflicts of interest in s 175, CA 2006. You should understand that s 175 does not apply to a conflict of interest arising in relation to a transaction or arrangement with the company (s 175(3)). Such transaction or arrangement is governed by ss 177 and 182.

Corporate governance

5

How this topic may come up in exams

Corporate governance is mainly concerned with public companies and it is a popular topic, particularly in light of the recent financial crisis. Students often struggle with the breadth of information. You are expected to show a good knowledge of the basic corporate governance theories, such as the agency theory, shareholder primacy and stakeholder theory. The legal framework on corporate governance is frequently examined in relation to the board structure, non-executive directors, directors' remuneration and the increasingly important role of institutional shareholders. Your understanding of the UK Corporate Governance Code and its 'comply or explain' approach may also be tested. This topic overlaps with directors' duties and shareholders' remedies. As corporate governance is not covered in all company law courses, you are advised to check your syllabus before revising.

■ Attack the question

Question 1

'Shareholders are more likely to lose money because the relevant people in the firm are not up to the mark than merely because they are 'agents' bent on pursuing their own interests at the expense of others.' (Clarkham and Simpson, *Fair Shares: The Future of Shareholder Power and Responsibility* (Oxford University Press, 1999))

Undertake a critical discussion of the above statement in relation to the legal and regulatory framework in the United Kingdom in addressing the agency problems.

Answer plan

→ Discuss the separation of ownership and control in large public companies.

→ Explain the agency theory and agency costs.

→ Analyse the statutory framework of directors' duties and their enforcement.

→ Examine the self-regulatory code on corporate governance, in particular, the UK Corporate Governance Code ('The Code') and the 'comply or explain' approach.

Diagram plan

| The separation of ownership and control | The agency problems and agency costs | The legal and regulatory framework: the Companies Act 2006 and The Code |

A printable version of this diagram plan is available from www.pearsoned.co.uk/lawexpressqa

Answer

[1]You should identify the key legal issues which arise in the question. It gives your examiners a good impression that you know where your answer is going.

[2]Make sure you know who are the agents and principals. Some students get confused and make the mistake of stating that shareholders are the agents.

This question requires a discussion of the agency problems in corporate governance and the legal and regulatory framework in addressing them.[1] Corporate governance is defined in the Cadbury Report 1992 as the system by which a company is directed and controlled. A balanced relationship between the board of directors and shareholders is essential for good corporate governance.

The agency theory identifies the agency relationship between directors and shareholders; directors are the agents and shareholders are the principals.[2] Problems may arise when the agents do not act in the best interests of the principals; for example, the agents may misuse their power or take inappropriate risks when pursuing the principals' interests. When the agents have access to more

[3]The reference to Adam Smith and his work shows your sound knowledge. It is worth learning the title of his book.

[4]If you cannot remember the exact quotation, try to paraphrase it by stating that 'as directors are managing other people's money, they may not watch over it vigilantly as if it were their own'.

[5]This is another classic work on the separation of ownership and control and the agency problems. The reference to Berle and Means will gain you more marks.

[6]This sentence demonstrates your sound knowledge of corporate governance. The majority of students have a general understanding of the separation of ownership and control, but may wrongly believe that it applies to all types of companies in every country.

[7]The discussion of the influence of institutional shareholders will make your answer stand out because it shows your wider understanding of the corporate governance issues.

information than the principals, the latter may suffer from information asymmetry. These problems lead to the agency costs, which refer to the costs resulting from directors misusing their positions, as well as the costs of monitoring and disciplining them to ensure that they do not act in their own interests.

The agency problems are more acute in large companies where there is a separation of ownership and control. Adam Smith in *The Wealth of Nations* (1776)[3] made for the first time the observation that the directors of joint stock companies 'being the managers rather of other people's money than of their own, it cannot well be expected that they should watch over it with the same anxious vigilance [as if it were their own]'.[4] In order to expand, companies need to gain capital by issuing more shares to a diverse number of shareholders. This leads to a dilution of shareholders' powers and the controlling power is effectively vested in the majority shareholders. Later, Berle and Means, in *The Modern Corporation and Private Property* (1932),[5] identified the problem caused by the separation of ownership and control in US companies in the 1930s. They discovered that many of the large companies had such widely dispersed share ownership that no individual shareholder had an interest in controlling management. The board of directors, instead of shareholders, was therefore able to exert real control over the company. There was a great danger that directors would be free to run the company for their own benefit, rather than on behalf of the shareholders.

It should be noted that the separation of ownership and control is mostly applicable to the companies in the United States and the United Kingdom but not to those in many other countries.[6] As highlighted by La Porta *et al.* (1999), the most common form of ownership around the globe is the family firm with controlling shareholders, rather than a broad and dispersed shareholding. In addition, institutional shareholders, such as pension funds and insurance companies, hold a large number of shares in recent years. As a consequence, shareholdings in some major companies are no longer widely dispersed and the rise of institutional shareholders may to some extent mitigate the agency costs.[7]

In order to address the agency problems and reduce agency costs, it is important to ensure that directors do not abuse their power. Directors in both private and public companies are subject to various

8This sentence summarises
the recent reforms on
directors' duties and leads
to the detailed discussion of
directors' duties in the next
few paragraphs.

9Although the reference
to the section number is
not essential, it shows
your precise knowledge on
directors' duties and will add
more credit to your answer.

10The previous case law
on directors' duties is
still relevant despite the
codification in the Companies
Act 2006. A lack of reference
to case law will negatively
affect your marks.

11This is one of the key
aspects of s 172 and it is
also a significant theory in
corporate governance. You
will lose some marks if it is
not included in your answer.

duties in the Companies Act 2006. Directors in listed companies must also state whether The Code is complied with as required by the Listing Rules.

A director owes fiduciary duties to the company. The duties at common law and in equitable rules are now codified in the Companies Act 2006 (ss 170–177).[8] A director must act in accordance with the company's constitution and exercise his powers for proper purposes (s 171)[9] : **Hogg v Cramphorn** [1967] Ch 254.[10] He must also act in the way he considers, in good faith, would be most likely to promote the success of the company for the benefit of its members as a whole (s 172): **Re Smith & Fawcett** [1942] 1 All ER 542. In doing so, he must also have regard to other factors, such as the likely consequences of any decision in the long term, the interests of the company's employees, the impact on the community and environment, and the need for the company to act fairly as between members. Section 172 introduces the enlightened shareholder value,[11] whereby a company should be run not only to generate maximum wealth for shareholders but also to take a properly balanced view of the wider implications of decisions over time.

A director is required to exercise independent judgement (s 173): **Fulham Football Club and Others v Cabra Estates plc** [1994] 1 BCLC 363. He must exercise reasonable care, skill and diligence in carrying out his functions (s 174): **Dorchester Finance Co Ltd v Stebbing** [1989] BCLC 498. The subjective and objective tests at common law are also adopted. A director must avoid a situation in which he has a direct or indirect interest that conflicts with the interests of the company (s 175): **Regal (Hastings) Ltd v Gulliver** [1942] 1 All ER 378. He is prohibited from accepting a benefit from a third party conferred by reason of him being a director (s 176). If he is in any way interested in a proposed transaction or arrangement with the company, he must declare the nature and extent of any interest to other directors (s 177): **Aberdeen Railway Ltd v Blaikie** (1854) 1 Macq 461.

If a director breaches any of these duties, the company is the proper claimant to sue him: **Foss v Harbottle** (1843) 67 ER 189. Shareholders may apply for the court's permission to bring a statutory derivative action and challenge directors' breach of duties (ss 260–263). Shareholders may also bring an unfair prejudice petition if their interests have been unfairly prejudiced by the company's affairs (s 994).

[12]This sentence briefly summarises the main principles which are set out in the Code. It shows your sound knowledge of the Code and will add more credit to your answer.

[13]This is the distinctive feature of the Combined Code compared to the corporate governance in other countries. An explanation of the 'comply or explain' approach must be included in a good answer.

[14]The reference to the current events and the suggestions for future reforms in your conclusion will earn you more marks.

In addition to their statutory duties, directors in listed companies need to consider the UK Corporate Governance Code 2010 which consists of principles of good governance in relation to leadership, effectiveness, accountability, remuneration and relations with shareholders.[12] It adopts the 'comply or explain' principle,[13] whereby the board of a listed company is required by the Listing Rules to include a statement in its annual financial report of whether it has complied with The Code. If any provision of The Code has not been complied with, the reasons for non-compliance must be specified.

It can be argued that the company performance and shareholders' interests may be undermined if there is insufficient monitoring of directors' conduct. The recent financial crisis and corporate scandals indicate that the current legal and regulatory framework needs strengthening in order to sufficiently address the agency problems and ensure that directors act in the best interests of the company.[14]

✓ Make your answer stand out

- Assess the enlightened shareholder value in more detail.
- Evaluate in more detail the main principles in the Combined Code.
- Examine the corporate governance reports such as the Cadbury Report 1992, Greenbury Report 1995, Hampel Report 1998, Turnbull Report 1999, Myners Report 2001, Higgs Report 2003 and Smith Report 2003.
- Include more academic opinions in relation to the agency theory: Clark, T. *Theories of Corporate Governance* (Routledge, 2004), pp. 55–78; Mallin, C. *Corporate Governance*, 2nd ed. (Oxford University Press, 2007), pp. 12–13.

! Don't be tempted to...

- Ignore the enforcement of directors' duties by the company or shareholders. It is a powerful way to reduce the agency costs and therefore should be included in a good answer.
- Forget to discuss The Code. It is a very influential corporate governance code for listed companies and therefore should not be omitted in your answer.

📝 Question 2

'In light of the recent financial crisis, it is apparent that the UK Corporate Governance Code (the Code) is insufficient to promote good corporate governance in the United Kingdom. It is time to adopt a more robust approach similar to that in the United States.'

Critically analyse the above statement in relation to the development of the Code in the United Kingdom. Would the corporate governance in the United Kingdom be improved by following the approach of the Sarbanes-Oxley Act?

Answer plan

→ Discuss the development of the Combined Code by reference to the corporate governance reports, in particular, the Cadbury Report 1992, Greenbury Report 1995 and Hampel Report 1998.

→ Evaluate the effect of the 'comply or explain' approach in the Combined Code.

→ Analyse the key provisions of the Sarbanes-Oxley Act.

→ Examine the advantages and disadvantages of the mandatory approach in the United States.

Diagram plan

| The development of the Code in the UK | → | The effectiveness of the 'comply or explain' approach | → | The Sarbanes-Oxley Act in the US | → | Should the UK follow the US approach? |

A printable version of this diagram plan is available from www.pearsoned.co.uk/lawexpressqa

Answer

[1] A succinct introduction immediately gives examiners a good impression that your answer is well organised.

This question requires a critical evaluation of the historical development of The Code, the effectiveness of its 'comply or explain' approach and whether the mandatory approach to corporate governance in the United States should be adopted in the United Kingdom.[1]

[2] A few examples of the corporate scandals show your detailed knowledge and will add more credit to your answer.

[3] This sentence justifies the discussion of the Cadbury Report and other corporate governance reports in your answer.

In response to various corporate scandals such as Mirror Group Newspapers, Coloroll and Polly Peck,[2] the Cadbury Committee was set up to report into financial aspects of corporate governance. The Cadbury Report 1992 stresses the division of responsibilities of the board and the importance of non-executive directors. Its recommendations and those of subsequent reports form the framework for corporate governance in the United Kingdom.[3]

The first Combined Code 1998 drew upon the recommendations of the Cadbury, Greenbury and Hampel Reports. The Cadbury Report created the Code of Best Practice and introduced the philosophy of 'comply or explain'. It is adopted by the London Stock Exchange, which requires that the boards of all listed companies comply with The Code but, if they cannot comply with any particular aspect of it, they should explain their reasons for non-compliance. This approach is based on the assumption that the market will monitor compliance with The Code and will either penalise non-compliance through lowering share prices or accept that non-compliance is justified in the circumstances.[4] The disclosure provides investors with detailed information on a company's non-compliance and enables them to decide whether non-compliance is justified. It can be an influential factor in making their investment decisions. The Combined Code is a self-regulatory code and therefore no legal sanction will arise for non-compliance with it. Failure to include it in the company's annual report, however, leads to penalties for non-compliance with the Listing Rules.[5]

The Greenbury Report 1995 focuses on strengthening account-ability and enhancing the performance of directors. It recommends setting up a remuneration committee comprising independent non-executive directors and linking rewards of directors to the performance of both the company and individual directors. The Hampel Report 1998 endorses the majority of the findings of both the Cadbury and the Greenbury Reports and goes further by considering the relationships of the company with stakeholder constituencies. It states that 'the directors as a board are respon-sible for relations with stakeholders; but they are accountable to the shareholders'.[6]

The application and interpretation of different aspects of the Combined Code are addressed in various reports.[7] The Turnbull Report 1999 is concerned with the implementation of the internal control requirements in The Code. It requires the board to periodically assess the control measures in place and report on them annually. The Myners Report 2001 promotes shareholder activism and encourages institutional investors to be more proactive. The Higgs Report 2003 focuses on the independence of the non-executive director whilst the Smith Report 2003 considers the functions of the audit committee.

[4]This sentence explains the rationale of the 'comply or explain' approach. It will gain you more marks than simply explaining what the approach means.

[5]Although no penalties are imposed for non-compliance of The Code itself, you should understand that a failure to include a statement in the company's annual report breaches the Listing Rules. You may lose marks if this issue is not addressed.

[6]A short quotation like this is easy to remember. It may impress your examiners by showing such detailed knowledge of the Hampel Report.

[7]This sentence shows your good understanding of the relationship between the Combined Code and other corporate governance reports.

[8]The reference to the UK Corporate Governance Code 2010 demonstrates your up-to-date knowledge and will make your answer stand out.

[9]Although this sentence seems to repeat the previous explanation of the 'comply or explain' approach, it does reaffirm its application in the most recent Code and therefore emphasises the importance of this approach.

[10]This sentence echoes the statement in the question and shows that you are engaging with the question.

[11]The Enron scandal should be referred to in your answer because it was so influential in leading to the passing of the Sarbanes-Oxley Act.

[12]This sentence demonstrates the sharp contrast between the approach in the United States and the voluntary approach of The Code in the United Kingdom.

[13]These sentences analyse the problems associated with implementing the Sarbanes-Oxley Act. It will add more credit to your answer than simply describing the main sections of this Act.

The Combined Code has been constantly revised and the current version is the UK Corporate Governance Code 2010.[8] It sets out the standards of good practice in relation to issues such as leadership, effectiveness, accountability, remuneration and relations with shareholders. It adopts the 'comply or explain' principle and requires listed companies, in their annual reports and accounts to report on how they apply the principles, and confirm that they comply with The Code's provisions or, where they do not, provide an explanation.[9] The effectiveness of The Code as a corporate governance control mechanism has been widely debated. It has been criticised as a purely cosmetic box-ticking exercise that companies adhere to only in name. Although the scale of compliance has increased over time, there remains a significant incidence of non-compliance. The disclosures of non-compliance made by companies are often extremely brief and uninformative; this may defeat the purpose of the 'comply or explain' approach. Moreover, the research by Dedman (2002) shows that there is no clear link between compliance with The Code and superior performance of the company. It is argued, therefore, that corporate governance issues are too important to be left to The Code and the soft obligations should be replaced by statutes following the mandatory approach to corporate governance in the United States.[10]

In response to major corporate and accounting scandals such as Enron[11] and Worldcom, the Sarbanes-Oxley Act was passed in 2002 in the United States in order to strengthen corporate governance and restore investor confidence. It establishes enhanced standards for boards and management of public companies. Compliance with the 2002 Act is mandatory.[12] Section 302 requires that the CEO and CFO of a company that files reports must certify in each annual and quarterly report. Section 906 requires that every periodic report containing financial statements must be accompanied by written statements by the company's CEO and CFO. The statements must certify that they have reviewed the report, the information contained in the report fairly presents the financial condition of the company, and the report does not contain any untrue statements or omissions of material facts. Failure to comply with these provisions is a criminal offence. Although the possibility of criminal sanctions for directors may deter their misuse of power, it is difficult to attract international companies to list in the United States. In fact, the extra costs for compliance with the Sarbanes-Oxley Act have led to some listed companies delisting in the United States.[13]

The legislative approach in the United States requires higher standards of transparency, direct accountability on the part of the CEO and a greater degree of independence in the boardroom. The rigidity of this legislative approach, however, is costly to implement and may not foster trust or improve corporate performance. By comparison, the 'comply or explain' approach in the United Kingdom has the advantage of flexibility and discretion. It can be more easily amended and less administratively burdensome than legislation. Moreover, it is impossible to adopt a 'one size fits all' approach to corporate governance codes, primarily because companies differ in terms of size and structure. The Company Law Review (*Completing the Structure*, 2000) considered the high level of compliance with The Code and found no support for putting it on a statutory basis. It concludes that The Code strengthens awareness of the importance of an effective board structure and creates a climate of openness and accountabilities. It is therefore preferable that The Code should remain on a non-statutory basis.

✓ Make your answer stand out

- Discuss in more detail the main principles in the UK Corporate Governance Code 2010.
- Evaluate in more detail the effect of the Sarbanes-Oxley Act in the United States.
- Make reference to more academic opinions on the effectiveness of the Code: Abarca, 'The need for substantive regulation on investor protection and corporate governance in Europe: does Europe need a Sarbanes-Oxley?' (2004) *Journal of International Banking Law and Regulation* 419; MacNeil I. and Li, X. '"Comply or explain", market discipline and non-compliance with the Combined Code' (2006) *Corporate Governance* 486.

! Don't be tempted to...

- Apply The Code to all types of companies. Although private companies are encouraged to follow its recommendations, The Code only applies to listed companies which are public companies listed on the London Stock Exchange.
- Only discuss the old versions of The Code. You should also make reference to the latest Code – the UK Corporate Governance Code 2010.
- Only focus on The Code. You should also discuss the corporate governance reports which are important for the development of The Code.
- Misunderstand the 'comply *or* explain' approach. Some students tend to make the mistake by writing 'comply *and* explain'.

📝 Question 3

'Effective and robust boards are an essential feature of successful companies. Within the unitary board, non-executive directors have a crucial part to play.' (*Review of the role and effectiveness of non-executive directors* (The Higgs Review 2003, para 1.1))

Discuss the role and effectiveness of non-executive directors in corporate governance by reference to the Higgs Review 2003 and the UK Corporate Governance Code (the Code).

Answer plan

→ Discuss the board structure and the role of the board.

→ Consider the role of non-executive directors by reference to the Combined Code and the Higgs Review.

→ Examine the requirements for independent non-executive directors.

→ Analyse the appointment procedure and the required number of non-executive directors.

→ Evaluate whether the existence of non-executive directors is effective in promoting good corporate governance.

Diagram plan

A printable version of this diagram plan is available from www.pearsoned.co.uk/lawexpressqa

[1]This sentence identifies the key issues. Try to interpret the question in your own words and avoid repeating the question. It shows that you understand what this question is about.

Answer

This question requires an evaluation of the role of non-executive directors, in particular, whether they are effective in promoting good corporate governance and preventing corporate scandals.[1] The role

²The reference to the current
version of the Code shows
your up-to-date knowledge
and will add more credit to
your answer.

³The reference to the
general management clause
emphasises the important role
of the board of directors.

⁴Some students have only a
vague understanding of the
functions of non-executive
directors. The explanation
of the differences between
executive and non-executive
directors is essential for
a good answer because it
shows that you understand
what non-executive directors
do.

⁵This sentence relates
the corporate governance
issues to directors' duties
in the Companies Act
2006. It shows your sound
understanding of the legal
framework that applies to
non-executive directors.

⁶If you cannot remember
the exact numbering of
the paragraph, a general
reference to the Higgs Review
should suffice.

⁷This sentence explains the
'comply or explain' approach,
which is the basis of The
Code. You will lose some
marks if it is omitted in your
answer.

of non-executive directors has been subject to detailed consideration in the UK Corporate Governance Code 2010[2] and the Higgs Review 2003.

The board of directors plays an extremely important role in good corporate governance because it is effectively in charge of the management of the company. The general management clause in the Model Articles (art 3) states that subject to the articles, the directors are responsible for the management of the company's business, for which purpose they may exercise all the powers of the company.[3] The board consists of executive and non-executive directors. Executive directors are concerned with the actual management of the company. Non-executive directors do not have executive management responsibilities but are concerned with general management policy and the monitoring of executive directors.[4] Both executive and non-executive directors are all required to act to promote the success of the company and owe the same duties to the company (ss 170–177, Companies Act 2006).[5] Such a unitary board structure brings the benefit of the executive knowledge within the board and the wider experience brought by non-executive directors (Higgs Review, para 4.2[6]).

The Combined Code sets out standards of good practice in relation to board leadership and effectiveness, remuneration, accountability and relations with shareholders. It is a voluntary code and adopts the 'comply or explain' approach. Listed companies are required to report on how they have applied the main principles of The Code (B1), and either to confirm that they have complied with it or, if they have not complied, to provide an explanation.[7] The Combined Code recommends that every company should be headed by an effective board which is collectively responsible for the long-term success of the company. The board should include an appropriate combination of executive and non-executive directors so that not any individual or small group of individuals dominates the board's decision taking. It should also have the appropriate balance of skills, experience, independence and knowledge of the company to enable them to discharge their respective duties and responsibilities effectively.

The Higgs Review 2003 emphasises the essential role of non-executive directors in monitoring executive activity and

[8]The discussion of the Combined Code 1998 shows your good understanding of the historical development of the Code and will gain you more marks.

[9]This is one of the main principles in relation to non-executive directors in the Code and therefore it should be included in a good answer.

[10]The independence of non-executive directors is the significant issue in this question. It should be addressed in detail in your answer.

contributing to the development of strategy (para 6.1). It argues that the Combined Code 1998[8] offered little guidance on the role of non-executive directors and the lack of clarity affected their performance in corporate governance. It therefore suggests that the non-executive directors' powers and responsibilities for monitoring should be clarified. This recommendation is embodied in the Code; for instance, non-executive directors should constructively challenge and help develop proposals on company strategy as part of their role as members of a unitary board (The Code, A4).[9] With respect to the appointment procedure, non-executives should be selected through a formal process and be appointed for specific terms. Any term beyond six years should be subject to particularly rigorous review and should take into account the need for progressive refreshing of the board (The Code, B 2.3).

Non-executive directors play a significant role in monitoring executive activity and contributing to the development of strategy (Higgs Review, para 6.1). They not only play a supervisory role in controlling conflicts of interest, but also provide a broader view and bring a fresh perspective to strategic matters. To ensure that they fulfil their roles, non-executive directors should be capable of providing an independent and impartial view of the board's consid-erations and challenging or questioning the executive decisions.[10] The presence of independent non-executive directors on the board may mitigate the agency costs through their mutual monitoring functions.

The Combined Code 1998 required the majority of non-executive directors to be independent of management; however, the board was left to determine whether a non-executive director was independent and there was little guidance to the companies as to what the independence should entail. In order to address this problem, the Higgs Review therefore recommends that the independence should be clearly defined and it is desirable if a definition is provided in The Code which addresses relationships or circumstances that would affect the directors' independence. A checklist which identifies the level of independence was put forward in the Higgs Review and later incorporated into the Combined Code 2003.

The Code (B.1.2) recommends that at least half of the members of the board, excluding the chairman, should be independent non-executive directors (Combined Code, B.1.2).[11] A smaller company should have at least two independent non-executive directors. The board is now required to identify in the annual report each non-executive director it considers to be independent. It should determine whether the director is independent in character and judgement and whether there are relationships or circumstances which are likely to affect the director's judgement. Moreover, it should state its reasons if it determines that a director is independent notwithstanding the existence of relationships or circumstances which may appear relevant to its determination. For instance, if the director has been an employee of the company within the last five years; or has had, within the last three years, a material business relationship with the company; or has received or receives additional remuneration from the company apart from a director's fee; or has close family ties with any of the company's advisers, directors or senior employees; or holds cross-directorships or has significant links with other directors through involvement in other companies or bodies; represents a significant shareholder (The Code, B 1.1). Although it is impractical comprehensively to list all possible criteria in defining what independence really means, this check-list approach provides some guidance on developing best practice and increasing the accountability of the boards of listed companies.[12]

[12]This sentence demonstrates your analytical skills by examining the advantages of the check-list approach. It will make your answer stand out from those which only describe the check-list.

Independent non-executive directors are perceived to play a monitoring role on executive directors and enhance corporate governance; however, they have not effectively prevented corporate scandals, as revealed by the collapse of Enron in the United States and the scandals at Equitable Life and Maxwell Communications in the United Kingdom, all of which had independent non-executive directors.[13] It may be difficult to ensure complete independence of non-executive directors; nevertheless, it is essential that they follow the recommendations in The Code and have suitable skills, experience and knowledge in performing their functions.

[13]The reference to the specific examples of corporate scandals shows your excellent knowledge of corporate governance. It will gain you more marks.

✓ **Make your answer stand out**

- Consider whether the dual board structure such as that in Germany, which consists of directors and supervisors, should be adopted in the United Kingdom.
- In your discussion of the appointment of non-executive directors, make reference to the Tyson Report on the Recruitment and Development of Non-Executive Directors.
- Explain the agency problems and agency costs in more detail.
- Further reading on the role of non-executive directors: Burke, 'The Higgs Review' (2003) 24 *Company Lawyer* 162; Griffin, S. 'Corporate collapse and the reform of boardroom structures – Lessons from America' (2003) 6 *Insolvency Law Journal* 214.

! **Don't be tempted to...**

- Only discuss the recommendations in the Combined Code. You should also make reference to the Higgs Review 2003, as required by the question.
- Only focus on the role of non-executive directors. You should also discuss the role of the board and that of executive directors.

Question 4

'Institutional investors play an important monitoring role in corporate governance. There are, however, concerns over their reluctance to tackle corporate underperformance in the companies in which they invest.'

Critically analyse the above statements by reference to the Combined Code and the UK Stewardship Code 2010.

Answer plan

→ Discuss the important monitoring roles that institutional shareholders play in corporate governance.

→ Analyse the recommendations in the Combined Code in relation to institutional shareholders.

→ Examine the main principles in the UK Stewardship Code 2010.

→ Assess the advantages and disadvantages of institutional shareholders using 'voice' or 'exit'.

Diagram plan

A printable version of this diagram plan is available from www.pearsoned.co.uk/lawexpressqa

Answer

[1]These sentences are helpful in showing the examiner that you are engaging with the question.

[2]The examples demonstrate that you know who institutional shareholders are. They form the basis of your discussion of their role in corporate governance.

[3]Many students understand that institutional shareholders can use their voice in voting at general meetings but may not appreciate that one-to-one meeting with the companies is another way of using their voice.

[4]This phrase shows that you are aware that institutional investors may misuse their power. It will add more credit to your answer.

This question requires an examination of the role of institutional shareholders in corporate governance by reference to the recommendations in the Combined Code and the UK Stewardship Code 2010. The benefits and problems of institutional shareholders using the 'voice' or 'exit' are also analysed.[1]

The main types of institutional shareholders are insurance companies, pension funds, unit trusts and investment trusts.[2] As the largest block of shareholders in listed companies in the United Kingdom, institutional shareholders are in a significant position to monitor company management and improve company performance. The forms of actions that institutional investors can take when faced with poor corporate governance are often referred to as the 'voice' and 'exit'. By using their voice, institutional shareholders remain with the company and use their influence to change corporate behaviours; for instance, they can vote on shareholder resolutions at companies' general meetings or engage with the company through one-to-one meetings with the company management.[3] By using the 'exit', institutional investors sell their shares and invest somewhere else.

Institutional shareholders are more sophisticated investors than individual shareholders. They are less likely to suffer from the problems of information asymmetry and therefore more likely to make informed choices about how they exercise their votes in general meetings. The block vote of an institutional investor, if used appropriately,[4] can enforce a significant change in company policy and make their involvement in monitoring meaningful and effective. Shareholders who own over 50% of the company's shares can dismiss directors and appoint new management (s 168, Companies Act 2006). Shareholders with 75% of the shares can alter the company's articles of association (s 21, CA 2006).[5] The active role of institutional shareholders in corporate governance can alleviate the agency problems by aligning the interests of management with those of the shareholders.[6] The use of voice by institutional shareholders has been highly recommended in the United Kingdom, although it does have its own drawbacks.

The role of institutional investors received significant attention in the Cadbury Report (1992).[7] It states that, given the weight of their votes, the way in which institutional shareholders use their power to influence the standards of corporate governance is of fundamental importance. They should act as responsible owners to use such power and bring about changes in companies rather than selling their shares. This emphasis on the active role of institutional shareholders is reflected in the Combined Code 2008 and the Stewardship Code 2010.[8]

The Combined Code 2008[9] encourages institutional investors to enter into a dialogue with companies based on the mutual understanding of objectives (E1). When evaluating companies' governance arrangements, particularly those relating to board structure and composition, institutional shareholders should give due weight to all relevant factors drawn to their attention (E2). They should consider carefully explanations given for departure from this Code and make reasoned judgements in each case. If they are not satisfied with the company's position, they should give an explanation to the company and be prepared to enter a dialogue. A box-ticking approach should be avoided when assessing a company's corporate governance. In relation to voting, institutional shareholders have a responsibility to make considered use of their votes (E 3). Major shareholders should attend AGMs where appropriate and practicable and should, on request, make available to their clients information on the proportion of resolutions on which votes were cast and non-discretionary proxies lodged.

The Stewardship Code 2010 aims to enhance the quality of engagement between institutional investors and companies and to

---

[5] These sentences show your wider understanding of company law and will gain you more marks.

[6] The reference to the agency problems shows your good knowledge of the corporate governance theories.

[7] The discussion of the Cadbury Report will help your answer stand out because it is a very important corporate governance report.

[8] This sentence leads onto your discussion of the Combined Code and the Stewardship Code in the next two paragraphs. It shows your ability to clearly signpost your answer.

[9] Although the Combined Code 2008 is not the latest version, it contains detailed recommendations on the role of institutional shareholders. The latest version of the Combined Code – the UK Corporate Governance Code 2010 contains very few principles in this respect because detailed recommendations are now contained in the Stewardship Code.

The 'comply or explain' approach is the essence of the Combined Code. Your understanding of the voluntary basis will gain you more marks.

[11]This phrase demonstrates your knowledge of the inconclusive evidence that the active role of institutional shareholders will improve corporate performance. It may impress your examiners.

[12]An examination of the potential problems caused by the active role of institutional shareholders shows your excellent analytical skills. It will make your answer stand out from those narrative answers which focus only on the recommendations of the Combined Code and the Stewardship Code.

[13]This discussion of short-termism is often omitted in students' answers.

help improve long-term returns to shareholders and the efficient exercise of governance responsibilities. It adopts the principle of 'comply or explain' in the Combined Code.[10] It recommends that institutional investors should publicly disclose their policy on how they will discharge their stewardship responsibilities and have a robust policy on managing conflicts of interest in relation to stewardship. They should monitor their investee companies and establish clear guidelines on when and how they will escalate their activities as a method of protecting and enhancing shareholder value. Moreover, they should have a clear policy on voting and disclosure of voting activity and report periodically on their stewardship and voting activities.

There are perceived benefits[11] of shareholder activism that more efficient monitoring of company management aligns the interests of shareholder and those of directors and therefore helps to maximise shareholders' wealth. Although institutional shareholders are encouraged to take an active role, there are concerns that this approach is not necessarily beneficial to the company for a number of reasons.[12] First, institutional investors owe fiduciary duties to their own shareholders, not to the companies (investee companies) in which they invest. In some circumstances they may find that it is in the best interests of their own shareholders to exit the company. Secondly, institutional investors may only be interested in short-term maximisation of profits and therefore pressure the investee companies to focus on short-term rather than long-term profits.[13] This can be detrimental to the long-term survival of the investee companies because they need to invest in long-term projects in order to maintain a sustainable growth. Thirdly, the action by institutional shareholders may lead to adverse media publicity which results in a fall in share price of the investee companies and a reduction in the value of their investment. Moreover, it can be difficult for institutional shareholders to take legal actions such as the derivative claims (s 260, CA 2006) and unfair prejudice petitions (s 994, CA 2006). The litigation may be costly in terms of time and money. Fourthly, institutional shareholders may lack sufficient incentives to initiate proceedings due to the free-rider problems when other shareholders benefit from their monitoring roles. Finally, although institutional shareholders are more sophisticated than individual investors, the pension fund managers may not be professionally trained or qualified in corporate governance or financial management. If they become

14 The discussion of insider
dealing and market abuse
shows your wider knowledge
and will gain you more marks.

too involved in the affairs of the investee companies and receive price-sensitive information that has not been publicly disclosed, they may become insiders and be restricted from dealing with the company's shares according to the Financial Services and Market Act 2000.[14] In the light of the problems associated with using their voice, institutional investors may prefer the use of exit which clearly avoids the free rider problems. The use of exit, however, may be expensive because institutional shareholders have to accept substantial discounts to liquidate their holdings. In conclusion, it is argued that institutional investors should take an active interest in their investment and act as responsible owners of the investee companies, which will in turn improve the corporate governance and enhance the financial performance of their investee companies.

✓ Make your answer stand out

- Consider the main guidelines on corporate governance and shareholder activism, such as *The Responsibilities of Institutional Shareholders and Agents – Statement of Principles* (Institutional Shareholders' Committee, 2007).
- Provide examples of institutional shareholders using their voice by engaging in constructive dialogue with its investee companies. Kingfisher plc, for instance, changed some aspects of its directors' remuneration packages following criticisms from its institutional shareholders (see Mallin, C. *Corporate Governance*, Oxford University Press, 2007, p. 95).

! Don't be tempted to...

- Ignore the main principles in the Stewardship Code 2010. This is the most recent and important document on the role of institutional investors and it should not be omitted in your answer.
- Only describe what is meant by the use of 'voice' or 'exit'. You should also analyse the advantages and disadvantages of both mechanisms.

❓ Question 5

Urban Bank plc is listed on the London Stock Exchange. Its recent annual report shows that it has suffered heavy losses. It reveals that each of its executive directors is paid an annual salary of £800,000 plus £1 million bonus; the chief executive director has been appointed as the chairman of the board. There are only two non-executive directors on the board; both are family members of the executive directors and both lack banking expertise and experience.

River Pension Ltd, who owns 30% of the shares in Urban Bank plc, is unhappy with these business practices.

Advise River Pension Ltd as to whether Urban Bank plc has complied with the UK Corporate Governance Code (the Code) and what actions it should take to improve the corporate governance of Urban Bank plc.

Answer plan

→ Consider the main principles in The Code in relation to directors' remuneration.

→ Examine the board structure and whether the chief executive director and the chairman of the board can be the same person.

→ Discuss the requirements in The Code in relation to the independence and competence of non-executive directors as well as the number of non-executive directors on the board.

→ Evaluate the role of institutional shareholders which is recommended by The Code and the Stewardship Code.

→ Analyse whether River Pension Ltd should use its voice or exit Urban Bank plc.

Diagram plan

Is the Combined Code complied with?	→	Is the remuneration of executive directors excessive?
	→	Should the chief executive director and the chairman be the same person?
	→	Is the number of non-executive directors sufficient?
	→	Are the non-executive directors independent or competent?

If it is not complied with, is there any explanation given for the non-compliance?

What action(s) can the institutional shareholder (River Pension Ltd) take if it is unhappy with the non-compliance with the Combined Code?

A printable version of this diagram plan is available from www.pearsoned.co.uk/lawexpressqa

[1]You should point out in your introduction that River Pension Ltd is an institutional shareholder because it indicates that your answer is going in the right direction.

[2]This part of the sentence summaries the key legal issues that arise in the problem scenario. It will give your examiners a good impression that you know what this problem question is about.

[3]The reference to the problem scenario shows that you are engaging with the question.

[4]The precise section number shows your excellent knowledge of the Combined Code and makes your answer stand out.

Answer

In order to advise River Pension Ltd, which is an institutional shareholder,[1] it is essential to examine whether Urban Bank plc has complied with the UK Corporate Governance Code 2010 (The Code) in relation to directors' remuneration, board structure and the role of non-executive directors.[2] It is also important to weigh the advantages and disadvantages of any action that River Pension Ltd may take to improve the corporate governance of Urban Bank plc.

Despite the failure in company performance, as indicated by the heavy losses, the executive directors of Urban Bank plc are paid generously in terms of base salary and bonus.[3] The Code (s D)[4] recommends that the remuneration committee should be set up to recommend and monitor the level and structure of remuneration for senior management. It should consist of at least three independent non-executive directors. There should be a formal and transparent procedure for fixing the remuneration packages of individual directors. In particular, the levels of remuneration should be sufficient to retain and motivate directors to run the company successfully. A company, however, should avoid paying more than is necessary for this purpose. A significant proportion of executive directors' remuneration should be structured so as to link rewards to corporate and individual performance.[5] This performance-related element of executive directors' remuneration should be designed to promote the long-term success of the company. It can be argued that the directors' remuneration in Urban Bank plc is not linked to either corporate or individual performance.

[5]This is the key recommendation in the Combined Code in relation to directors' remuneration. You will lose marks if it is omitted in your answer.

[6]This sentence shows that you are moving on to the next issue. Try to use a new paragraph to address a different legal issue. The use of clear paragraphs helps examiners follow your answer and allocate marks.

The annual report of Urban Bank plc reveals that its chief executive director also acts as the chairman of the board.[6] The Combined Code 2010 (Section A) recommends that there should be a clear division of responsibilities at the head of the company between the running of the board and the executive responsibility for the running of the company's business. No one individual should have unfettered powers of decision. In particular, the roles of chairman and chief executive should not be exercised by the same individual. The division of responsibilities between the chairman and chief executive should be clearly established, set out in writing and agreed by the board. It is therefore argued that Urban Bank plc does not comply with the Combined Code in this respect.

[7]Pay attention to the recommended number of non-executive directors on the board. It is often missing in exam answers.

[8]The Enron scandal is the classic case to illustrate the importance of independent non-executive directors. The reference to Enron will gain you more marks.

In relation to the number of non-executive directors, the Combined Code 2010 (Section B) recommends that at least half the board, excluding the chairman,[7] should comprise independent non-executive directors. The board should have the appropriate balance of skills, experience, independence and knowledge of the company to enable them to discharge its duties and responsibilities effectively. The independence and competence of non-executive directors are essential for an effective board as illustrated by the Enron scandal.[8] The non-executive directors in Urban Bank plc are family members of the executive directors and lack finance or banking expertise. It is apparent that they lack independence and expertise.

[9]Note here that the independence of non-executive directors is decided by the board, instead of shareholders.

Moreover, the board should identify in the annual report each non-executive director it considers to be independent (The Code, Section B). It should determine whether the director is independent in character and judgement and whether there are relationships or circumstances which are likely to affect the director's judgement.[9] The board should state its reasons if it determines that a director is independent, notwithstanding the existence of relationships or circumstances which may appear relevant to its determination; for example, if the director has close family ties with any of the company's directors as is the case in Urban Bank plc. The board of Urban Bank plc should, in its annual report, justify the independence of these non-executive directors who are family members of executive directors.

Urban Bank plc is a listed company, to which the Combined Code applies.[10] The Code adopts the principle of 'comply or explain'. It requires that the boards of all listed companies should comply with The Code but, if they cannot comply with any particular aspect of it, they should explain their reasons for non-compliance. It is a voluntary code and no legal sanction will arise for non-compliance with it. Failure to include it in the annual report, however, is a breach of the Listing Rules and penalties may be imposed for such non-compliance. As some aspects of The Code are not complied with, the board of Urban Bank plc should provide explanations for such non-compliance in its annual report.

Due to the large block of shares it holds, River Pension Ltd has the potential to influence the company management and monitor the board. It may use its voice by voting on shareholder resolutions at general meetings or engaging with the company through one-to-one meetings with the board. Alternatively, it may choose to exit by selling its shares in Urban Bank plc. The Combined Code 2008 (Section E)[11] recommends that institutional investors are encouraged to enter into a dialogue with companies. They should consider carefully explanations given for departure from this Code and make reasoned judgements in each case. If they are not satisfied with the company's position, they should give an explanation to the company and be prepared to enter a dialogue. In relation to voting, institutional shareholders have a responsibility to make considered use of their votes and should attend AGMs where appropriate and practicable.

[11]The Combined Code 2008 is discussed here instead of the latest Code 2010 because the former contains detailed recommendations on the role of institutional shareholders.

The Stewardship Code 2010 recommends that institutional investors should publicly disclose their policy on how they will discharge their stewardship responsibilities and have a robust policy on managing conflicts of interest in relation to stewardship. They should monitor their investee companies and establish clear guidelines on when and how they will escalate their activities as a method of protecting and enhancing shareholder value. Moreover, they should have a clear policy on voting and disclosure of voting activity and report periodically on their stewardship and voting activities.

As River Pension Ltd is unhappy with the management arrangement in Urban Bank plc, it is encouraged by the Combined Code and the Stewardship Code to enter into dialogue with the board or vote at the company's general meeting. Any action, however, may lead to adverse media interests that result in a fall in share price and a reduction in the value of its investment.[12] River Pension Ltd may also consider the use of exit; however, it could be expensive because of the substantial discounts to liquidate its entire shareholdings. After balancing the advantages and disadvantages of both options, River Pension Ltd is advised to take an active role by entering into a dialogue with the board and if it is not satisfied with the response, using their voting power at the general meeting of Urban Bank plc.[13]

[12]This sentence discusses the disadvantages of using voice. It will gain you more marks than only focusing on the perceived benefits of the active role of institutional shareholders.

[13]Clearly answer the question in your conclusion by stating your advice to River Pension Ltd.

✓ Make your answer stand out

- Discuss the recommendations in the *Walker Review of Corporate Governance of UK Banking Industry* in relation to directors' remuneration, board structure and the role of institutional shareholders in corporate governance of banks.
- Consider the legal actions that River Pension Ltd may take to challenge directors such as the derivative actions (ss 260–264, Companies Act 2006).
- Assess in more detail the benefits and problems with regard to the use of voice by River Pension Ltd.

! Don't be tempted to...

- Treat the Combined Code as law. You must understand that it is only a self-regulatory code and the compliance with it is not mandatory.
- Make no reference to the Stewardship Code 2010 in your discussion of the role of institutional shareholders.

Question 6

'Despite the collapse of banks and other large public companies, their directors still receive generous pay packages. It seems that remuneration committees have not made any significant changes in the amount of remuneration awarded.'

Analyse the above statements by reference to directors' remuneration and the role of remuneration committee in corporate governance.

Answer plan

→ Consider the agency problems and directors' remuneration.

→ Examine the role of remuneration committees in deciding directors' pay by reference to the Greenbury Report and the UK Corporate Governance Code (the 'Code').

→ Discuss the recommended levels of remuneration for non-executive directors.

→ Analyse the legal requirements for the disclosure of directors' remuneration in the Companies Act 2006.

Diagram plan

A printable version of this diagram plan is available from www.pearsoned.co.uk/lawexpressqa

Answer

Directors' remuneration has attracted considerable public attention and media publicity in light of the recent financial crisis and corporate scandals. One high-profile example is the controversy behind the pension entitlement of Sir Fred Goodwin, the former chief executive officer of the Royal Bank of Scotland.[1] He was awarded a very generous pension despite the failure in company performance. In order to align the interests of directors with those of shareholders, it is essential to assess the role of the remuneration committee in corporate governance and the appropriate levels of remuneration

[1] A specific example shows your good knowledge of the recent events from the national press. It makes your answer stand out from the start.

[2]This sentence identifies
the key legal issues that
arise in this essay question.
It demonstrates to the
examiners that you know
clearly what this question is
asking.

[3]The reference to the book by
Berle and Means shows your
excellent knowledge of the
agency problem. It will gain
you more marks than simply
explaining agency problems.

[4]This sentence leads
to the discussion of the
two important corporate
governance documents.
It also shows that you are
engaging with the question
by referring back to the core
issues raised in the question.

[5]Note the differences in the
recommended number of
non-executive directors in a
remuneration committee in
the Greenbury Report and the
Combined Code.

[6]Your reference to the exact
section number of the
recommended principle in
an exam answer will impress
your examiners.

for directors.[2] It can be argued that the remuneration committee has a significant role to play in maintaining the appropriate levels of directors' remuneration.

Directors' remuneration mainly comprises base salary, bonus, stock options, restricted share plans, pension and other benefits. It is closely linked to the agency problems that the principals (shareholders) have in monitoring the agents (directors). Berle and Means in *The Modern Corporation and Private Property* (1932) identified the problem caused by the separation of ownership and control in US companies in the 1930s.[3] They discovered that many large companies had such widely dispersed share ownership that the board of directors, instead of the shareholders, was able to exert real control over the company. This could lead to a great danger that directors would run the company for their own benefit, rather than on behalf of the shareholders; for example, directors were likely to award themselves large pay packages. In order to address this problem, directors' remuneration and the role of remuneration committee have been subject to detailed examination by the Greenbury Report and The Code.[4]

The Greenbury Committee was formed after widespread public concerns over the excessive amounts of remuneration paid to directors of quoted companies and newly privatised companies. When the Greenbury Report was published in 1995, it dealt specifically with the question of directors' remuneration and many of its recommendations were developed from the earlier Cadbury Report. The Greenbury Report recommends that directors' remuneration should be linked to company performance. It also addresses the problem of the rewards for failure for directors whose performance had not been successful but still managed to leave the company with generous compensation for loss of office.

The establishment of remuneration committees aims to prevent executive directors from deciding their own remuneration levels. The Greenbury Report recommends that the remuneration committee should consist exclusively[5] of non-executive directors who have no personal financial interest, no potential conflicts of interest arising from cross-directorships and no day-to-day involvement in running the business. According to The Code (D.2.1),[6] the remuneration committee should consist of at least three, or in the case of smaller companies two, independent non-executive directors. In addition, the company chairman may also be a member of the committee if he was considered independent on appointment as chairman. The remuneration committee should recommend and monitor the level and structure of remuneration for senior management and no director should be involved in deciding his own remuneration. Moreover, there should be a formal and transparent procedure for developing policy on executive remuneration and for fixing the remuneration packages of individual directors (The Code 2010, D2).

It is inappropriate for the remuneration committee to decide non-executive directors' pay because it is made up of non-executives. In this regard, the Combined Code 2010 recommends that the remuneration of non-executive directors should be decided by the board itself or, where required by the articles of association, the shareholders. Levels of remuneration for non-executive directors should reflect the time commitment and responsibilities of the role.

The performance measures are important for aligning directors' performance and their remuneration. The Code recommends that levels of remuneration should be sufficient to attract, retain and motivate directors of the quality required to run the company successfully, but a company should avoid paying more than is necessary for this purpose. A significant proportion of executive directors' remuneration should be structured so as to link rewards to corporate and individual performance (The Code, D.1). The performance-related elements of executive directors' remuneration should be designed to promote the long-term success of the company.

[7] A consideration of the compensation schemes for directors should be included in your answer because it is an important component of directors' pay packages.

In order to avoid rewarding poor performance, the remuneration committee should carefully consider what compensation commitments their directors' terms of appointment would entail in the event of early termination.[7] It should take a robust line on reducing compensation to reflect departing directors' obligations to mitigate loss (The Code, D.1.4). The compensation contracts, if designed appropriately, may help to ensure that the objectives of directors and shareholders are aligned.

The disclosure of directors' remuneration is essential to ensure a transparent and fair remuneration. The former Department of Trade and Industry published the Directors' Remuneration Report

[8]Many students are not aware of this piece of regulation. Although the provisions are now contained in the Companies Act 2006, the reference to the 2002 Regulations shows your sound knowledge and will gain you more marks.

[9]Adding your own analysis makes your answer stand out from a pure narrative account.

[10]A discussion of academic argument shows your broader knowledge and will add more credit to your answer.

[11]This sentence demonstrates your analytical skills. It gains you more marks than simply describing the requirements in The Code.

[12]This sentence shows that you appreciate the complicated issues associated with directors' pay. A balanced view also enhances your critical analysis and helps your answers to stand out.

Regulations 2002, which are now contained in the Companies Act 2006 (ss 420–422).[8] Its main aim is to promote greater transparency and accountability of companies' remuneration policies of listed companies. The key requirement is that directors of a listed company must prepare a directors' remuneration report for each financial year of the company (s 420). The requirements on the contents of such report are listed in s 421. The directors' remuneration report must be approved by the board of directors and signed on behalf of the board by a director or the secretary of the company (s 422). It is debatable to what extent the disclosure of directors' remuneration has achieved the aim of improving the accountability of companies' remuneration policies.[9]

The remuneration committee, composed of independent non-executive directors, plays a key role in ensuring that executive directors' remuneration packages are linked with company performance. Sykes (2002), however, is sceptical of the functions of remuneration committees. It is argued that although remuneration committees predominantly consist of a majority of non-executive directors, they are effectively chosen by, or only with the full agreement of, senior management.[10] It is therefore doubtful how effective the remuneration committee is in ensuring a fair pay package for directors.[11] A fine balance needs to be struck between incentivizing directors on the one hand and aligning directors' interests with those of shareholders on the other.[12] The difficulties, however, lie on how to ensure that the directors' pay matches up with their performance and how to establish an appropriate pay structure for this purpose.

 Make your answer stand out

- Consider the important roles that institutional shareholders play in restraining directors' pay.
- Make reference to the provisions in Schedule A to the Combined Code 2010 on designing schemes of performance-related remuneration for executive directors.

Question 7

'[P]ublic opinion, which ultimately makes law, has made and is today making substantial strides in the direction of the view of the business corporation as an economic institution which has a social service as well as a profit-making function, that this view has already had some effect upon legal theory, and that it is likely to have a greatly increased effect upon the latter in the near future.' (Dodd, 'For whom are corporate managers trustees?' (1932) 45 *Harvard Law Review* 1145, p. 1148)

Critically analyse the above statement with reference to the recent statutory development in the United Kingdom.

Answer plan

→ Discuss the Berle and Dodd debates in relation to shareholder primacy and stakeholder theory.

→ Analyse the theory of shareholder primacy.

→ Evaluate the stakeholder theory.

→ Examine the enlightened shareholder value which is adopted in the Companies Act 2006.

Diagram plan

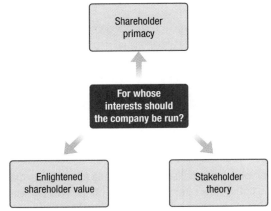

A printable version of this diagram plan is available from www.pearsoned.co.uk/lawexpressqa

Answer

[1]This sentence not only refers to the question but also analyses the underlying issue in corporate governance. It shows that you know what this question is about.

[2]The discussion of the corporate governance issues in other countries demonstrates your broad knowledge of international corporate governance. It will impress your examiners.

[3]It is worth learning the title of Berle's article because it is a significant argument for shareholder primacy.

Dodd's statement reflects the ongoing debate on the fundamental question in corporate governance: for whose interests the company should be run.[1] Traditionally, there are two influential theories: shareholder primacy (or shareholder value theory) and stakeholder theory (or the pluralist approach). Shareholder primacy has historically been the dominant company law philosophy in the United Kingdom and the United States, whilst the stakeholder theory operates in many continental European and East Asian countries such as Germany and Japan.[2] A new approach is adopted in the Companies Act 2006 in the United Kingdom.

The debate on shareholder primacy and stakeholder theory started from as early as 1932. Advocates of shareholder primacy such as Berle (1931)[3] argued that a company should be run to maximise profits for shareholders who invested in the company. It would be inappropriate to release directors from a strict accountability to shareholders. This theory reflects the view that shareholders are owners of the company and bear the residual risks.

Supporters of the stakeholder theory, such as Dodd (1932), are concerned that concentration on share price and profits encourages short-termism. They argue that the company should be run not only for the interests of shareholders but also for all their stakeholders. Stakeholders refer to any individual group on which the activities

[4]This word demonstrates
that you are analysing Dodd's
argument rather than simply
stating it.

[4]This word demonstrates
that you are analysing Dodd's
argument rather than simply
stating it.

[5]This sentence shows your
analytical skills by evaluating
the problems associated with
the stakeholder theory. It
will add more credit to your
answer.

[6]The reference to *Hutton*
shows your good knowledge
of case law and will gain you
more marks.

[7]The CLRSG's criticisms
of the stakeholder theory
demonstrate your excellent
understanding of the
company law reform. It will
make your answer stand out
from those without detailed
analysis of the reasons for
the rejection of stakeholder
theory.

[8]Make sure that you can
write this phrase accurately.
Some students have a vague
idea of this concept and
often make the basic mistake
of writing 'enlightening
shareholder value'.

of the company have an impact. Dodd challenged the shareholder primacy and convincingly[4] argued that public opinion in the United States increasingly regarded companies as economic institutions which have a social service as well as a profit-making function. He identified that employees, customers and the general public also had a valid interest in how the company should be run. Although the stakeholder theory is beneficial in the wider context and in the long term, it inevitably involves a fine balance of stakeholders' potentially competing interests.[5]

The traditional approach in the United Kingdom is the shareholder primacy whereby a company should be run for the wealth maximisation of its shareholders above those of other parties such as customers and suppliers. Directors were under a duty to act in the interests of the company: **Percival *v* Wright** [1902] 2 Ch 421. Such interests were interpreted as the best interests of present and future shareholders: **Hutton *v* West Cork Railway Company** (1883) LR 23 ChD 654.[6] During the recent company law reform, the stakeholder theory was considered but not adopted in the Companies Act 2006, mainly because of the difficulties faced by directors in balancing interests of different groups and the concerns in enforcing these duties. The Company Law Review Steering Group (*The Strategic Framework*, 1999) rejected the stakeholder approach as neither workable nor desirable.[7] It argued that it was impractical to identify all the stakeholders and redefine the nature and extent of the directors' responsibilities. If the pluralist approach was adopted, the directors would not be effectively accountable to anyone since there would be no clear yardstick for judging their performance. There was also a lack of a proper measure for the enforcement of the pluralist approach. Additionally, it put forward a strong philosophical argument against the pluralist approach – it would turn directors from being business decision-makers into being moral, political and economic arbiters.

The new concept of enlightened shareholder value[8] is introduced into the Companies Act 2006. Section 172 not only codifies the common law duty to act *bona fide* in what a director considers is in the interests of the company (**Re Smith & Fawcett Ltd** [1942] 1 All ER 542) but also introduces the enlightened shareholder value. A director must act in a way he considers, in good faith, would be most likely to promote the success of the company for the benefit of

[9]You should pay attention to the non-exhaustive list because it reflects the essence of the enlightened shareholder value. Although you do not need to learn the exact provision of s 172 by heart, a good understanding of this provision is essential for your answer.

its members as a whole. In doing so, he must also have regard to a number of factors in s 172(1),[9] including the likely consequences of any decision in the long term, the interests of the company's employees, the need to foster the company's business relationship with suppliers, customers and others, the impact of the company's operations on the community and the environment, the desirability of the company maintaining a reputation for high standards of business conduct; and the need to act fairly as between members of the company.

The enlightened shareholder value is perceived to better achieve wealth generation and competitiveness for the benefit of all because it requires a long-term approach and permits directors to consider other interests as the best way of securing prosperity and welfare overall. It appears to be a compromise between shareholder primacy and stakeholder theory by maintaining the primacy of shareholders whilst considering other stakeholders' interests.[10] Despite the introduction of the non-exhaustive list in s 172(1) that a director has to consider, it is clear that shareholder primacy is still dominant because a director must act to promote the success of the company for the interests of members as a whole.

[10]This sentence analyses the relationship between the enlightened shareholder value with the other two theories. It will gain you more marks.

The enlightened shareholder value provides some guidance for businesses faced with the task of balancing different interests among employees, communities, environment and their own reputation. It is unclear, however, whether a director would breach this duty if he considered all the factors, except the one relating to the environment or community. It is also problematic when there is a conflict between two or more of the factors, for example, if a decision benefits the employees but is detrimental to its customers.[11] While shareholders may bring a derivative action against directors for breach of this duty, there is a lack of procedure for other stakeholders such as employees or the community to hold directors accountable if the directors fail to consider their interests set out in s 172(1).[12] As derivative actions are only available to *members* of the company (s 260), it is most likely that directors will continue to ensure they exercise their power in good faith and promote the success of the company for the benefit of its members.

[11]These sentences demonstrate your analytical skills by examining the problems associated with the enlightened shareholder value. They will make your answer stand out.

[12]The lack of enforcement of directors' duties by stakeholders is one of the main problems with the stakeholder theory. It should not be omitted in a sound answer.

It is argued that the English company law has moved closer to the stakeholder theory. A company is still run to generate maximum

[13]This sentence summarises the current position in the United Kingdom in relation to the shareholder and stakeholder debate. It shows your excellent understanding of the enlightened shareholder value.

wealth for shareholders but directors should take a properly balanced view of the implications of decisions over time and foster effective relationships with employees, customers, suppliers and the wider community.[13] In the light of recent financial crisis and corporate failures, which have had a drastic impact, not only on shareholders, but also on stakeholders of the companies such as employees and communities, there may be more support for a stakeholder-orientated approach and corporate social responsibility.[14]

[14]You will gain more marks by expressing your views with reference to the current affairs in your conclusion.

✓ Make your answer stand out

- Discuss the problems associated with s 172; for instance, it is unclear which criteria should be used to assess objectively whether the action of the directors has led to success of the company.

- In relation to the test for the duty to act in good faith in s 172, consider *Fulham Football Club* v *Cabra Estates plc* [1992] BCLC 863 and *Re Southern Counties Fresh Foods Ltd* [2008] All ER (D) 195.

- Further reading on shareholder primacy, stakeholder theory and enlightened shareholder value: Keay, A. R. 'Enlightened shareholder value, the reform of the duties of company directors and the corporate objective' [2006] LMCLQ 335; Keay, A. R. 'Section 172(1) of the Companies Act 2006: an interpretation and assessment' (2007) 28 *Company Lawyer* 106; Kiarie, S. 'At crossroads: shareholder value, stakeholder value and enlightened shareholder value: which road should the United Kingdom take?' [2006] ICCLR 329.

! Don't be tempted to...

- Undertake no discussion of the debates by Dodd and Berle. You must not ignore these influential debates when answering an exam question with respect to shareholder primacy and stakeholder theory.

- Provide a detailed discussion of directors' duties. This is not a question on directors' duties; you should focus on the enlightened shareholder value in s 172 instead of discussing directors' statutory duties in general.

Shares and share capital

How this topic may come up in exams

Shares and share capital are complex topics and many students struggle to apply the large number of complicated statutory provisions. You are expected to show a good understanding of class rights, pre-emption rights, allotment of shares, payment of shares and transfer of shares. The procedures governing the reorganisation of share capital and the doctrine of capital maintenance are popular exam questions. The prohibition of financial assistance by a public company for the acquisition of its own shares is also frequently examined. These topics may overlap with other areas of law such as articles of association, shareholders' rights and directors' duties.

■ Attack the question

? Question 1

Pesto Ltd has an issued share capital of £40,000. Peter, Jim and Emily hold 60%, 30% and 10% of the company's shares respectively. Peter and Jim are directors of the company. Its articles of association, which otherwise follow the Model Articles for private companies limited by shares, state that: 'Any member who intends to transfer shares to an outsider must give notice of his intention in writing to the board. The directors reserve the right to refuse to register the transfer of shares by any member for whatever reason.'

Emily has agreed to sell her shares to John. One month after the transfer was lodged with the company, the board of directors refused to register the transfer without giving any reasons for the refusal.

Advise Emily and John as to their legal positions and any possible action against the directors.

Answer plan

→ Discuss whether the shares of Pesto Ltd are freely transferable.

→ Consider whether the board of directors can refuse to register the transfer of shares without giving any reasons.

→ Examine the legal positions of Emily and John when the registration is refused.

→ Evaluate the possible legal actions against the directors.

Diagram plan

Are the shares in Pesto Ltd transferable?

Yes, subject to the restrictions in the articles of association.

Can directors refuse to register the transfer?

Yes, but only when they are granted the power by the articles and give reasons for refusal within two months (s 771).

Have the directors breached any of their statutory duties in exercising this power (ss 171 and 172)?

If so, Emily can bring a derivative action against directors (ss 260–263) or an unfair prejudice petition (s 994).

A printable version of this diagram plan is available from www.pearsoned.co.uk/lawexpressqa

Answer

[1]This sentence identifies the key legal issues and shows that you are engaging with the problem question.

[2]Shares are not well defined. The reference to this common law illustration shows your good understanding of the definition of shares and will gain you more marks.

In order to advise Emily and John, it is essential to analyse whether the shares in Pesto Ltd are freely transferable and whether the board of directors has the power to refuse to register the transfer of shares.[1] Shares are personal property (s 541). Farwell J in **Borland's Trustee v Steel Bros & Co Ltd** [1901] 1 Ch 279 explained that: 'A share is not a sum of money ... but is an interest measured by a sum of money, and made up of various rights contained in the contract.'[2] A share represents a bundle of contractual rights conferred by the company's constitution and the Companies Act 2006, such as the

[3]Most students understand
that shares are transferable
but are not aware of the
conditions – subject to
the company's articles of
association. The reference to
the statutory provision shows
your precise knowledge.

[4]This sentence explains why
there may be restrictions
on the transfer of shares in
private companies. It adds
more credit to your answer
than simply stating the
restrictions.

[5]Make sure that your answer
refers back to the problem
question.

[6]The explanation of the
rationale for pre-emption rights
will earn you more marks.

[7]This is the key phrase in s
771. When directors refuse to
register the transfer, reasons
must be given.

[8]The consequences for failure
to comply with s 771 have
important implications in
a problem question. They
are often omitted in exam
answers.

[9]This sentence indicates that
you are answering the part
of the question in relation to
the legal positions of Emily
and John.

right to vote, to declared dividends and a return of capital on winding up of the company. Shares are transferable in the manner provided by the company's articles (s 544).[3] It is common for the articles in a private company to impose restrictions on the transfer of shares because the existing members may wish to control the membership of the company.[4] Any restrictions of the right to transfer must be clearly expressed in the articles: **Re Smith & Fawcett Ltd** [1942] 1 All ER 542.

The articles of Pesto Ltd state that any member who intends to transfer shares must give notice of his intention in writing to the board.[5] This triggers the pre-emption rights which provide the existing shareholders with the opportunity to buy the shares for sale before they are offered outside the company. It ensures that a shareholder is able to protect his proportion of the total equity of a company.[6] As a company's articles of association create contractual rights between members (s 33); the provisions regarding the pre-emption rights are enforceable by members: **Rayfield v Hands** [1958] 2 All ER 194.

Although Emily and John have agreed on the sale of shares, John will not become a member of the company until he is registered. A share certificate is *prima facie* evidence that the named member has title to the shares (s 768). When a transfer of shares has been lodged, the company must either register the transfer or give the transferee notice of refusal to register the transfer, together with its reasons for the refusal (s 771).[7] This must be done as soon as practicable and in any event within two months after the date on which the transfer is lodged with it. If the company refuses to register the transfer, it must provide the transferee with further information about the reasons for the refusal as the transferee may reasonably request (s 771(2)). If a company fails to comply with this section, an offence is committed by the company and every officer of the company who is in default (s 771(3)).[8] Since the board of Pesto Ltd has not given any reasons for the refusal, Emily can apply to the court for rectification of the Register and the issue of a share certificate (s 125).

It is important to clarify the legal positions of Emily and John before the transfer of shares is registered.[9] If a transfer of shares is refused, the equitable title to the shares passes to the purchaser once the contract of sale is made and the legal title passes on completion and registration by the company: **Roots v Williamson** (1888) 38

Ch D 485. Such refusal will not affect John's beneficial interest in a share; for example, he is still entitled to the dividends declared on the shares and a return of capital on winding up. John, however, is not able to exercise all the membership rights; for example, he may not vote at shareholder meetings until the transfer is registered and his name is entered in the register of members. The legal title does not pass to him until his name is on the members' list but he can instruct Emily on how to vote because Emily still holds the shares as trustee for John: **Re Rose, Rose v IRC** [1952] 1 All ER 1217. If Emily did not promise to secure registration of transfer of shares, she would not be liable for damages for breach when the registration was refused.[10]

[10]This sentence analyses the terms of the contract of sale. It goes further than a discussion of the board's power to register the transfer of shares and adds more credit to your answer.

Although directors in Pesto Ltd are given absolute discretion to refuse registration of transfer of shares by its articles, they are not totally free to exercise such power. In **Re Smith & Fawcett Ltd** [1942] 1 All ER 542,[11] the Court of Appeal held that, when directors exercise such broad discretion, they must act *bona fide* in what they consider to be in the interests of the company and not for any collateral purpose. Emily and John may argue that directors' refusal to register the transfer is not made *bona fide* for the success of the company and therefore in breach of their duties in s 172. This duty, however, is very subjective in nature: **Bristol & West Building Society v Mothew** [1998] Ch 1. It is what a director considers, not what a court considers, would be most likely to promote the success of the company. Moreover, they can argue that the directors breached their duties in s 171 by exercising their power for improper purposes: **Howard Smith Ltd v Ampol Petroleum** [1974] AC 821.[12]

[11]This case law is very important here because it is directly relevant to the exercise of directors' power in registering the transfer of shares. The absence of this case law will negatively affect your mark.

[12]Although directors' duties are now codified in the Companies Act 2006, you should still refer to case law which is relevant in the application and interpretation of the statutory duties.

Emily may consider bringing a derivative action to challenge directors' breach of duties. She needs to establish a *prima facie* case and go through the two-stage procedure in s 261. The court will take into account a number of factors in s 263 when considering whether to give or refuse permission to continue the derivative claim. This procedure, however, is subject to tight judicial control. The court has taken a restrictive approach; for instance, it refused to grant permission if the judges did not believe that the hypothetical director would attach much importance to the claim, or if all that the claimant was seeking could be recovered by means of an unfair prejudice petition: **Mission Capital plc v Sinclair** [2008] BCC 866; **Franbar Holding Ltd v Patel** [2008] BCC 885.[13] A more practical option for

[13]These sentences analyse the merits of a derivative claim. They will gain you more marks than simply stating the possibility of bringing a derivative claim.

Emily is the unfair prejudice petition under s 994 whereby she can claim that her interests as a member have been unfairly prejudiced by the conduct of the company's affairs. If the court is satisfied that the petition is well founded, it may make any order it thinks fit for giving relief in respect of the matters complained of; for example, the court may order the board of Pesto Ltd to register the transfer of shares and issue a share certificate to John (s 996).

✓ Make your answer stand out

- Discuss the relevant clauses in the Model Articles, for example, the general management clause in Article 3 which provides that 'subject to the articles, the directors are responsible for the management of the company's business, for which purpose they may exercise all the powers of the company'.
- Point out that John also has *locus standi* in the unfair prejudice petition because s 994 also applies to a person who is not a member of a company but to whom shares in the company have been transferred.

! Don't be tempted to...

- Ignore the time limit for the refusal to register the transfer of shares. This must be done as soon as practicable and in any event within *two months* after the date on which the transfer is lodged with it.
- Undertake no discussion of directors' breach of duties. As this question asks about the legal actions available to Emily, an examination of directors' duties and shareholder remedies is essential.
- Get confused with the legal positions of Emily and John when the transfer of shares is refused. John has the *equitable* title to the shares when the contract of sale is made but Emily still has the *legal* title.

🖎 Question 2

'The doctrine of capital maintenance is designed to protect the interests of creditors. It has been relaxed in the Companies Act 2006 to accommodate modern business needs and now offers little protection for creditors.'

Undertake a critical analysis of the above statements in relation to the regime of capital maintenance in the Companies Act 2006.

Answer plan

→ Consider the rationale of the doctrine of capital maintenance.

→ Analyse the historical development of the doctrine of capital maintenance: *Trevor* v *Whitworth* (1887) 12 App Cas 409.

→ Examine the statutory provisions in the CA 2006 in relation to: reduction of share capital; company's distribution (such as dividends); purchase by a company of its own shares and redemption of shares; and prohibition of providing financial assistance in public companies.

Diagram plan

A printable version of this diagram plan is available from www.pearsoned.co.uk/lawexpressqa

Answer

[1]Your answer should start with an explanation of the doctrine of capital maintenance. The reference to the landmark case of *Trevor* v *Whitworth* is essential here.

[2]This part of the sentence summaries the main aspects of the doctrine of capital maintenance. It also sets a clear structure for your answer.

It was established in **Trevor v Whitworth** (1887) 12 App Cas 409 that a company could not return its capital to its members other than on a proper reduction of capital duly approved by the courts.[1] This doctrine of capital maintenance was originally designed to protect the interests of creditors and is now reflected in the Companies Act 2006 in relation to the company's distribution to shareholders, the reduction of capital, the redemption or purchase of a company's own shares, and the prohibition of financial assistance to others for purchase of its shares.[2]

The rules on distribution are important aspects of the doctrine of capital maintenance because they protect creditors from asset-stripping by directors and shareholders of the company: **It's a Wrap (UK) Ltd v Gula** [2006] 2 BCLC 634.[3] A company may only make a distribution (such as dividends) to shareholders out of profits available (s 830). Such profits are defined as its accumulated, realised profits less its accumulated, realised losses. An unlawful distribution of profits is *ultra vires* and a director who knew or ought to know that the payment amounted to a breach is liable to repay the dividends: **Bairstow v Queens Moat Houses plc** [2002] BCC 91.[4]

[3] The explanation as to why the rules on distribution are part of the doctrine of capital maintenance adds more credit to your answer than simply stating the statutory rules on distribution.

[4] Some students may forget to discuss the legal consequences for unlawful distribution. The reference to case law gains you more marks.

Historically, the law was strict in relation to reduction of capital for the protection of the company's creditors. The statutory rules in the Companies Act 1985 were criticised as complex by the White Paper 2005. The Companies Act 2006 seeks to deregulate this area of law for private companies by removing some burdensome measures whilst the rules for public companies remain mostly the same.[5] A private company[6] may reduce its capital by a special resolution supported by a solvency statement (s 641). The directors should make a statement of the solvency of the company not more than 15 days before the date on which the resolution is passed (s 642). A solvency statement is defined in s 643[7] as a statement that each of the directors has formed the opinion, as regards the company's situation at the date of the statement, that there is no ground on which the company could then be found to be unable to pay its debts. If it is intended to commence the winding up within 12 months of that date, each of the directors has formed the opinion that the company will be able to pay its debts in full within 12 months of the commencement of the winding up. If the directors make such statements without having reasonable grounds for the opinions expressed in it, an offence is committed by every director who will be liable to imprisonment on conviction and/or a fine (s 643(4)).

[5] The historical background for the rules on the reduction of share capital shows your sound knowledge and adds more credit to your answer.

[6] You should pay attention to the type of companies here. Only a private company can reduce share capital by a special resolution and a solvency statement; a public company must follow the procedure in s 645.

[7] A further explanation of a solvency statement demonstrates your good understanding and will earn you more marks.

Both private and public companies may reduce its share capital by a special resolution confirmed by the court (s 645). The court has wide discretion as to whether to confirm a reduction or not; its main concerns are the protection of the interests of creditors and the fair treatment of different classes of shareholders: **Re Ratners Group plc** [1988] BCLC 685. The creditors are given the opportunities to object to the reduction of capital (s 646).[8]

[8] This provision is important for the protection of creditors and therefore it should not be left out in your answer.

A limited company may not acquire its own shares whether by purchase or subscription (s 658). In case of an infringement of s 658, the company will be liable to a fine and every officer of the company who is in default is liable to imprisonment or a fine, and the purported acquisition will be void (s 658(2)). This reflects the judgment by the House of Lords in **Trevor v Whitworth** that a company could not purchase its own shares under the Companies Act, even if it was authorised by its articles of association. In the light of the modern business needs, these rigid requirements have been relaxed and some exceptions to this general rule are developed.[9] For instance, purchase by a company of its own shares is not prohibited in a reduction of capital duly made or in pursuance of an order of the court (s 659).

[9]This sentence refers back to the statement in the question and shows that you are engaging with the question.

A company may issue shares which are to be redeemed or are liable to be redeemed at the option of the company or the shareholder under s 684. A public company must be authorised by its articles to issue redeemable shares; such authorisation is not required for private companies although the articles may exclude or restrict their issue.[10]

[10]Note that the rules which apply to private and public companies are different.

The law in relation to the financial assistance by the company for purchase of its own shares has been significantly reformed by the Companies Act 2006. The general rule that a company may not give financial assistance for the purchase of its own shares has been abolished for private companies but it still applies to public companies.[11] The scope of financial assistance is wide, including by way of gift, guarantee, security or indemnity, release or waiver. It also includes financial assistance given by way of a loan or any other agreement under which any of the obligations of the person giving the assistance are to be fulfilled (s 677). It is unlawful for a public company or its subsidiary to give financial assistance for the acquisition of its own shares (s 678); an infringement of this provision is a criminal offence (s 680). A company, however, is not prohibited from doing so if its principal purpose in giving the assistance is not for the purpose of any such acquisition, or the giving of the assistance for that purpose is only an incidental part of some larger purpose of the company; and the assistance is given in good faith in the interests of the company (s 678(2)). Despite the House of Lords' interpretation of this 'principal purpose' exception in **Brady v Brady** [1988] BCLC 20, it is still difficult to ascertain exactly what sort of

[11]This sentence demonstrates your excellent knowledge of the recent reforms introduced by the Companies Act 2006 and will impress your examiners.

[12]This brief analysis of the 'principal purpose' exception by reference to case law makes your answer stand out from a pure description of the statutory provisions.

situations would fall within its scope: **Dyment v Boyden** [2005] 1 WLR 792.[12] The courts may take into account the commercial reality in deciding whether financial assistance has been given: **Chaston v SWP Group plc** [2003] 1 BCLC 675.

[13]Summarise your main arguments and directly refer back to the question in your conclusion. The comments on future reforms may gain you more marks.

It is argued that the doctrine of capital maintenance still plays an important role in protecting the interests of creditors, despite the recent relaxation of the rules for private companies to accommodate modern business needs. The current rules, however, are still complex and wide-ranging; further reforms are desirable to clarify this area of law and reduce the costs in complying with them.[13]

✓ Make your answer stand out

- Discuss the rules in relation to the issue of shares. Shares may not be allotted at a discount (s 580).
- Examine the payment of shares for non-cash consideration. If shares are issued for a non-cash consideration in a public company, the assets must be valued before allotment (s 593).
- Further reading on the doctrine of capital maintenance: Armour, J. 'Share capital and creditor protection: efficient rules for a modern company law' (2000) 63 *Modern Law Review* 355; Milman, D. 'Share capital maintenance: current developments and future horizons' (2007) *Company Law Newsletter* 1.

! Don't be tempted to...

- Treat private companies and public companies in the same way. You should be aware that different rules may apply to these two types of companies.
- Only focus on the reduction of share capital. Your answer should include other main aspects of the doctrine of capital maintenance, including making distributions to shareholders and purchasing its own shares by a company.
- Provide an answer without reference to the relevant statutory provisions. Although the common law rules are still important, they have been modified by the statutory provisions in the Companies Act 2006.

❓ Question 3

Supreme Cotton Ltd has an issued share capital of £40,000, divided into 15,000 £2 ordinary shares and 10,000 £1 preference shares. Its articles of association provide that: 'The directors have unrestricted power to allot shares.' The board of directors has decided to issue another 8,000 £2 ordinary shares and 5,000 £1 preference shares.

Advise the board as to the legal procedures to achieve these.

Answer plan

→ Consider the legal procedures for the allotment of shares in a private company limited by shares.

→ Discuss the implications of pre-emption rights.

→ Examine whether an allotment of preference shares amounts to a variation of class rights.

→ Assess the procedures required for a variation of class rights.

→ Evaluate directors' duties and possible legal actions by shareholders.

Diagram plan

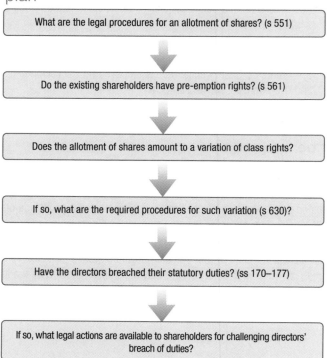

A printable version of this diagram plan is available from www.pearsoned.co.uk/lawexpressqa

Answer

[1]The introduction identifies the two key legal issues that arise from the problem question. It immediately demonstrates that you understand what are asked by the question.

This question concerns the legal procedures in relation to the allotment of shares and the variation of class rights in a private company.[1] There are two classes of shares in Supreme Cotton Ltd: ordinary shares and preference shares with the latter carrying class rights. A company may alter its share capital subject to the statutory procedures in the Companies Act 2006 (s 617). Directors may exercise their power to allot shares in the company if they are authorised to do so by the articles or by resolution of the company (s 551). Authorisation may be given for a particular or general exercise of the power; it may be conditional or unconditional. It must state the maximum amount of shares that may be allotted and specify the date on which it will expire. Directors in Supreme Cotton Ltd can allot shares because they are given unrestricted power to do so by the articles.[2]

[2]This sentence shows that you are engaging with the problem scenario instead of providing a general answer to an essay question on the allotment of shares.

When allotting shares, the directors need to consider whether the existing shareholders have pre-emption rights. These rights ensure that a shareholder is able to protect his proportion of the total equity of a company by having the opportunity to subscribe for any new issue of shares.[3] According to s 561, a company must not allot shares to a person unless it has made an offer to each person who holds ordinary shares in the company and allot to him on the same or more favourable terms a proportion of those shares that is as nearly as practicable equal to the proportion in nominal value held by him of the ordinary share capital of the company. The offer must state a period during which it may be accepted and the offer shall not be withdrawn before the end of that period (s 562). If these provisions on pre-emption rights are not complied with, the company and every officer of it who knowingly authorised or permitted the non-compliance are jointly and severally liable to compensate any person to whom an offer should have been made (s 563).

[3]The rationale for pre-emption rights will add more credit to your answer because it goes beyond a simple description of these rights.

The issue of pre-emption rights, however, may not always arise.[4] Pre-emption rights are subject to exceptions; for instance, they do not apply in the allotment of bonus shares (s 564) or issue for non-cash consideration (s 565). Pre-emption rights may be excluded by the articles of a private company (ss 567–568); moreover, they may be disapplied by the articles or a special resolution of a

[4]Some students may have the wrong understanding that pre-emption rights always apply. It is important to appreciate that such rights are subject to exceptions, exclusions and dis-applications.

[5]These sentences demonstrate your skills of analysing the problem scenario and applying the relevant law. They will gain you more marks.

[6]This sentence explains the significance of class rights because it is more difficult to alter. It shows your good understanding of class rights and will add more credit to your answer.

[7]You should pay attention to this phrase here. It refers to the holders of the issued shares with class rights instead of the holders of ordinary shares.

[8]This sentence clearly states the judicial approach to the variation of class rights. It will make your answer stand out from those which only describe the procedure in s 630 for the variation of class rights.

[9]This case is very important here for two reasons. First, it illustrates what amounts to a variation of class rights by making the distinction between class rights and the enjoyment of such rights; secondly, it is the common law authority on whether an allotment of shares amounts to a variation of class rights.

[10]This provision is often missing in students' answers. It is important for the protection of class rights and therefore should be included in a good answer.

company (ss 569–573). It is unclear whether pre-emption rights are excluded or disapplied by the articles of Supreme Cotton Ltd. If they are not excluded or disapplied, the new shares must be first offered to the existing holders of ordinary shares.[5]

In relation to the procedure for the allotment of shares, it is essential to consider whether an allotment of preference shares varies the class rights of existing preference shareholders. Class rights confer greater security on the holder of preference shares than rights conferred merely by the articles because the latter can be altered by a special resolution under s 21.[6] Class rights may only be varied in accordance with provisions in the company's articles, or, where the company's articles contain no such provisions, if the holders of shares of that class consent to the variation (s 630). The consent must be in writing from the holders of at least three-quarters in nominal value of the issued shares of that class[7] or a special resolution passed at a separate general meeting of the holders of that class sanctioning the variation.

The court has interpreted restrictively what amounts to a variation of class rights. A distinction is made between matters affecting the rights attached to each share and matters affecting the enjoyment of these rights.[8] If only the enjoyment of the right is affected, it does not attract the protection under s 630 for the variation of class rights because the right remains the same. In **White v Bristol Aeroplane Co Ltd** [1953] Ch 65[9] it was held that an issue of preference shares to the existing ordinary shareholders was not a variation of class rights although it would dilute the control of the existing preference shareholders. It was concluded that the new issue did not affect the rights of the existing preference shareholders which remained exactly as they were before. As the court is very likely to follow the approach in **White v Bristol Aeroplane Co Ltd**, the board of directors in Supreme Cotton Ltd, when allotting preference shares, does not need the consent of the holders of preference shares as required by s 630.

It should be noted that even when a majority of the class has consented to a variation, the holders of not less than 15% of the issued shares of the class in question may apply to the court to have the variation cancelled, provided that they did not consent to or vote in favour of the resolution for the variation (s 633).[10] If the

[11]The evaluation of the practicality of s 633 will gain you more marks because it shows your sound analysis.

[12]Although directors have unrestricted power to allot shares according to the articles, it does not mean they can exercise this power in any way they like. The discussion of directors' duties is essential here and helps your answer stand out.

[13]Some students may forget to discuss s 171 on the directors' duty to exercise power for proper purposes. The reference to case law is also important because it is still relevant to the interpretation and application of the codified duties.

court is satisfied that the variation would unfairly prejudice the shareholders of the class represented by the applicant, it may disallow the variation; otherwise, it must confirm it and the decision of the court is final. This provision is rarely used in practice because it is unlikely that the court would overturn a decision which was made by a majority of the class. It may be easier to bring an unfair prejudice petition under s 994 if a member of the class feels that his rights have been unfairly prejudiced.[11]

When directors exercise the power to allot shares, they must ensure that they do not breach their statutory duties to the company.[12] In particular, the exercise of this power must be made *bona fide* in a way that is likely to promote the success of the company (s 172). It adopts a subjective test in the sense that directors are not in breach of this duty if they honestly believe that they are acting properly: **Re Smith and Fawcett** [1942] 1 All ER 542. Directors must also ensure that the power is exercised for a proper purpose for which it is conferred (s 171): **Howard Smith Ltd v Ampol Petroleum Ltd** [1974] AC 821.[13] If the allotment is for improper purposes such as diluting the control of existing shareholders, an unfair prejudice petition may be brought under s 994: **Dalby v Bodilly** [2005] BCC 627.

 Make your answer stand out

- Consider that shareholders can also bring a derivative action against directors' breach of duties (ss 260–263, CA 2006).
- Further reading on pre-emption rights and class rights: MacNeil, I. 'Shareholders' pre-emptive rights' [2002] JBL 78 and Reynolds, B. 'Shareholders' class rights: a new approach' [1996] JBL 554.

! Don't be tempted to…

- Apply the procedure in s 550 to the allotment of shares in Supreme Cotton Ltd. Section 550 applies to a private company with only one class of shares. It is not applicable here because the company has two classes of shares.
- Forget to discuss whether an allotment of preference shares varies the class rights of existing preference shareholders. This is an important issue raised in the question and therefore should be sufficiently addressed.

🕮 Question 4

Nottinghill plc issued 400,000 £1 ordinary shares in November 2009. Ella was allotted 100,000 shares for her services as an IT consultant for six years at the rate of £20,000 per annum. Ella then transferred all her shares to her friend Lisa.

In January 2010, the board of directors paid a dividend of 50p per share although they were aware that the company had no profits for distribution.

Advise the board of directors as to the validity of these arrangements.

Answer plan

→ Consider the rules on payment of shares for non-cash consideration in a public company (s 593).

→ Discuss the restrictions on the issue of shares against performance of future personal services (s 585).

→ Examine the rules with regard to payment of dividends (s 830).

Diagram plan

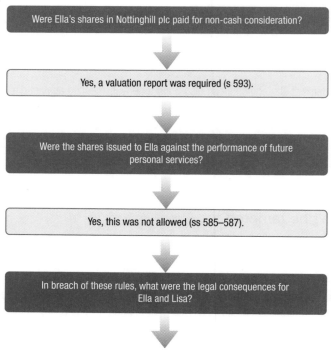

They should be held jointly and severally liable unless Lisa was a purchaser for value without notice of the shares (s 588). The court may grant her relief from liabilities (s 589).

Was the payment of dividends a lawful distribution?

No, it was in violation of s 830 because the company had no distributable profits.

A printable version of this diagram plan is available from www.pearsoned.co.uk/lawexpressqa

Answer

[1]The introduction identifies the key issues and shows that you know what this question is about.

In order to advise the board of directors in Nottinghill plc, it is essential to examine whether the allotment of shares to Ella for non-cash consideration is legal and whether the payment of dividend is a lawful distribution.[1]

Shares must not be issued at a discount to their nominal value (s 580). Shares allotted by a company may be paid up in money or money's worth, including goodwill and know-how (s 582). If shares are paid in non-cash consideration such as goods or services, there may be a danger that they are undervalued. At common law, the courts make little inquiry into the value of non-cash consideration unless it is illusory or manifestly inadequate. Lord Waton in **Ooregum Gold Mining Co of India v Roper** [1892] AC 125 held that 'so long as the company honestly regards the consideration given as fairly representing the nominal value of the shares in cash, its estimate ought not to be critically examined'.[2] In **Re Wragg Ltd** (1897) 1 Ch 796, it was alleged that the defendant directors sold their business to the company they had incorporated at an overvalue and these shares should be treated as unpaid. The court held that the directors made the decision in good faith and the benefit received in return for the shares was worth their nominal value and therefore not open to challenge. Lindley LJ held that the agreements by a limited company to pay for property or services were valid and

[2]The reference to Lord Waton and his judgment shows your precise knowledge. It will gain you more marks than only stating the name of the case.

6 SHARES AND SHARE CAPITAL

[3]This sentence shows that you appreciate the different requirements for private companies and public companies. The reference to Nottinghill plc indicates that your answer focuses on the rules applicable to public companies.

[4]Section 593 is very important for any question on payment of shares for non-cash consideration. You will lose some marks if it is omitted in your answer.

[5]Apply to the question after discussing the relevant law.

[6]Some students may forget to discuss s 587 in relation to the restrictions on long-term undertaking. The application of s 587 to the problem question will make your answer stand out.

[7]The legal consequences for breach of these provisions on the allotment against non-cash consideration (s 593) and the restrictions on undertaking (s 587) are the same. You do not need to repeat them or state them separately.

[8]An analysis of the circumstances where the transferee is not jointly and severally liable will gain you more marks.

binding on the company and its creditors, provided that the company 'does so honestly and not colourably and that it has not been so imposed upon as to be entitled to be relived from its bargain'. This common law approach still applies to a private company; however, more restrictions are imposed on a public company such as Nottinghill plc.[3]

A public company must not allot a share except as paid up at least as to one quarter of its nominal value and the whole of any premium on it (s 586). It must not allot shares as fully or partly paid up otherwise than in cash unless it meets the following three requirements in s 593.[4] First, the consideration for the allotment has been independently valued; secondly, the valuer's report has been made to the company during the six months immediately preceding the allotment of the shares; and thirdly, a copy of the report has been sent to the proposed allottee. A copy of the valuation report must also be filed by the company with the registrar of companies. As Nottinghill plc allotted shares to Ella for her services instead of in cash, the board of directors had to ensure these conditions in s 593 were met.[5]

Moreover, in payment of its shares, a public company must not accept an undertaking given by any person that he should do work or perform services for the company (s 585). In particular, it must not allot shares for a non-cash consideration which includes an undertaking which is to be performed more than five years after the date of the allotment (s 587).[6] As it accepted an undertaking from Ella to perform services as a consideration for the allotment of shares and the services would be provided over six years (longer than five years), Nottinghill plc was in breach of the requirements in s 585 and s 587. Moreover, the company and its officers committed criminal offences for contravention of these provisions and they are liable to a fine on conviction (s 590 and s 607). The allottee, Ella, is liable to pay the company in respect of those shares an amount equal to the aggregate of the nominal value of the shares, with interest at the appropriate rate which is fixed at 5% per annum (s 592).[7]

As Ella transferred her shares to Lisa, both will be jointly and severally liable in respect of the amount for which Ella is liable unless Lisa was a purchaser for value without notice of the shares (s 588).[8] The court has the power to grant relief from liability of Ella and Lisa where it is just and equitable to do so (ss 589 and 606):

156

Re Bradford Investments plc (No. 2) [1991] BCLC 688. In **Re Ossory Estates plc** [1988] BCLC 213,[9] the property was sold to the company as part of the consideration for the purchase of shares. It was not valued as required by s 103, CA 1985 (now s 593, CA 2006) and a claim was made against the allottee for payment for the price of the shares. The court granted relief under s 113, CA 1985 (now s 606, CA 2006) on the grounds that the company had sold the property at a substantial profit and received at least money or money's worth equal to the aggregate nominal value of the shares and any premium. There was therefore manifestly no issue at a discount. If the agreement between Nottinghill plc and Ella is likely to be honoured, Ella and Lisa may be exempt from their liabilities provided that they can prove that the company has received total or partial consideration for the share allotment.[10]

10Again, apply the law to the problem scenario.

Another legal issue is whether Nottinghill plc has made unlawful distribution by paying dividends when it had no distributable profits. A company may pay dividends only out of distributable profits (s 830). A breach of these rules makes a payment unlawful and *ultra vires*; a director who knew or ought to know that the payment amounted to a breach is liable to repay the dividends. In **Bairstow v Queens Moat Houses plc** [2002] BCC 91, directors were held liable for unlawfully paying dividends that exceeded the distributable reserves.[11] In **Re Exchange Banking Co, Flitcroft's case** (1882) 21 Ch D 519, the former directors of the company were sued for paying half-yearly dividends when they knew that some items in the accounts were bad debts and that the company had no distributable profits. The directors were held jointly and severally liable for the amount of the dividends. The distribution of dividends in Notthinghill plc was unlawful because directors knew that the company had no distributable profits. Thus the directors should be liable to repay the dividends. If, at the time of the distribution, the shareholders know or have reasonable grounds for believing that it is so made, they should also be liable to repay it to the company (s 847).[12]

11The case law illustration is essential for a good answer because it shows your sound knowledge of the common law approach.

12A discussion of the potential liabilities of other shareholders goes beyond the liabilities of the directors, Ella and Lisa. It will add more credit to your answer.

✓ Make your answer stand out

- Show your wider understanding by relating the rules on payment of shares to the doctrine of capital maintenance.
- Point out that your answer will be different if it is a private company. If the shares are paid in non-cash consideration, there is no requirement for valuation report and the court will treat such consideration as fully paid unless it is manifestly inadequate or illusory (*Re Wragg Ltd* (1897)).

! Don't be tempted to...

- Fail to discuss whether Lisa should be held jointly and severally liable for the repayment of dividends.
- Forget to examine the court's power to grant relief for Ella and Lisa where it is just and equitable to do so under s 589.
- Only focus on the issue in relation to the payment of shares for non-cash consideration. You should address all the issues that arise from the question and discuss whether the payment of dividends amounts to unlawful distribution.

? Question 5

John and Peter are directors of Johnson plc. Peter, who owns 15% of the company's shares, wishes to sell them. John is interested in purchasing them but does not have sufficient funds. In order to purchase Peter's shares, John has authorised a private loan with the bank which is guaranteed by Johnson plc.

Emma, who owns 1% of the company's shares, is unhappy about the arrangement in relation to the guarantee.

Advise Emma.

Answer plan

- → Discuss the statutory provisions on the prohibition of financial assistance by a public company for the acquisition of its own shares (ss 677–683).
- → Analyse whether the 'principal purpose' exception applies.
- → Examine the consequences of a breach of the statutory provisions on financial assistance.
- → Consider whether John has breached his director's duties in authorising the arrangement.
- → Evaluate what actions Emma can take to challenge the arrangement.

Diagram plan

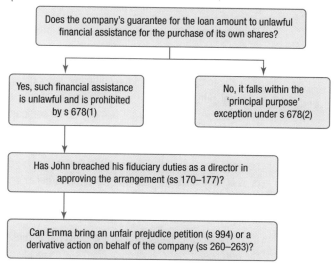

Does the company's guarantee for the loan amount to unlawful financial assistance for the purchase of its own shares?

↓

Yes, such financial assistance is unlawful and is prohibited by s 678(1)

No, it falls within the 'principal purpose' exception under s 678(2)

↓

Has John breached his fiduciary duties as a director in approving the arrangement (ss 170–177)?

↓

Can Emma bring an unfair prejudice petition (s 994) or a derivative action on behalf of the company (ss 260–263)?

A printable version of this diagram plan is available from www.pearsoned.co.uk/lawexpressqa

---

[1]The introduction clearly identifies the important issues that you are going to address in your answer. It immediately shows that you know this question is in relation to financial assistance, directors' duties and shareholders' remedies.

[2]By pointing out that Emma is a minority shareholder here, it indicates that your answer will deal with the issues in relation to minority shareholder remedies.

[3]This is the main provision on the prohibition of financial assistance in a public company. You will lose some marks if it is not referred to.

Answer

In order to advise Emma on any legal action against the guarantee provided by the company, it is essential to consider three key issues:[1] first, whether the guarantee for the private loan amounts to unlawful financial assistance by the company for the purchase of its own shares; secondly, whether John has breached his statutory duties as a director; and, thirdly, what legal actions are available to Emma, who is a minority shareholder of the company.[2]

The guarantee, which is provided by the company for the loan for John's purchase of shares, falls within the definition of financial assistance in s 677. It states that financial assistance can be given by way of gift, guarantee, security or indemnity, a loan or any other agreement. The assistance must also be given for the purpose of the acquisition or to reduce or discharge a liability incurred for the purpose of the acquisition: **Dyment v Boyden** [2005] 1 BCLC 163. Where a person is acquiring or proposing to acquire shares in a public company, it is unlawful for that company or its subsidiary, to give financial assistance directly or indirectly for the purpose of the acquisition (s 678(1)).[3] As John is purchasing shares in Johnson

4This sentence demonstrates your ability to apply the relevant law to the problem scenario.

plc, the financial assistance is given directly for the purpose of the purchase and therefore it is unlawful.[4]

There are, nevertheless, exceptions to the prohibition in s 678(1). Financial assistance is not prohibited in a public company if both the requirements in s 678(2) are met.[5] First, if it is given in good faith and in the interests of the company; secondly, if the company's principal purpose is not the acquisition of shares or it is only an incidental part of some larger purpose of the company. Thus, if John can convince the court that the guarantee is given in good faith and in the interests of the company and that the company's principal purpose in granting the guarantee is not for the purchase of shares or it is only an incidental part of some larger purpose, it is likely that the court will not consider the guarantee as unlawful financial assistance.

5Note here that both requirements must be met for the exception to apply. This is another essential provision on financial assistance and it must not be omitted in your answer.

6This sentence shows that you appreciate the complicated nature of the principal purpose exception. It also demonstrates your analytical skills and makes your answer stand out.

It is difficult to determine what the principal purpose is or whether the purpose of an acquisition of shares is an incidental part of some larger purpose.[6] In **Brady v Brady** [1988] BCLC 20,[7] the House of Lords interpreted the principal purpose narrowly and distinguished between a purpose and the reason why a purpose was formed. This approach appears to restrict unduly the scope of the principal purpose exception; it also makes it very difficult to ascertain exactly what sort of situations would fall within its scope. Nevertheless, it appears that in some cases a more pragmatic approach is adopted towards the prohibition by looking at the commercial realities surrounding a financial assistance claim: **Charterhouse Investment Trust Ltd v Tempest Diesels Ltd** [1986] BCLC 1; **Anglo Petroleum Ltd v TFB (Mortgages) Ltd** [2008] 1 BCLC 185.[8] In **Chaston v SWP Group plc** [2003] 1 BCLC 675, it was alleged that Chaston, as a director of a subsidiary company, had breached his fiduciary duties by giving financial assistance for the purpose of the acquisition by the purchaser of the shares in its parent company. The alleged financial assistance was that the subsidiary paid the accountants' fees for the reports in respect of the transaction.[9] Arden LJ considered the commercial substance of the transaction and held that the transaction amounted to unlawful financial assistance and Chaston was liable for damages for breach of his statutory duties.

7This case is important here because it is the House of Lords' interpretation of the principal purpose exception. It will gain you more marks.

8A discussion of the judicial approach of respecting commercial realities demonstrates your excellent understanding of the common law on financial assistance. It adds more analysis and more credit to your answer.

9Although the facts of a case are not usually required, a brief summary of the facts of *Chaston* here illustrates the court's pragmatic approach and shows your sound knowledge.

If the court is of the opinion that the guarantee by Johnson plc amounts to unlawful financial assistance by looking at the commercial realities

[10]Some students forget to discuss the legal consequences for the company and its officers as well as the validity of the guarantee agreement.

[11]This sentence refers back to the problem question and leads on to the discussion of directors' duties. It shows that your answer is clearly structured.

[12]The reference to common law will gain you more marks because it demonstrates that you are aware of its relevance in the interpretation of the statutory duties.

[13]Most students are familiar with the duties under s 171 and s 172 but not s 175. Your sound knowledge of s 175 may impress your examiner.

[14]Although the most popular remedy for the unfair prejudice petition is the buy-out order, the court has very wide discretion and can make any order it thinks fit under s 996, in particular, to 'require the company to refrain from doing or continuing an act complained' under s 996(2)(b).

behind the arrangement, the company is liable to a fine and every officer who is in default is liable to imprisonment or a fine or both (s 680); the guarantee agreement will be unenforceable by either party to it: **Heald v O'Connor** [1971] 2 All ER 1105.[10]

John, as a director of Johnson plc, has authorised the giving of unlawful financial assistance, so it can be argued that he has breached his fiduciary duties to the company in ss 171, 172 and 175.[11] A director must exercise powers for the purposes for which they are conferred (s 171): **Howard Smith Ltd v Ampol Petroleum** [1974] AC 821.[12] He must also act in the way he considers, in good faith, would be most likely to promote the success of the company for the benefit of its members as a whole (s 172): **Re Smith & Fawcett** [1942] 1 All ER 542. Moreover, a director must avoid a situation in which he has, or can have, a direct or indirect interest that conflicts, or possibly may conflict with the interests of the company (s 175): **Aberdeen Rly Co v Blaikie Bros** (1854) 1 Macq 461.[13] It appears that John did not exercise his power of authorising transactions for proper purposes or act in the interests of the company. Besides, he did not avoid a situation where there was a conflict of interest between him and the company in relation to the guarantee agreement. John is therefore liable to account for the full amount of the financial assistance: **JJ Harrison (Properties) Ltd v Harrison** [2002] 1 BCLC 162.

Emma may bring an unfair prejudice petition under s 994 and claim that her interests as a member have been unfairly prejudiced by the guarantee agreement. If the court is satisfied that the petition is well founded, it may issue an injunction to restrain the giving of financial assistance in breach of the statutory provisions (s 996(2)(b)).[14] Emma may also bring a derivative action on behalf of the company under ss 260–263 to challenge John's breach of duties. She needs to establish a *prima facie* case and go through the two-stage procedure in s 261. The court will take into account a number of factors in s 263 when considering whether to give or refuse permission to continue the derivative claim. It should be noted that the court has taken a restrictive view towards this procedure and it is likely that permission to continue the claim would be refused if all that the claimant was seeking could be recovered by means of an unfair prejudice petition: **Mission Capital plc v Sinclair** [2008] BCC 866.

Make your answer stand out

- Consider the issue of pre-emption rights. Peter's shares may need to be offered to all of the existing shareholders if there is a pre-emption clause in the company's articles of association.
- Point out that the answer would be different if it is a private company limited by shares. The rules on the prohibition of financial assistance by a private company for the acquisition of its own shares are abolished by the Companies Act 2006.

Don't be tempted to...

- Jump to the conclusion that the guarantee arrangement amounts to unlawful financial assistance under s 678(1). You must discuss the 'principal purpose' exception in s 678(2).
- Only focus on the legal issue of financial assistance. Your answer must also include an analysis of directors' duties and shareholder remedies by reference to case law and statutory provisions.

 Question 6

'A public company is prohibited from providing financial assistance to a purchaser of its own shares. The prohibition is wide-ranging but it appears that the courts have adopted a pragmatic approach in defining financial assistance.'

Critically analyse the above statements by reference to the common law and statutory provisions.

Answer plan

→ Consider the rationale and historical background of the rules on the prohibition of financial assistance by a company for the acquisition of its own shares.

→ Examine the circumstances where financial assistance is prohibited (s 678).

→ Analyse the 'principal purpose' exception in s 678(2).

→ Evaluate the House of Lords' judgment in *Brady* v *Brady* [1988] BCLC 20.

Diagram plan

Financial assistance by a company for the acquisition of its own shares (ss 677–683)

| Rationale and historical development | The definition of financial assistance: s 677 | The rules on the prohibition of financial assistance: s 678 | The 'principal purpose' exception: s 678 |

A printable version of this diagram plan is available from www.pearsoned.co.uk/lawexpressqa

[1]The reference to the doctrine of capital maintenance shows your understanding of the wider context. It will impress your examiner at the beginning of your answer.

[2]This sentence explains the main reasons why the financial assistance is prohibited. It demonstrates your good understanding of its rationale.

[3]The detailed understanding of the whitewash procedure will gain you more marks than simply referring to the procedure without explaining it.

[4]The reference to the *Modern Company Law for a Competitive Economy* demonstrates your excellent knowledge of the problems in relation to the provisions in the CA 1981. It will add more credit to your answer.

[5]This shows your knowledge of the relevant EU legislation and helps your answer stand out.

Answer

As a general rule, a company is prevented from providing financial assistance in purchasing its own shares. This reflects the doctrine of capital maintenance that a company must maintain its share capital in order to protect the interests of creditors: **Trevor v Whitworth** (1877) 12 App Cas 409.[1] The prohibition on financial assistance aims to prevent the abuse of asset-stripping whereby a bidder, after taking control of the company, uses the assets of the company to pay for the price of the shares.[2] Such abuse may prejudice the interests of the creditors of the company and the interests of any shareholder who does not accept the offer to acquire the shares.

The prohibition on financial assistance was first introduced by s 45 of the Companies Act 1929 as a result of the recommendations of the Greene Committee (1926). The whitewash procedure was then introduced for private companies in the Companies Act 1981, where financial assistance was permitted subject to certain conditions (ss 155–158). It essentially required a special resolution and a directors' statement backed up by an auditors' statement.[3] These statutory procedures were criticised as expensive and time-consuming because substantial professional fees were incurred when the company attempted to ensure that innocent and worthwhile transactions did not breach the rules (*Modern Company Law for a Competitive Economy*, 1998).[4] It was proposed that these rules should be abolished completely for private companies. This proposal is adopted in the Companies Act 2006 but the rules on financial assistance still remain for public companies as a result of the implementation of the Second Company Law Directive (art 23).[5]

Financial assistance can be given by way of gift, guarantee, security or indemnity, or by way of release or waiver, a loan or any other agreement. It also includes any other financial assistance given by a company where the net assets of the company are reduced to a material extent by the giving of the assistance (s 677). In addition, the assistance must be given for the purpose of the acquisition or to reduce or discharge a liability incurred for the purpose of the acquisition: **Dyment v Boyden** [2005] 1 BCLC 163.

[6]This sentence echoes the statement in the question and demonstrates that you are engaging with the question.

The scope of the prohibition is wide but it appears that the courts have adopted a pragmatic approach by looking at the commercial realities surrounding a financial assistance claim instead of focusing on whether a transaction may technically be classified as financial assistance.[6] Hoffmann J[7] in **Charterhouse Investment Trust Ltd v Tempest Diesels Ltd** [1986] BCLC 1 emphasised that the commercial realities of the transaction as a whole must be considered when deciding whether a transaction could properly be described as the giving of financial assistance by the company. This view has been accepted by the Court of Appeal in **MT Realisations Ltd v Digital Equipment Co Ltd** [2003] 2 BCLC 117 and **Chaston v SWP Group plc** [2003] 1 BCLC 675. The emphasis on commercial realities has enabled the courts to narrow the scope of the prohibition.

[7]The name of the leading judge shows your detailed and precise knowledge of this case.

[8]Note that there are three main provisions in relation to the prohibition. Many students only make reference to the first one.

In relation to the statutory provisions in the Companies Act 2006, there are three main rules in relation to the prohibition on financial assistance.[8] First, where a person is acquiring or proposing to acquire shares in a public company, it is unlawful for that company or its subsidiary to give financial assistance directly or indirectly for the purpose of the acquisition (s 678(1)). Secondly, where a person has acquired shares in a company and a liability has been incurred for the purpose of the acquisition, it is unlawful for that company, or its subsidiary, to give financial assistance directly or indirectly for the purpose of reducing or discharging the liability (s 678(3)). Thirdly, where a person is acquiring or proposing to acquire shares in a private company, it is not lawful for a public company that is a subsidiary of that company to give financial assistance directly or indirectly for the purpose of the acquisition (s 679(1)).

[9]You must pay attention to the word 'both' instead of 'either'. Students tend to make the careless mistake of stating that financial assistance is allowed in a public company if one of the requirements in s 678(2) is met.

Financial assistance is not prohibited in a public company if both of the requirements in s 678(2) are met:[9] first, if it is given in good faith and in the interests of the company; and secondly, if the company's principal purpose is not the acquisition of shares or it is only an incidental part of some larger purpose of the company. The exceptions are designed to ensure that genuine commercial transactions which are in the interests of the company are not prohibited. It is, however, often difficult to determine what the company's principal purpose is or whether the purpose of an acquisition of shares is an incidental part of some larger purpose.[10]

[10]It is important to point out the problems with these exceptions here because they are the main difficulties faced by the courts in interpreting this provision.

The 'principal purpose' exception is illustrated in **Brady v Brady** [1988] BCLC 20[11] where the House of Lords held that the purpose of the transaction was to assist in financing the acquisition of the shares and the acquisition of the shares was not incidental to the reorganisation but the essence of it. It interpreted the principal purpose narrowly and distinguished between a purpose and the reason why a purpose was formed. It found that the purpose of the transaction in this case was to assist financing the acquisition of the shares although the reason for the transaction was to facilitate the division of the business. The financial assistance was not incidental to a larger purpose and therefore illegal. This interpretation of the principal purpose exception has been criticised, as it appears to restrict its scope of application unduly and makes it very difficult to ascertain exactly what sort of situations would fall within its scope.[12]

[11]The case of *Brady* v *Brady* (1988), which was decided by the House of Lords, should not be omitted in your answer.

[12]This sentence shows your analytical skills and will gain you more marks.

A breach of these provisions is a criminal offence and the company is liable to a fine and every officer in default is liable to imprisonment or a fine or both (s 680).[13] An agreement which provides unlawful financial assistance is unenforceable by either party to it: **Heald v O'Connor** [1971] 2 All ER 1105. Moreover, a director who authorises the giving of unlawful financial assistance is in breach of his duties and liable for the full amount of the improper financial assistance: **JJ Harrison (Properties) Ltd v Harrison** [2002] 1 BCLC 162.

[13]The discussion of the consequences for the breach of the statutory provisions is essential for a sound answer.

It can be concluded that the pragmatic approach in defining financial assistance by looking at the commercial realities is helpful in ensuring that genuine commercial transactions are not prohibited. The current rules on the prohibition of financial assistance, however, are still complex despite the reform in the Companies Act 2006.[14]

[14]Your conclusion should refer back to the question and summarise the main arguments.

✓ Make your answer stand out

■ Consider the exceptions to the prohibition where certain transactions do not amount to unlawful giving of financial assistance: conditional exceptions (s 682) and unconditional exceptions (s 681).

■ Make reference to academic opinions on financial assistance, in particular, in relation to the interpretation of the 'principal purpose' exception: Ferran, E. 'Corporate transactions and financial assistance: shifting policy perceptions but static law' (2004) *Cambridge Law Journal* 225; Ho, L. C. 'Financial assistance after *Chaston* and *MT Realisations*' (2003) JIBLR 424; Hirt, 'The scope of prohibited financial assistance after *MT Realisations Ltd* v *Digital Equipment Co Ltd*' (2004) 25 *Company Lawyer* 9; Luxton, P. 'Financial assistance by a company for the purchase of its own shares – the principal or larger purpose exception' (1991) *Company Lawyer* 18.

! Don't be tempted to...

■ Wrongly believe that the rules on the prohibition of financial assistance apply to a private company in the same way as they do to a public one. These rules have been abolished for a private company and now only apply to a public company and its subsidiary (which may be a private company).

■ Only focus on the statutory provisions. You must also discuss the common law in the interpretation of the 'principal purpose' exception.

? Question 7

Sunshine Ltd has an issued share capital of £40,000, divided into 30,000 £1 ordinary shares and 10,000 £1 preference shares. Its articles of association provide that: 'The holders of preference shares are entitled to a 5% fixed dividend and prior repayment of capital on a winding up of the company.'

Advise the board of directors as to the procedures required to achieve the following schemes:

1. Reducing the preferential dividend from 5% to 3%.

2. Paying off the whole preference shares.

Answer plan

→ Examine whether a reduction of the dividend attached to the preference shares constitutes a variation of class rights.

→ Consider the procedure for the reduction of share capital.

→ Evaluate whether the cancellation of the whole class of preference shares amounts to a variation or abrogation of class rights.

Diagram plan

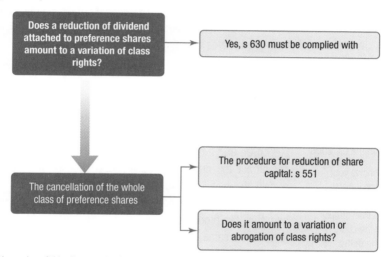

A printable version of this diagram plan is available from www.pearsoned.co.uk/lawexpressqa

Answer

[1]This sentence explains the presumption that any rights attached to a share are deemed to be exhaustive. It is a good starting point to discuss class rights.

This question concerns the legal procedures required for a variation of class rights and the reduction of share capital. The rights attached to preference shares as stated in the articles are class rights and they are presumed to be exhaustive: **Re National Telephone Co [1914] 1 Ch 755.**[1]

1. A reduction of dividend from 5% to 3%[2]

[2]In an exam question like this, the use of headings may help examiners follow your answer and allocate marks accordingly.

If the board decides to reduce the dividend of the preference shares from 5% to 3%, it needs to consider whether the reduction constitutes a variation of class rights. If it is not a variation of class

[3]Section 630 is a very
important provision for the
protection of class rights. It
must not be omitted in your
answer.

rights, a special resolution is required for an alteration of the articles of association (s 21); otherwise, the procedure in s 630 must be followed for a variation of class rights.[3] Class rights may only be varied in accordance with provisions in the company's articles, or where the articles contain no such provisions, if the holders of shares of that class consent to the variation (s 630(1)). The consent must be in writing from the holders of at least three-quarters in nominal value of the issued shares of that class[4] or a special resolution passed at a separate general meeting of the holders of that class sanctioning the variation (s 630(4)). It appears that the articles of Sunshine Ltd do not contain provisions on the variation of class rights; thus, the consent of the holders of at least three-quarters in nominal value of the issued shares of that class is required.[5]

[4]You need to pay attention to the requirement here. Three-quarters in nominal value refers to the issued shares of 'that class', instead of 'ordinary shares'.

[5]In a problem question, it is important to apply to the problem scenario after analysing the relevant law.

Section 630 only applies to variation or abrogation of class rights; however, there is no definition of variation or abrogation of class rights. A distinction is made at common law between matters affecting the rights attached to each share and matters affecting the enjoyment of these rights: **White v Bristol Aeroplane Co Ltd** [1953] Ch 65.[6] If only the enjoyment of the right is affected, it does not attract the protection under s 630 because the class rights remain the same. Moreover, the courts have adopted a narrow[7] view by comparing the right which would attach to a share before and after the proposed amendment of the class right. If the right remains the same, no variation occurs: **Re Mackenzie and Co Ltd** [1916] 2 Ch 450. The dividend of preference shares in Sunshine Ltd is reduced from 5% to 3% and it is clearly a variation of class rights.

[6]The judicial interpretation of a variation of class rights is essential here because it is not defined in the CA 2006.

[7]This word shows your analysis of the judicial approach. It will gain you more marks than simply stating how the court compares the rights.

It should be noted that where a class has consented to a variation, the holders of not less than 15% of the issued shares of the class in question may apply to the court to have the variation cancelled, provided that they did not consent to or vote in favour of the resolution for the variation (s 633(2)).[8] If the court is satisfied that the variation would unfairly prejudice the shareholders of the class represented by the applicant, it may disallow the variation (s 633(5)). This provision is rarely used in practice because it is unlikely that the court would overturn a decision which was made by a majority of the class. An unfair prejudice petition under s 994 may be preferable if a member of the class feels that his rights have been unfairly prejudiced.[9]

[8]Students often forget to discuss this right of objection by the holders of the preference shares. It can be a useful tool for minority holders of preference shares.

[9]This analysis demonstrates your excellent knowledge of s 633 and shareholder remedies. It will make your answer stand out.

2. Cancellation of the whole class of the preference shares

[10]The reference to the rule of capital maintenance shows your wider understanding of the reduction of share capital. It may impress your examiners.

The cancellation of the preference shares involves a reduction of share capital. A reduction of share capital is subject to strict conditions because it goes against the doctrine of capital maintenance which is designed to protect the interests of creditors.[10] A private company may reduce its capital by special resolution supported by solvency statement (s 641(a)). The directors should make a solvency statement not more than 15 days before the date on which the resolution is passed (s 642). If they make such statements without having reasonable grounds for the opinions expressed in it, an offence is committed by every director who will be liable to imprisonment on conviction and/or a fine (s 643(4)). A private company may also reduce its share capital by special resolution confirmed by the court (s 645).[11] The court has discretion to confirm or reject a proposed reduction of capital. Its main concern in approving reduction is the protection of creditors and fair treatment of different classes of shareholders: **Re Ratners Group plc** [1988] BCLC 685. Creditors are given the opportunities to object to the reduction of capital if a reduction involves any diminution of liability or any repayment of capital (s 646).

[11]Most students are aware of the requirements of special resolution and solvency statement in s 641 but many forget to discuss the alternative procedure in s 645.

[12]The reference to case law here will gain you more marks because it shows your good understanding of the general rule by illustrating how it works.

The general rule on the repayment of capital is that money should be paid in the order in which the classes of shares would rank on a winding up. In **Re Chatterley-Whitfield Collieries Ltd** [1948] 2 All ER 593,[12] the company decided to reduce its capital by paying off preference capital but keeping its ordinary shareholders. It was held that the reduction was fair because it was carried out in accordance with the rights of the two classes of shareholders on a winding up.

When considering whether a reduction of capital amounts to a variation of the class rights of preference shareholders, the courts will compare the rights of the preference shareholders on a winding up with their rights under the proposed reduction. If the proposed reduction is in accordance with the class rights on a winding up, there is no variation of the class rights: **Re Saltdean Estate Co Ltd** [1968] 3 All ER 829.[13] Buckley J in this case noted that although the preference shareholders hoped to retain their interest in the company, this expectation was always vulnerable to a future winding up or a reduction of capital.

[13]This analysis is essential for a good answer because it addresses one of the core issues raised in the problem question. The reference to the case law authority should not be omitted.

[14]This sentence shows that your analysis has progressed from a reduction of share capital generally (which is discussed in the previous paragraph) to an abolition of the whole class of preference shares.

[15]This is a House of Lords authority on whether a cancellation of a whole class of shares amounts to variation of class rights. It will add more credit to your answer.

In relation to the abolition of the whole class of preference shares, the courts have been generally reluctant to treat it as a variation of class rights.[14] In **House of Fraser plc v ACGE Investments Ltd** [1987] AC 387,[15] the ordinary shareholders passed a special resolution which approved the paying off of the whole preference shares of the company. The House of Lords held that the proposed reduction of capital which led to the extinction of the preference shares was not a variation of the class rights attached to these shares and therefore the consent of the preference shareholders was not required. The preference shareholders had a right to a return of capital prior to other shareholders and that right was not affected. As the preference shareholders in Sunshine Ltd are entitled to prior repayment of capital on a winding up, the capital of the preference shares should be repaid first and a proposed cancellation is not a variation of class rights.

✓ Make your answer stand out

- Consider whether directors have breached their duties in s 171 and s 172 in exercising their power to reduce the dividend and to pay off the whole class.
- Discuss in more detail the protection of shareholders' rights by way of unfair prejudice petition under s 994 or a derivative claim under s 260 against a director's breach of duties.
- Explain the solvency statement as defined in s 643 in more detail.

! Don't be tempted to...

- Only answer part of the question. Although the first part of the question on the reduction of dividend from 5% to 3% appears simple and straightforward, it still requires a detailed analysis of class rights and the procedures for a variation of class rights.
- Reach the wrong conclusion that a cancellation of a whole class of preference shares amounts to a variation of class rights. Contrary to what many students may think, the abolition of a whole class does not vary class rights in this question.

Loan capital

7

How this topic may come up in exams

Students often find the questions on loan capital complex and confusing. The legal distinctions between fixed charges and floating charges are often examined in an essay question; in particular, you should focus on the nature of charges over book debts. Other popular areas for examination include the requirements for the registration of charges, the conclusive nature of the registration certificate, and the consequences and remedies for non-registration or late registration. This topic overlaps with corporate insolvency where the liquidator needs to consider the validity of charges and their order of priority when the company goes into liquidation.

■ Attack the question

🖋 Question 1

Critically evaluate the distinctions between fixed charges and floating charges, in particular, the nature of charges over book debts.

Answer plan

➜ Explain the definitions of a fixed charge and a floating charge.

➜ Examine the differences between a fixed charge and a floating charge.

➜ Analyse the nature of charges over the company's book debts.

Diagram plan

A printable version of this diagram plan is available from www.pearsoned.co.uk/lawexpressqa

Answer

This question requires an examination of the legal distinctions between a fixed charge and a floating charge with particular reference to the nature of the charge over book debts. A fixed charge is created over a specific asset of a company such as its land and buildings. It gives the charge holder an immediate proprietary interest in the assets and restricts the company's ability to deal with the asset; for example, the company would not be able to sell the asset without the consent of the charge holder.[1]

[1] The example here highlights the feature of a fixed charge and demonstrates your good knowledge of a fixed charge.

A floating charge is not attached to any particular assets and it is typically taken over the entire undertaking of the company, including removable plant and equipment, stock-in-trade, work in progress and book debts. It is an extremely flexible device because it enables the company to deal with the charged assets without the need to obtain the consent of the charge holder.[2] Its main characteristics are illustrated by Romer LJ in **Re Yorkshire Woolcombers Association** [1903] 2 Ch 284: a floating charge is a charge on a class of assets of a company, present and future; that class of assets would be changing from time to time in the company's ordinary course of business; and the company may carry on its business in the ordinary way until some future step is taken such as crystallisation.[3] Once it is crystallised, the floating charge becomes a fixed charge and the company is no longer free to deal with the assets in the normal course of business. When the company is in liquidation, a floating charge is still treated as a floating charge notwithstanding it has been crystallised. A floating charge may crystallise in the events expressly specified in the charge document, or upon the appointment of a receiver or administrator (**Evans v Rival Granite Quarries Ltd** [1910] 2 KB 979), or upon a winding up order (**Wallace v Universal Automatic Machines** [1894] 2 Ch 547), or the company's ceasing to carry on business (**Re Woodroffes (Musical Instruments) Ltd** [1986] Ch 366).[4]

It is more advantageous for a creditor to hold a fixed charge than a floating charge for four main reasons.[5] First, a fixed charge offers greater security. Although the holder of a floating charge has considerable control over the company's affairs and can take steps to enforce the charge, there is always the danger that the assets will be dissipated. Secondly, a floating charge is open to challenge by a liquidator or an administrator under s 245 of the Insolvency Act 1986 whilst a fixed charge is not subject to this provision.[6] Thirdly, when the company goes into liquidation, a floating charge ranks before unsecured creditors but is subject to the prior claims of the expenses of liquidation, the preferential debts and the prescribed part of the floating charge assets. By contrast, the fixed charge holder ranks above all other creditors, including the expenses of the liquidation. Finally, the holder of a floating charge over a company's assets is vulnerable to the company granting another lender a fixed charge over the same assets at a later date. In order to prevent this,

[2]This is the most important feature of a floating charge. You will lose some marks if it is omitted in your answer.

[3]The reference to the case law and Romer LJ's classic statement of the characteristics of a floating charge will make your answer stand out because they go beyond a simple description of a floating charge.

[4]A discussion of the events for crystallisation with the support of relevant case law shows your sound understanding. It will add credit to your answer.

[5]Your answer should go beyond a basic description of the definitions of fixed charges and floating charges. An analysis of the advantages of a fixed charge over a floating one is essential for a sound answer. Also try to adopt a clear and logical list rather than stating everything you know about the differences between the two types of charges.

[6]The discussion of the avoidance of floating charges adds more credit to your answer. It is often ignored by students when comparing fixed and floating charges.

[7]Some students do not understand, or are not aware of, the negative pledge clause. It is very common in relation to a floating charge and therefore should be included in your answer.

[8]This shows your understanding of the complicated issues in relation to book debts. It also indicates that your answer is moving on to the legal issues of book debts. Try to signpost your answer so that it is easier for your examiners to follow.

[9]These are the two most important cases on the nature of charges over book debts. They should be discussed in detail in a good answer.

[10]The two-stage process for determining the nature of the charge enhances your understanding of the judgment of Re Brumark. It will gain you more marks.

it is common to include a negative pledge clause[7] in the charge instrument, which states that the company will not grant another charge over the same assets or any attempt to grant another charge will be regarded as a crystallising event for the first floating charge.

The nature of a charge over the proceeds of book debts has been subject to a considerable amount of litigation.[8] Book debts are sums due to the company by its debtors and they would ordinarily be entered in the books of the company for accounting purposes. The nature of the charge is determined by who has control of the proceeds of the book debts, as demonstrated by **Agnew v IRC (Re Brumark)** [2001] 2 BCLC 188 and **National Westminster Bank plc v Spectrum Plus Ltd** [2005] 2 BCLC 269 **(Re Spectrum Plus Ltd)**.[9]

In **Re Brumark** the dispute arose in relation to the nature of the charge on the book debts which were uncollected at the time of the appointment of the receivers. The New Zealand Court of Appeal considered that the company was free to collect the book debts and deal with the proceeds in the normal course of business and therefore held that it was a floating charge. This decision was confirmed by the Privy Council, where a two-stage process was established: first, the court must construe the charge instrument and seek to ascertain the intention and the rights of the parties; and then it is a matter of law for the courts to determine whether the charge is fixed or floating.[10] Thus, neither the intention of the parties nor the terms which they use to describe the charge are conclusive in determining whether a charge is fixed or floating. The key issues are whether the company has control of the asset and whether it is free to remove it from the security without the consent of the bank. This approach was adopted by the House of Lords in **Re Spectrum Plus**.

In **Re Spectrum Plus** the company collected its book debts and paid them into a bank account. It was free to draw on the account for its business purposes, provided that the overdraft limit was not exceeded. At first instance, the court held that it was a floating charge over book debts. The Court of Appeal overturned this decision and held that it was a fixed charge because the bank was in control of the proceeds. The House of Lords concluded that it was only a floating charge because the company was free to withdraw the proceeds of the book debts in the ordinary course of business despite the

[11]Some students only focus on the decision by the House of Lords. As this is a very important case, you should also discuss the judgments by the court of first instance and the Court of Appeal which will demonstrate your excellent knowledge of this case.

[12]The reference to this case demonstrates your sound understanding of the case law in relation to the nature of charges over book debts. It will gain you more marks.

restrictions.[11] The decision in **Siebe Gorman & Co Ltd v Barclays Bank Ltd** [1979] 2 Lloyd's Rep 142 was overruled.[12]

In most cases charges on book debts are floating charges; nevertheless, it is still possible to create a fixed charge over book debts. In **Re Keenan Bros Ltd** [1986] BCLC 242 the funds collected by the company were required to be paid into a blocked account with the charge holder and the consent of the bank was required for each withdrawal from that account. It was held that the charge was a fixed charge as the debts were unavailable to the company. It can be concluded from the above discussion that a charge over book debts is a floating charge if the company is free to collect the debts and deal with the proceeds without the consent of the holder of the charge.

 Make your answer stand out

- Discuss the effect of the negative pledge clause. Registration of a floating charge does not by itself give constructive notice of the negative pledge clause: *Wilson* v *Kelland* [1910] 2 Ch 306.
- Examine in detail the judgments in *Re Spectrum Plus* (2005).
- Analyse in more detail the avoidance of a floating charge under s 245 of the Insolvency Act 1986.
- Explain the judgment in *Siebe Gorman & Co Ltd* (1979), where it was held that the charge was a fixed charge over book debts because the restrictions on the book debts and on their proceeds gave the lender some control.
- Make reference to academic opinions on fixed charges and floating charges: Capper, D. 'Fixed charges over book debts – the future after *Brumark*' [2003] 24 *Company Lawyer* 325; Smart, P. 'Fixed or floating? Siebe Gorman post-Brumark' [2004] 25 *Company Lawyer* 331; Sheehan D. and Arvind, T. T. 'Prospective overruling and the fixed-floating charge debate' (2006) 122 *Law Quarterly Review* 20; Pennington, 'Recent developments in the law and practice relating to the creation of security for companies' indebtedness' [2009] 30 *Company Lawyer* 163.

! Don't be tempted to...

- Forget to discuss the nature of a charge over book debts. You need to show a good understanding of the circumstances when it is categorised as a fixed charge or a floating one.

- Provide an answer without reference to cases such as *Re Brumark* [2001] 2 BCLC 188 and *Re Spectrum Plus Ltd* [2005] 2 BCLC 269. These are very influential cases and should not be ignored in your answer.

❓ Question 2

Park Ltd obtained a loan of £10,000 from M Bank plc and a floating charge was created on 5 January 2011 in favour of M Bank plc over its entire undertakings, both present and future, to secure the loan. The charge instrument prohibits the creation of any subsequent charges which rank in priority to the floating charge. It was discovered on 25 February 2011 that the charge was not registered with the Registrar.

In March 2011, Park Ltd borrowed £20,000 from N Bank plc. On 2 May 2011, a fixed charge was created over Park Ltd's office buildings in favour of N Bank plc for this loan and it was registered on 20 May 2011. Park Ltd went into insolvent liquidation on 3 October 2011.

Discuss the validity of both charges and their order of priority.

Answer plan

→ Analyse the legal requirements for the registration of both charges (s 860, CA 2006).

→ Examine the remedies for late registration or non-registration of the floating charge in favour or M Bank plc (s 873, CA 2006).

→ Evaluate the effect of the negative pledge clause in the floating charge instrument.

→ Consider whether the floating charge in favour of M Bank plc can be avoided under s 245, IA 1986.

→ Discuss whether the floating charge or the fixed charge can be set aside as a preference under s 239, IA 1986.

Diagram plan

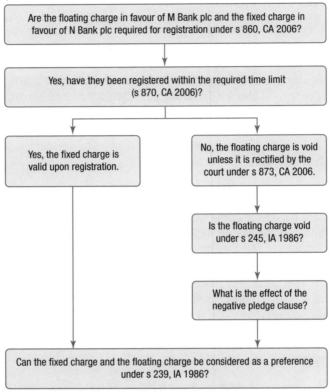

Are the floating charge in favour of M Bank plc and the fixed charge in favour of N Bank plc required for registration under s 860, CA 2006?

↓

Yes, have they been registered within the required time limit (s 870, CA 2006)?

Yes, the fixed charge is valid upon registration.

No, the floating charge is void unless it is rectified by the court under s 873, CA 2006.

Is the floating charge void under s 245, IA 1986?

What is the effect of the negative pledge clause?

Can the fixed charge and the floating charge be considered as a preference under s 239, IA 1986?

A printable version of this diagram plan is available from www.pearsoned.co.uk/lawexpressqa

[1] This sentence identifies the main legal issues that arise in the problem question. It clearly indicates that your answer is going in the right direction.

[2] Note that this statutory provision is included in the Companies Act 2006, not the Insolvency Act 1986.

[3] Some students may assume that all fixed charges must be registered. You should understand that registration is only required for those charges listed in s 860(7).

Answer

This question concerns whether both charges are registered according to s 870 of the Companies Act 2006, whether the charges are valid under s 245 and s 239 of the Insolvency Act 1986, and whether the floating charge has priority over the fixed charge in light of the negative pledge clause.[1] Two charges were created by Park Ltd, one is a floating charge over its entire undertakings and the other is a fixed charge over its office buildings. Both charges are required for registration with the registrar. According to s 860 of the Companies Act 2006,[2] all floating charges must be registered; fixed charges need only be registered if they are over one of the specified classes of assets listed in s 860(7).[3] The list covers most classes of charges commonly given by companies, such as a charge on land, book debts, or any intellectual property; the charges on shares are not required to be registered. The purpose of registration is to give potential lenders more accurate information about the company and warn other creditors of the company's charged assets.[4]

The particulars and the instrument of a charge must be delivered to the registrar of companies within 21 days beginning with the day after the day on which the charge is created[5] (s 870(1)). If a company fails to comply with it, an offence is committed by the company and every officer in default who is liable to a fine (s 860(4)) and the charge is void against the liquidator or administrator and any creditor of the company (s 874(1)). It loses all priority it would otherwise possess and the charge holder will become an unsecured creditor. The charge, however, is still valid against the chargee and the money secured by it immediately becomes payable (s 874(3)).[6] The fixed charge in favour of N Bank plc was registered within the 21-day limit. The floating charge in favour of M Bank plc, however, was not registered within 21 days of its creation and was therefore void unless it was successfully registered out of time.[7] This may have some implications in relation to the priority of the charges which have been registered in the period during which the floating charge was void.

The court, on the application of Park Ltd or M Bank plc, may order that the period allowed for registration shall be extended on such terms and conditions as seem to the court just and expedient (s 873). The court will only make the order if it is satisfied with one of the following three conditions:[8] first, the failure to register a charge on time was accidental or due to inadvertence or to some other sufficient cause; secondly, the failure to register is not of a nature to prejudice the position of creditors or shareholders of the company; thirdly, it is just and equitable to grant relief. The jurisdiction of the court is very wide; however, the chargee must act expeditiously once the failure to register is discovered: **Re Teleomatic** [1994] 1 BCLC 90. Moreover, the court will not normally make an order under s 873 once a winding up has commenced: **Barclays Bank Plc *v* Stuart London Ltd** [2001] 2 BCLC 316.[9]

It should be noted that a floating charge on the company's undertaking or property shall be invalid if it is created in favour of an unconnected person within 12 months (two years for a connected person) ending with the onset of insolvency, unless the company was

[10]Not all charges created within the specified period of time are invalid. It is essential that you know the exception.

able to pay its debts at the time the charge was created[10] (s 245, IA 1986). A person is connected with the company if he is a director, a shadow director or an associate of such a director or shadow director, or if he is an associate of the company (s 249, IA 1986). It appears that M Bank plc does not fall within this definition of a connected person. The floating charge in favour of M Bank plc was created within 12 months of the commencement of the winding up; it was therefore invalid unless Park Ltd was solvent when granting the floating charge.

The floating charge or the fixed charge may be avoided under s 239 of the IA 1986 on the basis that the transaction has given one of the company's creditors an unfair advantage to increase their chances of repayment over the other creditors. The liquidator can apply to the court challenging the alleged preference, if a company has, within six months prior to the onset of insolvency (two years for connected person) given a preference to an unconnected person.[11] The court may make such order as it thinks fit for restoring the position to what it would have been if the company had not given that preference. It shall not make an order unless the company which gave the preference was influenced in deciding to give it by a desire to put that person in a better position. The floating charge in favour of M Bank plc was not created within six months prior to the onset of insolvency and therefore s 239 does not apply to it. As the fixed charge in favour of N Bank plc was created within six months before the commencement of the winding up, it should be set aside if the court is satisfied that Park Ltd was influenced in deciding to give it by a desire to give N Bank plc an unfair advantage over other creditors.

[11]Some students are not aware of the different time limits which apply to the connected and unconnected persons. You will lose some marks in case of failure to make this important distinction.

The priority between charges is subject to common law. In principle, a fixed charge takes priority over the equitable floating charge on the assets concerned. This means that a floating charge will be postponed to any subsequently created fixed charge over the same assets. In order to prevent this, a negative pledge clause is often included in the floating charge instrument which expressly prohibits the creation of charges in priority to the floating charge, which is the case with the floating charge in favour of M Bank plc.[12] Although registration is held to give constructive notice of the charge, it does not constitute notice of the terms and conditions contained in the charge document: **Wilson v Kelland** [1910] 2 Ch 306.[13] Thus,

[12]This part of the sentence identifies the negative pledge clause in the problem question.

[13]A discussion of the effect of this clause by reference to case law gains you more marks.

registration of a floating charge does not by itself give constructive notice of the negative pledge clause. It appears that N Bank plc did not know this clause and therefore the fixed charge, (if it is not considered as a preference under s 239, IA 1986), ranks in priority to the floating charge in the event of insolvency (even if the floating charge was allowed to be registered out of time).

✓ Make your answer stand out

- Discuss that the charge which is caught by s 245 is valid only to the extent of any new value in the form of cash, goods or services supplied to the company, or the discharge of any liability of the company, if these take place at the same time as, or after, the creation of the charge (s 245(2), IA 1986).
- In your discussion of s 245, IA 1986, make reference to the case of *Power* v *Sharpe Investments Ltd* [1994] 1 BCLC 111, where it was held that the new value must be provided at the same time with the creation of the charge.
- Consider the order of priority of charges when the company goes into insolvency. The fixed charge holder ranks above all other creditors, including the expenses of the liquidation and the preferential debts. By contrast, the floating charge ranks in a lower position, just above the unsecured creditors.

! Don't be tempted to...

- Assume that the floating charge was void because it was not registered within 21 days under s 870, CA 2006. You should discuss the possibility of a court order for registration out of time under s 873, CA 2006.
- Come to the conclusion that the fixed charge ranks after the floating charge because of the negative pledge clause. You should be aware that the negative pledge clause does not take effect unless the holder of the later charge has actual notice of it, in other words, unless he knows the clause in the charge instrument.
- Only focus on the requirements for registration of charges in the Companies Act 2006. You should also examine whether the floating charge can be avoided and whether the fixed charge or the floating charge can be considered as a preference in the Insolvency Act 1986.

❓ Question 3

Bamboo Ltd has granted a charge over its book debts in favour of H Bank plc. The charge instrument provides that the proceeds of the book debts shall be paid into its bank account with H Bank plc. It also states that Bamboo Ltd is free to withdraw monies in the account.

Bamboo Ltd went into liquidation. H Bank plc claimed that the proceeds over the book debts were subject to a fixed charge in its favour.

Advise H Bank plc as to the nature of the charge over the book debts.

Answer plan

→ Discuss the differences between a fixed charge and a floating one.

→ Examine earlier authorities in relation to the nature of charges over book debts in *Siebe Gorman & Co Ltd* v *Barclays Bank Ltd* [1979] 2 Lloyd's Rep 142 and *Re New Bullas Trading Ltd* [1994] 1 BCLC 485.

→ Analyse recent authorities in relation to charges over book debts in *Agnew* v *Commissioner of Inland Revenue (Re Brumark)* [2001] 2 BCLC 188 and *National Westminster Bank plc* v *Spectrum Plus Ltd (Re Spectrum Plus Ltd)* [2005] 2 BCLC 269.

→ Apply the relevant law to the problem question.

Diagram plan

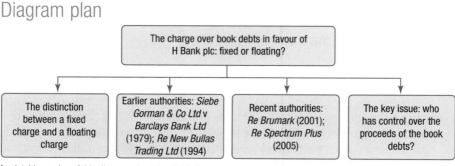

The charge over book debts in favour of H Bank plc: fixed or floating?

| The distinction between a fixed charge and a floating charge | Earlier authorities: *Siebe Gorman & Co Ltd* v *Barclays Bank Ltd* (1979); *Re New Bullas Trading Ltd* (1994) | Recent authorities: *Re Brumark* (2001); *Re Spectrum Plus* (2005) | The key issue: who has control over the proceeds of the book debts? |

A printable version of this diagram plan is available from www.pearsoned.co.uk/lawexpressqa

[1] In a problem question, you need to engage with the problem scenario in your introduction.
[2] Some students do not understand what is meant by book debts. This explanation shows that you know the basic concept of this topic.

Answer

H Bank plc may have difficulties in seeking to enforce the fixed charge over the book debts of Bamboo Ltd.[1] Book debts are sums due to the company by its debtors and would ordinarily be entered in the books of the company.[2] The nature of a charge over book debts has been subject to a considerable amount of litigation. This

[3]These two sentences succinctly summarise the development of common law. They immediately demonstrate that you are very familiar with this area of law and make your answer stand out from the start.

complex area of case law has recently been clarified by the Privy Council in **Re Brumark** [2001] 2 BCLC 188 and the House of Lords in **Re Spectrum Plus Ltd** [2005] 2 BCLC 269. Earlier authorities such as **Siebe Gorman & Co Ltd v Barclays Bank Ltd** [1979] 2 Lloyd's Rep 142 and **Re New Bullas Trading Ltd** [1994] 1 BCLC 485 were overruled.[3]

A fixed charge is created over a specific asset of a company, for example, its land and buildings and fixed plant. The charge restricts the company's ability to deal with the asset. By contrast, a floating charge is not attached to any particular assets identified when the charge is created; the company is free to deal with the charged assets in the ordinary course of business without the need to obtain the consent of the chargee: **Re Yorkshire Woolcombers Association** [1903] 2 Ch 284.

[4]Although *Siebe Gorman & Co Ltd* has been overruled, a discussion of the judgment is still essential because it shows how the law has developed. It will gain you more marks.

In **Siebe Gorman & Co Ltd** (above),[4] the charge instrument required that the proceeds of the book debts be credited to a specific account held with the lender. This effectively prevented the company from withdrawing the monies in the course of its business. It was held that the charge was a fixed charge over book debts because the restrictions on the proceeds gave the lender some control. In **Re New Bullas Trading Ltd** (above) the Court of Appeal accepted the arrangement which created a fixed charge over the uncollected book debts and a floating charge over their collected proceeds in the bank account. It was overruled by the House of Lords in **Re Spectrum Plus** on the basis that, since the company was free to deal with the book debts and their proceeds without the consent of the chargee, it was a floating charge.[5]

[5]The reason why *Re New Bullas Trading Ltd* was overruled shows your excellent understanding. It will add more credit to your answer.

[6]The facts of this case are complicated and a detailed description will add little to your answer. A brief summary, however, shows your good understanding of the case and may impress your examiners.

In **Re Brumark** a fixed charge was created in favour of a bank over all book debts of the company arising in its ordinary course of business. The dispute was in relation to the nature of the charge on the book debts which were uncollected at the time of the appointment of the receivers.[6] The Privy Council held that a charge over uncollected book debts was a floating charge because the company was free to collect the debts and use the proceeds in the ordinary course of its business. Lord Millett established a two-stage process: first, the court must construe the charge instrument and gather the intention of the parties from the language used in order to ascertain the nature of the rights and obligations which the parties

[7]The reference to the House
of Lords indicates that you
appreciate the significance of
this case.

[7]The reference to the House
of Lords indicates that you
appreciate the significance of
this case.

[8]The brief fact of this case
is included here because
it is similar to the problem
scenario.

[9]This sentence shows that
you understand the link
between *Re Spectrum Plus*
and *Siebe Gorman*. It also
lays the foundation for your
discussion of the overruling
of *Siebe Gorman* in the next
paragraph.

[10]Some students only discuss
the judgment of the House of
Lords. The decisions by the
court of first instance and the
Court of Appeal demonstrate
your excellent understanding
of this case and will improve
your grade.

[11]This part of the sentence,
although short, will add more
credit to your answer because
it analyses the reasons why
most charges over book debts
are floating charges.

intended to; second, it is a matter of law for the courts to determine
whether the charge is fixed or floating; neither the intention of the
parties nor the terms which they use to describe the transaction are
conclusive. The crucial question is therefore whether the company
has control of the asset and is free to remove it from the security
without the consent of the bank.

This approach was confirmed by the House of Lords[7] in **Re
Spectrum Plus**, where an overdraft had been secured by a charge
and the company was required to pay the proceeds from its book
debts into that bank account. The company, however, was free to
draw on the account for its business purposes provided the overdraft
limit was not exceeded.[8] The charge over book debts was expressed
in the same terms as that in **Siebe Gorman**, which had been
accepted as a fixed charge.[9] Upon the liquidation of the company,
the bank claimed that the proceeds of the book debts were the
subject of a fixed charge in its favour. The courts had to consider
whether the charge was fixed or floating.

At first instance, the court ruled that **Siebe Gorman** had been
wrongly decided and it was held that the charge was a floating
charge over book debts. The Court of Appeal, however, held that
it was a fixed charge because the bank was in control of the
proceeds.[10] The House of Lords confirmed that it was a floating
charge despite it was expressed to grant the bank a fixed charge
over the company's book debts. The restrictions imposed were insufficient because the company was still free to withdraw the proceeds
of the book debts in the ordinary course of business. The decision in
Siebe Gorman was overruled.

In most cases charges on book debts are floating charges because
it may be impossible in practice to give lenders complete control
over the company's book debts.[11] In **Re Brightlife Ltd** [1986]
BCLC 418 the company was free to collect the debts and pay the
proceeds into its bank account and use them in the ordinary course
of business. It was held that the charge was a floating charge despite
some restrictions on the company. In **Royal Trust Bank v National
Westminster Bank plc** [1996] 2 BCLC 682, the charge instrument
required that the company pay all the proceeds of the book debts
in a separate account. The charge was held to be a floating charge
because the company was free to withdraw the proceeds collected
which were deposited into the company's ordinary trading account.

It is still possible, nevertheless, to create a fixed charge over book debts if the lender prohibits the company from collecting the debts, for example, when there is requirement that the proceeds must be placed in a blocked account under the control of the lender. In **Re Keenan Bros Ltd** [1986] BCLC 242 the funds collected by the company were required to be paid into a blocked account with the charge holder and prior consent of the bank was required for each withdrawal from that account. The Privy Council held that the charge was a fixed charge because the debts were not available to the company.[12] Similarly, in **William Gaskell Group Ltd v Highley** [1994] 1 BCLC 197, it was held that a charge over a company's book debts was a fixed charge because the proceeds of the book debts were required to be paid into an account and the company could not make withdrawal without the chargee's consent.

[12]These two sentences illustrate the circumstances where fixed charges can be created over book debts. The reference to case law will gain you more marks.

It is concluded that the key issue in determining the nature of the charge over book debts is who has control of the proceeds of the book debts. In relation to the charge over the book debts of Bamboo Ltd, following **Re Spectrum Plus**, it is very likely that the court will consider it as a floating charge because Bamboo Ltd, instead of H Bank plc, is in control of the proceeds of the book debts.[13]

[13]Your conclusion should clearly state the legal position of the charge over the book debts of Bamboo Ltd.

 Make your answer stand out

- Consider the characteristics of a floating charge which were stated by Romer LJ in *Re Yorkshire Woolcombers Association* [1903] 2 Ch 284.

- Discuss whether the charge has been registered within the required time limit in s 860, CA 2006.

- Examine whether the floating charge over book debts can be avoided under s 245, IA 1986.

- Evaluate whether the floating charge can be set aside as a voidable preference under s 239, IA 1986.

- Analyse the circumstances where the floating charge crystallises.

> **! Don't be tempted to...**
>
> - Make no reference to the House of Lords' decision in *Re Spectrum Plus*. This is a highly significant case on the nature of a charge over book debts and it must be included in your answer.
> - Wrongly believe that the decisions in *Siebe Gorman & Co Ltd* v *Barclays Bank Ltd* [1979] 2 Lloyd's Rep 142 and *Re New Bullas Trading Ltd* [1993] BCC 251 are still valid. You should know that they have been overruled by *Re Spectrum Plus*.
> - Reach the wrong conclusion that all charges over book debts are floating charges. You should also examine the circumstances where they are considered as fixed charges.

? Question 4

David was the majority shareholder and director of WL Tea Ltd. In February 2009, David lent £50,000 to WL Tea Ltd. In April 2010, David was worried about the financial situation of the company and obtained a floating charge over the entire undertaking of WL Tea Ltd for his loan. WL Tea Ltd was wound up in September 2010.

Advise the liquidator as to the validity of the floating charge.

Answer plan

→ Consider the registration requirements for the floating charge in s 870, CA 2006.

→ Examine whether the floating charge can be avoided under s 245, IA 1986.

→ Analyse whether the floating charge can be set aside as a voidable preference under s 239, IA 1986.

Diagram plan

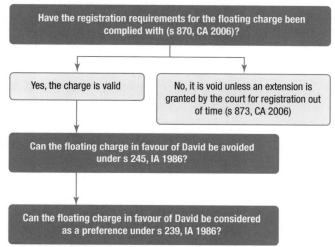

Have the registration requirements for the floating charge been complied with (s 870, CA 2006)?

Yes, the charge is valid

No, it is void unless an extension is granted by the court for registration out of time (s 873, CA 2006)

Can the floating charge in favour of David be avoided under s 245, IA 1986?

Can the floating charge in favour of David be considered as a preference under s 239, IA 1986?

A printable version of this diagram plan is available from www.pearsoned.co.uk/lawexpressqa

Answer

[1]These sentences not only identify the key legal issues arising from the question but also summarise the main areas of law which are relevant to the question. They immediately show your sound knowledge and clear structure of your answer. They will impress your examiners from the start.

[2]You should discuss the serious consequences for non-registration. Many students are not aware that the charge is still valid against the chargee and the debt becomes payable. You will lose some marks if this issue is not included in your answer.

This question concerns the validity of the floating charge created in favour of David, who was a director of WL Tea Ltd. A floating charge may be void if the registration requirements in s 870 of the Companies Act 2006 are not met. It may be avoided under s 245 of the Insolvency Act 1986 or set aside as a voidable preference by the liquidator under s 239, IA 1986.[1]

The floating charge over the company's undertaking must be registered with the registrar within 21 days, beginning with the day after the day on which the charge is created (s 870, CA 2006). If a company fails to comply with it, an offence is committed by the company and every officer in default who is liable to a fine (s 860) and the charge is void against the liquidator or administrator and any creditor of the company (s 874). It loses all priority it would otherwise possess and the charge holder will become an unsecured creditor. The charge is, however, not void against the chargee and the money secured by it immediately becomes payable (s 874).[2]

If the charge is not registered within the required 21 days of its creation, the company or a person interested may apply to the court for registration out of time (s 873, CA 2006). The court may order

[3] A discussion of the circumstances where the charge can be registered out of time shows your sound understanding. It will gain you more marks than only stating that the court may allow registration out of time.

that the period allowed for registration shall be extended on such terms and conditions as seem to the court just and expedient. The court will only make such an order if it is satisfied with one of the following three circumstances: first, the failure to register a charge on time was accidental or due to inadvertence or to some other sufficient cause; secondly, the failure to register is not of a nature to prejudice the position of creditors or shareholders of the company; thirdly, it is just and equitable to grant relief.[3] When the registration period is extended, the charge is regarded void until registered.

[4] The rationale of s 245 goes beyond a simple description of the statutory provision and will add credit to your answer.

[5] Try to apply the relevant law to the problem question as you go along. Some students discuss the law with little or no application to the problem question, or only start to apply to the question in the conclusion. Your examiners are keen to see not only your good understanding of the law but also your ability to apply the law.

David obtained a floating charge over his unsecured loan shortly before the company was wound up. It is likely that he had early warnings of the company going into insolvency. Section 245 of the Insolvency Act 1986 is designed to prevent this and protect the interests of other creditors.[4] If a floating charge on the company's undertaking or property is created in favour of a connected person within two years, ending with the onset of insolvency, it shall be invalid unless some value has been given to the company. The connected person is defined in s 249 and it includes a director, a shadow director and the associates of the director. David, who was the company director, is therefore a connected person.[5] The onset of insolvency refers to the commencement of the winding up or the making of an administration order (s 245). If the charge is created for an unconnected person within 12 months ending with the onset of insolvency, it shall be invalid unless the company is able to pay its debts at the time the charge was created (s 245(4)). The charge caught by s 245 is valid only to the extent of any new value in the form of cash, goods or services supplied to the company, or the discharge of any liability of the company, if these take place at the same time as, or after, the creation of the charge (s 245(2)).[6]

[6] Section 245(2) is often missing in students' answers. Many students have the wrong idea that the floating charge, if caught under s 245 of the IA 1986, will definitely be void. You need to understand that if any new consideration is provided, the charge is valid to the extent of the new value.

In **Power v Sharpe Investments Ltd** [1994] 1 BCLC 111, it was held that the new value must be provided at the same time with the creation of the charge. As the floating charge in favour of David was created within five months (less than two years) of the commencement of the winding up and new value was not provided either at the time or after the charge was created, it can be argued that the charge should be void.[7]

[7] Again, apply to the problem question after discussing the relevant law.

The floating charge may also be avoided under s 239 of the IA 1986 on the basis that the transaction has given one of the company's creditors a preference, for example, an unfair advantage in order to

8Note the different time
limits for connected and
unconnected persons.
Failure to show an accurate
understanding of this will lead
to a reduction of marks.

increase their chances of repayment over the other creditors. Where a company has, within two years prior to the onset of insolvency (six months for an unconnected person),[8] given a preference to a connected person, the liquidator can apply to the court challenging the alleged preference. If the court finds that a preference has been given, it can make such order as it thinks fit for restoring the position to what it would have been if the company had not given that preference.

9You need to pay more
attention here. 'Both' of
the conditions must be
met. If only one is met,
the transaction will not be
considered as a preference.

A company is considered to have given a preference if both of the following conditions are met.[9] First, if that person is one of the company's creditors or a surety or guarantor for any of the company's debts or other liabilities; secondly, in the event of the company going into insolvent liquidation, the person is put into a better position by what the company has done (s 239(4)). Both conditions are satisfied here, as David was the company's creditor and he was put into a better position by way of the creation of the floating charge.

10This is another condition
for the court to set aside the
preference. It is not often
discussed in exam answers.

11A discussion of the case
law which interprets the
application of the statutory
provisions makes your answer
stand out from those which
focus only on the statutory
provisions.

The court shall not make an order unless the company which gave the preference was influenced in deciding to give it by a desire to put that person in a better position (s 239(5)).[10] The essential element in establishing the existence of a preference is the desire to prefer that creditor on an insolvent liquidation. In **Re MC Bacon Ltd** [1990] BCLC 324,[11] the overdraft was secured by a debenture granted by the company within six months prior to the onset of insolvency when the company was unable to pay its debts. The court held that the company gave the security to the bank out of a desire to continue trading rather than positively wish to improve the bank's position; the debenture was not held void as a preference. This case emphasised that the key test was whether the company desired to improve the creditor's position in the event of its insolvency.

If a company has given a preference to a person connected with the company, it is presumed to have been influenced in deciding to give it by a desire to prefer that creditor unless the contrary is shown (s 239(6)). In **Re Exchange Travel (Holdings) Ltd** [1996] 2 BCLC 524 the company repaid loans made by the directors to the company two months before it went into administration. Such payments were held to be voidable preferences. It can therefore be presumed that WL Tea Ltd had been influenced in deciding to give the floating charge by a desire to prefer David because David is considered as a connected person. Unless the contrary is shown, the floating charge will be set aside as voidable preference.

✓ Make your answer stand out

- Consider whether David has breached any of his fiduciary duties owed to the company, in particular, the duty to act to promote the success of the company (s 172, CA 2006) and the duty to avoid conflicts of interests (s 175, CA 2006).
- Examine whether David may be liable for wrongful trading under s 214 of the Insolvency Act 1986. A director is liable to contribute to the assets of the company if, at some time before the commencement of the winding up of the company, he knew or ought to have concluded that there was no reasonable prospect that the company would avoid going into insolvent liquidation, and he did not take every step to minimise the potential loss to the company's creditors.
- Consider s 10 of the Company Directors Disqualification Act 1986 where the court can make a disqualification order against a director who has been liable for wrongful trading.

! Don't be tempted to...

- Mix up the reference to the Companies Act 2006 and the Insolvency Act 1986. The requirements for registration are contained in the CA 2006 whilst the provisions in relation to the avoidance of a floating charge and the voidable preference are contained in the IA 1986.
- Assume that the floating charge is duly registered and forget to discuss the legal requirements for registration of charges. The rules on registration, in particular with respect to registration of charges out of time, are an essential part of your answer because a failure to meet these requirements will make the charge void.
- Forget to discuss whether the floating charge can be set aside as a voidable preference in s 239 of the IA 1986.

Shareholder remedies

8

How this topic may come up in exams

Shareholder remedies are broad, complicated and important topics in company law and are often favoured by examiners. The main remedies are personal actions, unfair prejudice remedies, derivative actions and winding up remedies. Each type of remedy is likely to be examined by way of an essay or problem question on its own or with other types of remedies. You should pay special attention to statutory derivative actions and unfair prejudice remedies. In most problem questions, shareholder remedies are related to the topics on directors' duties. You should be able to apply the relevant law on directors' duties and shareholder remedies to complex problem questions.

■ Attack the question

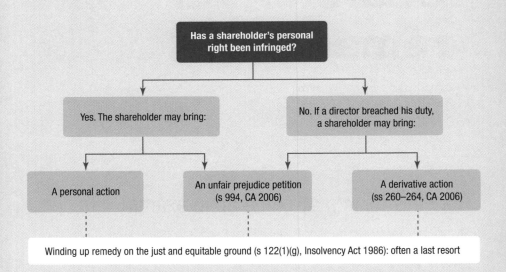

Has a shareholder's personal right been infringed?

Yes. The shareholder may bring:

No. If a director breached his duty, a shareholder may bring:

A personal action

An unfair prejudice petition (s 994, CA 2006)

A derivative action (ss 260–264, CA 2006)

Winding up remedy on the just and equitable ground (s 122(1)(g), Insolvency Act 1986): often a last resort

A printable version of this diagram plan is available from www.pearsoned.co.uk/lawexpressqa

🖋 Question 1

'Statutory derivative actions have been introduced by the Companies Act 2006 to replace those at common law. They have removed the obstacles which prevented shareholders from bringing derivative actions at common law. It is without doubt that they will open the floodgates for vexatious claims against directors by disgruntled minority shareholders.'

Critically analyse the above statements.

Answer plan

→ Discuss derivative actions at common law and the difficulties faced by shareholders in bringing such actions.

→ Focus on statutory derivative actions (ss 260–264) in relation to the procedure and the factors that the courts must take into account in granting permission to continue a derivative claim.

→ Compare derivative actions at common law and those in the Companies Act 2006.

→ Discuss whether the new rules provide shareholders with easier access to derivative actions and whether they will open the floodgates for vexatious litigation.

Diagram plan

A printable version of this diagram plan is available from www.pearsoned.co.uk/lawexpressqa

[1]These opening sentences set the context for the analysis which follows and reassure the examiner that you know exactly what the essay is about in terms of subject content.

[2]These sentences outline the essential points of the main arguments and demonstrate that you clearly understand what is being asked in the question. They also demonstrate immediately your critical analysis of the statements.

Answer

Derivative actions at common law were governed by the rule in **Foss v Harbottle** (1843) 67 ER 189 and the complicated rules effectively prevented vexatious suits. They were replaced by the statutory rules designed to provide a clearer procedure with more flexible criteria.[1] Whilst it can be asserted that they have modernised some aspects of derivative actions and removed some of the obstacles that existed previously, it is highly questionable as to whether the new procedures and criteria open floodgates for vexatious claims. It can be argued that there are still many obstacles in place and that any increase in the amount of litigation is debatable.[2]

This rule in **Foss v Harbottle** has two essential components: the majority rule and the proper claimant principle. This rule helps to prevent vexatious suits; however, it poses significant difficulties, especially when most or all of a company's directors have breached their duties. In order to protect the interests of minority shareholders, some exceptions were developed in **Edwards v Halliwell** [1950] 2 All ER 1064. Shareholders could bring an action in the case of an illegal or *ultra vires* act, or when there was a need for a special resolution, or when directors had committed fraud on the company. There was no clear definition of fraud; it was held in **Estmanco (Kilner House) Ltd v GLC** [1982] 1 WLR 2 that 'fraud in this context includes not only fraud and illegality at common law but also fraud in the wider equitable sense of an abuse or misuse of power by the directors'.[3] A mere negligent exercise of a director's powers did not constitute fraud if the directors had not benefited personally at the expense of the company: **Pavlides v Jensen** [1956] Ch 565. Nevertheless, it did amount to fraud if the directors had benefited from their negligence: **Daniels v Daniels** [1978] Ch 406.[4]

A shareholder also had to prove that the accused directors were in actual voting control of the company: **Prudential Assurance Co Ltd v Newman Industries Ltd (No. 2)** [1982] Ch 204. If an appropriate independent organ decided it was not in the commercial interests of the company to pursue the action, such a decision could prevent a derivative claim: **Smith v Croft (No. 2)** [1988] Ch 114. In addition, a derivative action would be barred if directors' breach of duties was only capable of ratification or had been actually ratified: **MacDougall v Gardiner** (1875) LR 1 Ch D 13.[5]

The Law Commission in 1997 concluded that the complex rules at common law were highly unsatisfactory and inadequate for minority shareholders.[6] In practice, there had been few cases, especially since the introduction of unfair prejudice remedies.[7] A new derivative procedure was recommended with more flexible and accessible criteria for determining whether a shareholder can pursue an action.

A shareholder can now bring a derivative action 'in respect of a cause of action arising from any actual or proposed act or omission involving *negligence, default, breach of duty or breach of trust by a director of the company*' (s 260(3)). Compared with that of derivative actions at common law, the scope has been extended to

[3] This quote shows your detailed knowledge of the important judgment in relation to the definition of fraud.

[4] These two sentences focus on whether directors' negligence amounted to fraud and demonstrate to an examiner your sound knowledge of derivative actions at common law.

[5] This paragraph shows your appreciation of the obstacles that a shareholder faced when bringing a derivative action at common law. It ties back to the question related to the obstacles at common law.

[6] The reference to the Law Commission's comments will gain you more marks because it demonstrates your wider understanding of the reform. This is also linked to the first two sentences in the question set.

[7] The brief comparison with the unfair prejudice remedy will gain you more marks as it demonstrates your awareness of the relationships between these two remedies.

cover a wider range of types of conduct including a director's mere negligence.[8]

Section 261 sets up a two-stage procedure for a derivative claim. At the first stage, the claimant is required to establish a *prima facie* case and the court considers only the application and evidence filed by the claimant. If it does not show a *prima facie* case the court must dismiss the application. If the court is satisfied at this stage it may give directions for evidence to be filed by the company. In this way, the court can dismiss unmeritorious cases at an early stage without involving the defendant directors or the company.[9]

[9] This shows your understanding of the reasons for such a procedure which will gain you more marks.

At the second stage, permission will be refused under s 263(2) if the claimant in accordance with s 172 (to promote the success of the company) would not seek to pursue the claim; or if the misconduct has been authorised or ratified by the company. In other situations, the court can exercise its discretion and must take into account a number of factors under s 263(3), in particular, whether the claimant is acting in good faith and the importance that a person acting in accordance with s 172 would attach to continuing it. Other relevant circumstances include whether the cause of action would be likely to be authorised or ratified, whether the company has decided not to sue and whether the shareholder can pursue a personal action. Section 263(4) also states that the courts should consider the views of members who have no personal interests in the matter.[10]

[10] A clear and comprehensive discussion of the factors that the courts take into account is an essential aspect of statutory derivative actions.

The current rules on derivative actions offer some guidance for a court in the exercise of its wide discretion and therefore provide greater clarity and certainty compared with those at common law. The scope has been widened as it fills a gap regarding directors' mere negligence. Moreover, the claimant no longer has to prove fraud and wrongdoer control. It appears, therefore, that shareholders may find it easier to bring such actions and the floodgates for litigation may be opened.[11]

[11] This sentence relates your discussion back to the issues raised in question in relation to the removal of obstacles at common law and easier access to derivative actions.

The court, however, is in control of litigation by way of the claimant's application for permission to continue the claim and, therefore, the amount of vexatious litigation can be controlled. The list of factors under s 263(2) and (3) also appears to be a set of hurdles that a claimant has to overcome. The Law Commission criticised the list of factors as a signal to adopt an over-restrictive approach and maintain a policy of not favouring a derivative action.[12] Effective

[12] These two sentences highlight the difficulties in bringing a derivative action and they will impress your examiners.

ratification, for example, still bars a derivative action; the court must also take into account the claimants' good faith, alterative remedies and the view of independent organ.

The Law Commission states that in all cases the new procedure will be subject to tight judicial control. These concerns are, to some extent, reflected in the judgments of **Mission Capital Plc v Sinclair** [2008] BCC 866 and **Franbar Holding Ltd v Patel** [2008] BCC 885. In both cases the claimant's application for permission to continue the derivative claim was refused. The procedures and factors, as well as the recent restrictive judicial attitudes towards derivative actions, therefore act as sufficient filters for vexatious claims. Moreover, shareholders may be deterred by the costs of litigation and the free-riding problem, as any recovery goes back to the company and shareholders cannot benefit directly. Hannigan (2009) is of similar view that there is unlikely to be any significant increase in the number of derivative claims because of the restrictive judicial attitude, the majority rule and a lack of incentive for shareholders.[13] It is therefore concluded that the statutory derivative actions are unlikely to open the floodgates for vexatious litigation.

[13]This section evaluates the problems associated with the new procedure and demonstrates your critical analysis skills by reference to the Law Commission's Report, case law and academic opinion. It will make your answer stand out by demonstrating your up-to-date knowledge and sound understanding of the current issues on this topic.

✓ Make your answer stand out

- Discuss the difficulties that shareholders still face in bringing statutory derivative actions by reference to academic opinions, such as: Almadani, M. 'Derivative actions: does the Companies Act 2006 offer a way forward?' (2009) 30 *Company Lawyer* 131; Keay and Loughrey, 'Derivative proceedings in a brave new world for company management and shareholders' (2008) JBL 151; and Hannigan, B. *Company Law* (Oxford University Press, 2009), pp. 460–2.

- Analyse the recent cases such as *Mission Capital plc* (2008) and *Franbar Holding Ltd* (2008) in greater detail. Explain why shareholders' application for permission to continue the derivative claim was refused in both cases.

- Examine the costs issue and the indemnity cost order as established in *Wallersteiner v Moir (No. 2)* [1975] QB 373.

- Evaluate the impact of the more popular unfair prejudice remedies on derivative actions. The court may refuse permission to continue a derivative claim when there is an alternative remedy available for shareholders.

- Consider more recent cases, such as *Kiani v Cooper* [2010] EWHC 557; *Stainer v Lee* [2010] EWHC 1539; *Iesini v Westrip Holdings Ltd* [2009] EWHC 2526; *Stimpson v Southern Landlords Association* [2009] EWHC 2072; *Kleanthous v Paphitis and Ors* [2011] EWHC 2287.

! Don't be tempted to...

- Focus only on the statutory derivative claim. You must also discuss the rule in *Foss* v *Harbottle* and the common law rules on derivative actions.
- Confuse the codification of derivative actions with the codification of directors' duties. Although these are related issues, you should not discuss directors' duties in great length in this question.
- Describe the detailed facts of some cases or apply case law which is not directly relevant. You should apply relevant case law, in particular, recent cases, in your answer.

? Question 2

Amelia and Tom set up Fine Chocolate Ltd in 2010. They are both directors of the company and hold 30% and 60% of shares respectively. Barry holds the remaining 10% of the company's shares.

Fine Chocolate Ltd was planning to upgrade its manufacturing equipment and recently was in negotiation with Choc Tec Ltd for purchase of the latest technology. Tom successfully persuaded Amelia to vote for the contract at a board meeting. A few days later, when talking to the employees of Choc Tec Ltd, Amelia found out that Tom had been the managing director of Choc Tec Ltd for two years and that Fine Chocolate Ltd had paid £10,000 more than the market price for the technology.

Amelia and Barry are furious with Tom and decide to challenge his misconduct and recover the losses suffered by Fine Chocolate Ltd.

Advise Amelia and Barry in relation to Tom's breach of director's duties and the possibility of bringing a derivative action against him.

Answer plan

→ Discuss whether Tom has breached any duty or duties as a director of Fine Chocolate Ltd.

→ Consider the procedure for derivative actions under ss 260–264 of the Companies Act 2006.

→ Examine the factors that a court will take into account when it considers granting Amelia and Barry permission to continue the action.

Diagram plan

A printable version of this diagram plan is available from www.pearsoned.co.uk/lawexpressqa

Answer

Shareholders may bring a derivative action against directors' breach of duty under ss 260–264 of the Companies Act 2006 (CA 2006). They replaced derivative actions at common law which were governed by the rule in **Foss v Harbottle** (1843) 2 Hare 461 and its exceptions.[1] The legal issues here are whether Tom has breached his duties as a director and whether Amelia and Barry as shareholders can successfully bring a derivative action against him.[2]

Directors' duties[3]

Directors' duties are codified in ss 170–177 of the Companies Act 2006; nevertheless, the previous case law and equitable principles are still relevant in the application and interpretation of the codified duties (s 170(4)). Tom, as a director, owes duties to the company: **Percival v Wright** [1902] 2 Ch 421 and s 170(1). As Tom failed to disclose the fact that he was a director in both companies before and after the transaction, it is argued that Tom breached his duties under ss 177, 182, 175 and possibly 172.[4]

If a director is in any way, directly or indirectly, interested in a *proposed* transaction with the company (s 177) or *existing* transaction with the company (s 182), he must declare the nature and extent of that interest to the other directors. A director need not declare an interest if the other directors are already aware of it. It is evident from the fact that Toms was directly interested in the transaction before and after it occurred. Moreover, Amelia was not aware of it and Tom did not disclose his conflict of interest. It is therefore argued that Tom breached his duties under ss 177 and 182.[5]

[5]Your knowledge of s 177 and s 182 may impress your examiners.

A director must avoid a situation in which he has, or can have, a direct or indirect interest that conflicts, or possibly may conflict with the interests of the company (s 175). This applies to the exploitation of any property, information or opportunity and it is immaterial whether the company could take advantage of the property, information or opportunity. Section 175 codifies the no-conflict rule and no secret profit rule at common law: **Aberdeen Rly Co v Blaikie Bros** (1854) 1 Macq 461 and **Regal (Hastings) Ltd v Gulliver** [1942] 1 All ER 378.[6] This duty is not infringed if the matter has been authorised by the directors and if nothing in this private company's constitution invalids such authorisation. Authorisation is effective only when the matter was agreed without the votes of these directors (s 175(6)). It appears that Tom's conflict of interest was not authorised by the board. Even if Tom tried to authorise it, authorisation would not be effective because Tom could not be counted towards the quorum and his votes would not be valid.[7]

[6]Discuss the duty to avoid conflicts of interest by reference to case law and apply it to the question.

[7]These sentences show your sound understanding of effective authorisation. It adds more credit to your answer because it is a key aspect of the duty to avoid conflicts of interest under s 175.

According to s 172, a director must act in the way he considers, in good faith, would be most likely to promote the success of the company for the benefits of its members as a whole, and in doing so have regard to other stakeholders' interests. Section 172 codified the duty to act in good faith at common law (**Re Smith & Fawcett Ltd** [1942] 1 All ER 542 and introduced the enlightened shareholder value. It adopts a subjective duty and emphasises what a director thinks. It may be difficult for Amelia and Barry to prove a breach of this duty, as Tom may argue that he acted in a way he considered would promote the success of the company.[8] The courts, however, have set some limits to the subjective test and will consider whether an intelligent and honest director could, in the whole of the circumstances, reasonably believe the transaction to be for the benefit of the company: **Charterbridge Corp Ltd v Lloyds Bank Ltd** [1970]

[8]These sentences analyse the problems associated with s 172 and will gain you more marks.

⁹A discussion of the objective test by reference to case law makes your answer stand out from a pure description of the statutory provision in s 172.

Ch 62.⁹ It is unclear whether such an objective approach would be considered by the court in interpreting s 172; however, it appears that an intelligent and honest director could not reasonably believe the purchase was for the success of Fine Chocolate Ltd, as the purchase price was considerably higher than the market price.

A derivative action

Amelia and Barry must apply to court for permission to continue the derivative claim and follow the two-stage procedure. At the first stage, the court considers only the application and evidence filed by Amelia and Barry and decides whether a *prima facie* case is established. If so, the court may order the company or defendant to provide evidence at the second stage. Permission will be refused if a person acting in accordance with s 172 would not seek to pursue the claim; or, if the misconduct has been authorised or ratified by the company (s 263(2)). It can be argued that the person acting to promote the success of the company would seek to pursue the claim and recover the company's loss of £10,000.

¹⁰A discussion of the law on ratification goes beyond a simple description of directors' duties and will make your answer stand out.

Moreover, Tom, as a majority shareholder, may try to ratify his breach of duties at a general meeting. The resolution for ratification is passed only if the necessary majority is obtained disregarding votes in favour of the resolution by the director and any member connected with him (s 239). Even though Tom holds 60% of the company's shares, it is unlikely that an effective resolution to ratify his misconduct could be passed.¹⁰ The court is therefore unlikely to refuse permission at this stage.

¹¹This section highlights the factors that the court must take into account. It adds more credit to your answer because it is very important for the assessment of the success of the derivative claim.

¹²This recent case law demonstrates to an examiner your excellent understanding of the problems associated with the derivative actions, in particular, the restrictive judicial approach. It will impress your examiners.

The court must then take into account all the factors under s 263(3), in particular, whether the claimant is acting in good faith, the importance that a person acting in accordance with s 172 would attach to continuing it, whether it would be likely to be authorised or ratified, whether the company has decided not to sue and whether the shareholder can pursue a personal action. It also considers the views of members who have no personal interests in the matter (s 263(4)).¹¹ It is likely that the court will take a restrictive approach as reflected in the judgments of two recent cases: **Mission Capital plc v Sinclair** [2008] BCC 866 and **Franbar Holding Ltd v Patel** [2008] BCC 885.¹² In both cases the court refused to grant permission to continue the derivative claims for two main reasons:

first, the judge did not believe that the hypothetical director as mentioned in s 263(2)(a) or (3)(b) would attach much importance to the claim; secondly, all that the claimants were seeking could be recovered by means of an unfair prejudice petition. As Amelia and Barry could bring an unfair prejudice remedy under s 994, it is most likely that the court would not grant permission to continue the derivative action against Tom despite the fact that Tom has breached his duties as a director.[13]

[13]In your conclusion, refer back to the question and clearly state your advice to Amelia and Barry.

✓ Make your answer stand out

- Comment on the judicial approach towards derivative actions by reference to the recent cases, such as *Kiani* v *Cooper* [2010] EWHC 577; *Stainer* v *Lee* [2010] EWHC 1539 (Ch); *Iesini* v *Westrip Holdings Ltd* [2009] EWHC 2526; *Stimpson* v *Southern Landlords Association* [2009] EWHC 2072 (Ch).
- Refer to academic opinions on the statutory derivative actions, such as Sykes, A. 'The continuing paradox: a critique of minority shareholder and derivative claims under the Companies Act 2006' (2010) *Civil Justice Quarterly* 205.
- Examine the costs problem and the possible indemnity cost order.
- Briefly discuss the courts' wide discretion and flexible reliefs under unfair prejudice remedies.

! Don't be tempted to...

- Give a detailed description of different types of directors (*de facto, de jure* and shadow directors). It will add very little credit to your answer.
- Provide a narrative account of directors' duties at common law. You should apply the relevant case law to the codified duties.
- Describe all directors' duties in the Companies Act 2006. You should focus on those duties which are relevant to this question.
- Concentrate on the director's breach of one duty. You should be aware that directors can breach more than one duty at the same time.
- Discuss in detail derivative actions at common law. Those rules at common law are replaced by the statutory derivative actions and therefore you should focus your discussion on the latter.
- Forget to relate your discussion back to the question. You should give specific advice to Amelia and Barry, as required by this question, as to whether Tom has breached his duties and whether their derivative claim against Tom would be successful.

Question 3

Discuss, by reference to case law, the application of unfair prejudice remedies in ss 994–996 of the Companies Act 2006.

Answer plan

→ Briefly explain the historical background of unfair prejudice remedy.

→ Discuss the meaning of 'conduct of company's affairs' and that of 'interests of members' in s 994 by reference to case law.

→ Evaluate what constitutes unfairly prejudicial conduct by reference to case law, in particular, *O'Neill* v *Phillips* [1999] 1 WLR 1092.

→ Consider the courts' wide discretion in granting relief in s 996, in particular, the purchase order.

Diagram plan

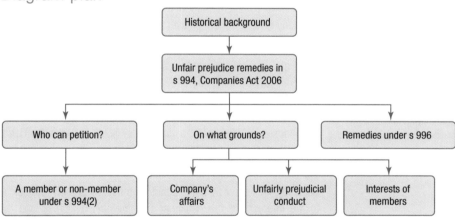

A printable version of this diagram plan is available from www.pearsoned.co.uk/lawexpressqa

Answer

[1]The introduction reassures the examiners that you know exactly what the question is about in terms of subject content.

Unfair prejudice remedy has evolved over a long period of time into an extremely valuable remedy for minority shareholders in England, particularly for those in small private companies. Whilst it has greatly enhanced minority shareholders' protection due to its broad scope of application and flexible reliefs, unfair prejudice remedy does have its own problems.[1]

Unfair prejudice remedy originated from the oppression remedy in s 210 of the Companies Act 1948, before the introduction of which aggrieved shareholders could either choose to bring derivative actions at common law or to petition for winding up the company on just and equitable grounds. Due to inadequacies of drafting and restrictive judicial interpretation of s 210, only two cases were successfully brought. The Jenkins Committee in 1962 recommended that a petition should be granted on the grounds of unfair prejudice rather than oppression. This was adopted in s 75 of the Companies Act 1980 and s 459 of the Companies Act 1985. This remedy is now restated in s 994 of the Companies Act 2006.[2]

[2]This paragraph demonstrates your clear understanding of the historical origins and the development of unfair prejudice remedy. It will add credit to your answer.

A petition under s 994(1) is made on the ground that the company's affairs are being, or have been, conducted in a manner which is unfairly prejudicial to the interests of its members generally or of some part of its members (including at least the petitioner) or that any actual or proposed act or omission of the company is or would be so prejudicial. It applies to a petition brought by a member or a person who is not a member of a company but to whom shares in the company have been transferred or transmitted by operation of law, for example, a personal representative and a trustee in bankruptcy.[3]

[3]The requirement for a s 994 petitioner is often ignored by students. Although it is a basic element of s 994, it is essential to include it in your answer.

There are three key elements in an unfair prejudice petition: conduct of a company's affairs, interests of a member and an unfairly prejudicial conduct.[4] First, the petition must relate to the conduct of the affairs of the company. It is not simply concerned with the conduct of an individual shareholder acting in a personal capacity: **Re Legal Costs Negotiators Ltd** [1999] BCC 547. It must be concerned with acts done by the company or those authorised to act as its organ.

[4]This sentence sets out a clear structure for the following discussion of the key elements of s 994. It also shows the examiners where you are going with your answer.

Secondly, the conduct complained of must be unfairly prejudicial to the interests of the petitioner *qua* member, which means the interests of the petitioner as a member as opposed to any other interests which the member might possess: **Re JE Cade & Son Ltd** [1991] BCC 360. It is recognised that the interests of members extend beyond their strict legal rights, which are usually contained in a company's constitution and the relevant company laws: **Re Blue Arrow plc** [1987] BCLC 585.

Lord Wilberforce in **Ebrahimi v Westbourne Galleries** [1973] AC 360 held that 'there are individuals, with rights, expectations and obligations *inter se* which are not necessarily submerged in the company structure'. His Lordship took the view that the strict legal rights of the parties could be subject to 'considerations ... of a personal character arising between one individual and another, which may make it unjust, or inequitable, to insist on legal rights or to exercise them in a particular way'. Hoffmann J in **Re A Company (No. 00477 of 1986)** [1986] BCLC 376 applied this reasoning to unfair prejudice petitions and recognised shareholders' legitimate expectations. This approach has strongly influenced the development of unfair prejudice remedy in a way that it has enabled the protection of members' wider interests and expectations beyond their strict legal rights.[5]

With regard to the unfairly prejudicial conduct, Hoffmann LJ in **Re Saul D Harrison & Sons plc** [1994] BCC 475 confirmed that the test of unfairness was objective in the sense that 'the focal point of the court's inquiry in determining whether conduct has been unfairly prejudicial is its impact and not its nature'. It was held in **O'Neill v Phillips** [1999] 1 WLR 1092[6] that a member would not ordinarily be entitled to complain of unfairness unless there had been some breach of terms on which the member agreed that the affairs of the company should be conducted; or some use of the rules in a manner which equity would regard as contrary to good faith. The application of equitable considerations depends on the nature of the company and the relationship among its shareholders.[7]

Where the company is purely a commercial relationship, as in a public company, the entire relationship of the parties is exhaustively determined by the constitution and there is no scope for equitable considerations to arise. Typical allegations include breach of company's articles of association, breaches of directors' duties involving misappropriation of corporate assets (**Re Little Olympian Each-Ways Ltd** [1995] 1 BCLC 636), improper allotments of shares (**Dalby v Bodilly** [2005] BCC 627) and allegations of mismanagement (**Re Macro (Ipswich) Ltd** [1994] BCC 781).[8]

Equitable considerations may make it unfair for those conducting the affairs of the company to rely upon their strict legal powers. This typically takes place in quasi-partnership companies, most of which are family-run businesses founded upon mutual confidence and trust.[9] Shareholders frequently play a role in the management of the company, based on the informal agreement that they should participate in management (**Re Saul D. Harrison & Sons plc**) and expect an investment return (**Re Kenyon Swansea** [1987] 3 BCC 259).

[5]The sentence analyses the impact of Hoffmann J's judgment on the functions of unfair prejudice remedies. It is significant for the understanding of this remedy and will gain you more marks.

[6]*O'Neill* v *Phillips* is the only House of Lords' judgment on the scope of unfairly prejudicial conduct. It should therefore be discussed in detail.

[7]This sentence sets the context for detailed discussion of unfairly prejudicial conduct in different types of companies.

[8]The reference to cases demonstrates your excellent understanding of the application of unfair prejudice remedies and it will add more credit to your answer.

[9]The discussion of quasi-partnership companies gains you more marks because it is important for your understanding of equitable considerations.

The most common examples are exclusion from management in small quasi-partnership companies whereby the exercise of removal of directors under s 168 would amount to unfairly prejudicial conduct in the absence of a fair offer by the majority to buy the petitioner's shares: **Brownlow v GH Marshall Ltd** [2000] 2 BCLC 655.

If the court is of the opinion that the petition is well grounded, it has wide discretion in granting remedies under s 996 and may make such order as it thinks fit. Based on its survey of unfair prejudice cases, the Law Commission Report has concluded that the relief most commonly sought was the order for the purchase of the petitioner's shares by the company or the respondents. When a court makes such an order, it has a choice as to the date and basis of the valuation of shares and the key requirement is *fairness*: **Re Bird Precision Bellows Ltd** [1984] Ch 419.[10]

[10]An evaluation of the purchase order by reference to case law shows your sound knowledge and will gain you more marks.

The unfair prejudice remedy is widely used by minority shareholders due to its broad scope of application and flexible reliefs. It has been a more attractive remedy for minority shareholders, compared with the complex procedures in derivative actions and the extreme consequences of a winding-up order. The Law Commission (1996), however, criticised the fact that its broad scope enables petitioners to include facts that may be remotely relevant to the case, which leads to complex, costly and cumbersome litigation.[11] There is a risk that it may be used as a means of oppression by minority shareholders because of its easy access. Thus, the courts face the challenge of balancing their wide discretion to protect shareholders from unfairly prejudicial conduct on the one hand and preventing malicious lawsuits on the other.[12]

[11]The Law Commission's criticisms demonstrate your excellent understanding of the weakness of unfair prejudice remedies. They will make your answer stand out.

[12]This sentence highlights your sound evaluation of unfair prejudice remedy and shows your analytical skills. It will impress your examiner.

✓ Make your answer stand out

- Discuss in detail the nature of quasi-partnership companies which was identified by Lord Wilberforce in *Ebrahimi* (1973).
- Evaluate the problems associated with unfair prejudice remedies by reference to academic literature, such as Payne, J. 'Sections 459–461 Companies Act 1985 in flux: the future of shareholder protection' (2005) 64 CLJ 647; Hirt, 'In what circumstances should breach of director's duties give rise to a remedy under ss 459–461 of the Companies Act 1985?' (2003) 24 *Company Lawyer* 100.

- Discuss *Clark* v *Cutland* [2003] 4 All ER 733 and consider its implications on the scope of unfair prejudice remedies. In this case, it was held that shareholders could bring unfair prejudice petitions and seek corporate remedies where the company had suffered losses, thereby circumventing the procedural requirements of derivative actions.
- Comment on the interrelationships between unfair prejudice remedy and other types of remedies, such as the statutory derivative actions (ss 260–264, Companies Act 2006) and the winding up remedy (s 122, Insolvency Act 1986).

! Don't be tempted to...

- Simply describe the provisions in ss 994–996. You must analyse the core elements of unfair prejudice remedies.
- Forget to discuss *O'Neill* v *Phillips* [1999] 1 WLR 1092. This is the only House of Lords authority on the scope of unfairly prejudicial conduct and therefore it is vital for your answer.
- Fail to examine the courts' wide discretion and the flexible reliefs in s 996.

? Question 4

David, James and Emma incorporated Oriental Delight Ltd in 2009. They are all directors and hold 50%, 30% and 20% of company's shares respectively. David and James recently found out that Emma secretly directed Oriental Delight Ltd's contracts to another company which her husband controlled. They felt that it was impossible to work with Emma and a resolution was passed at a shareholder meeting to remove her from the board.

Emma is unhappy about her removal and is considering bringing an unfair prejudice petition so that she can sell her shares to David and James at a fair price.

Advise Emma as to the merits of her unfair prejudice petition.

Answer plan

→ Discuss whether the shareholder resolution to remove Emma from the board of directors is unfairly prejudicial to her interests as a member.
→ Evaluate Emma's breach of duties as a director and the implications of this misconduct on her unfair prejudice petition.
→ Consider possible remedies that the court may grant under s 996.

Diagram plan

A printable version of this diagram plan is available from www.pearsoned.co.uk/lawexpressqa

Answer

[1]This sentence identifies the key legal issues that are raised in this problem question. It demonstrates to your examiners that you are able to engage with the question.

[2]Although a word-by-word citation is not often required in an exam, you should show a good knowledge of the statutory provision of s 994.

The key legal issues here are whether Emma can successfully bring an unfair prejudice petition under s 994 of the Companies Act 2006 and whether the court will think it fit to make an order for David and James to buy Emma's shares at a fair price under s 996.[1] A petition under s 994 is made on the ground that the company's affairs are being or have been conducted in a manner which is unfairly prejudicial to the interests of its members generally or of some part of its members (including at least the petitioner) or that any actual or proposed act or omission of the company is or would be so prejudicial.[2]

In order to assess whether a s 994 claim would be successful, it is essential to consider three important questions: first, whether Emma is a member of the company; secondly, whether Emma's removal

[3] This sentence sets the context and structure for your discussion of whether Emma's interests have been unfairly prejudiced by the decision to remove her.

[4] The discussion in relation to what constitutes a company's affair is often omitted in students' answers. Although this may appear a simple legal issue, you should discuss it by reference to case law.

[5] This sentence demonstrates that you understand the legal requirements for removal of directors under s 168. It will gain you more marks.

[6] The characteristics of quasi-partnership companies are important for your understanding of the concept of equitable considerations. The reference to Lord Wilberforce's classic definition of quasi-partnership companies will impress your examiners.

[7] This case is the House of Lords' authority on the scope of unfairly prejudicial conduct. Failure to discuss it in your answer will lead to a reduction of marks.

from the board is a company's affair; and finally, whether the removal is unfairly prejudicial to Emma's interests as a member.[3] It is clear from the scenario that Emma is a shareholder and therefore has the *locus standi* to bring a petition under s 994. The resolution to remove Emma from the board can be considered as a company's affair because it is connected with acts done by the general meeting of the company rather than the act of an individual shareholder acting in a personal capacity: **Re Legal Costs Negotiators Ltd** [1999] BCC 547.[4] It is then important to discuss whether the resolution to remove Emma is unfairly prejudicial to her interests *qua* member.

A company may by ordinary resolution at a shareholder meeting remove a director before the expiration of his period of office, notwithstanding anything in any agreement between it and him (s 168).[5] As David and James hold 80% of the company's shares, it is sufficient and legal to pass an ordinary resolution to remove Emma at general meeting. Whether this is unfairly prejudicial, nevertheless, depends on whether equitable considerations make it unfair to remove her.

Lord Wilberforce in **Ebrahimi v Westbourne Galleries** [1973] AC 360 held that 'there are individuals, with rights, expectations and obligations *inter se* which are not necessarily submerged in the company structure'. Hoffmann J in **Re A Company (No 00477 of 1986)** [1986] BCLC 376 applied this reasoning to unfair prejudice petitions and recognised shareholders' legitimate expectations. The interests of members therefore extend beyond their strict legal rights and include members' wider interests and expectations.

Such personal expectations are more likely to exist in quasi-partnership companies. As Lord Wilberforce stated in **Ebrahimi** (above), the personal relationship and mutual confidence form the basis of the business association in a quasi-partnership company; there is an understanding that all or certain shareholders will participate in management.[6] Hoffmann J in **O'Neill v Phillips** [1999] 1 WLR 1092[7] concluded that a member would not ordinarily be entitled to complain of unfairness unless there had been some use of the rules in a manner which equity would regard as contrary to good faith. This typically takes place in quasi-partnership companies. Oriental Delight Ltd appears to be a quasi-partnership company and it can be argued that the exclusion of Emma from management by s 168 would amount to unfairly prejudicial conduct in the absence of a fair offer by David and James to buy her shares: **Brownlow v GH Marshall Ltd** [2000] 2 BCLC 655.

The court will take into account the petitioner's own conduct in determining whether the respondent's behaviour is unfair.[8] In **Re A. Noble & Sons Ltd** [1983] BCLC 273, the petitioner's own conduct led to his exclusion from management and therefore the respondent's conduct was considered as not unfair, although prejudicial. Moreover, the petitioner's conduct may be material to the court in framing its remedy, particularly in relation to fixing the appropriate valuation date or price for the purchase order under s 996(2)(e): **Re London School of Electronics Ltd** [1986] Ch 211.

Emma diverted the company's contracts away for her husband's company and therefore she breached her duties as a director in ss 172 and 175. Section 172 requires a director to act in the way he considers, in good faith, would be most likely to promote the success of the company for the benefit of its members as a whole: **Re Smith & Fawcett Ltd** [1942] 1 All ER 542. It appears that Emma did not act in the best interests of the company and therefore breached s 172. Moreover, a director under s 175 must avoid a situation in which he has, or can have, a direct or indirect interest that conflicts, or possibly may conflict, with the interests of the company. This applies to the exploitation of any property, information or opportunity: **Cook v Deeks** [1916] 1 AC 554. David and James may argue that Emma breached s 175 because there was a clear conflict between her personal interests in securing the contract for her husband and her duty to secure it for the company.[9]

If it is satisfied that the petition is well founded, a court has wide discretion in granting remedies under s 996 and may make such order as it thinks fit. Without prejudice to the court's power, s 996(2) sets out in detail the types of order, including the purchase order which is most commonly sought by petitioners. When a court makes a purchase order, it has a choice as to the basis of the valuation of shares but the key requirement is fairness: **Re Bird Precision Bellows Ltd** [1984] Ch 419.[10]

As Emma has breached her duties under ss 172 and 175, if **Re A. Noble & Sons Ltd** is followed, it is mostly likely that Emma's own conduct led to her exclusion from management and therefore

[11]The conclusion should directly answer the question by providing specific advice to Emma. It should also include a reasoned assessment of the situation.

her removal from the board was not considered as unfair. As such, Emma may not have valid grounds for s 994 petition and a purchase order. Even if the court is satisfied that the removal is unfairly prejudicial, Emma's own misconduct may have a negative effect on the price for the purchase order (**Re London School of Electronics Ltd**).[11]

 Make your answer stand out

- Consider whether Emma may bring a personal action and claim damages for a breach of her service contract with the company if it is not complied with.
- Discuss the possibility of a winding up order on the just and equitable grounds under s 122(1)(g) of the Insolvency Act 1986, although it would be very unlikely for the court to grant this order due to its serious consequences on the company.

! Don't be tempted to...

- Describe all directors' duties at common law and in the Companies Act 2006. You should discuss the relevant duties by reference to case law and apply them to the problem question.
- Simply state the provisions in ss 994–996 without case law illustrations. This is not an essay question so you need to analyse the problem scenario and apply the appropriate law, in particular case law, in your answer.
- Jump to the conclusion that Emma's removal is unfairly prejudicial and Emma can successfully bring a s 994 petition and obtain a purchase order. You must demonstrate detailed knowledge of the application of unfair prejudice remedies.

Question 5

'In the light of the introduction of statutory derivative actions, it is likely that the unfair prejudice remedies will be rendered redundant in the near future.'
Discuss.

Answer plan

→ Examine the changes introduced by the statutory derivative actions by comparing them with derivative actions at common law.

→ Compare the statutory derivative actions with unfair prejudice remedies in relation to:
  - the scope of petitioners;
  - the grounds for the petition;
  - the procedure;
  - the remedies available; and
  - the issue of costs.

→ Evaluate whether the derivative actions will be more popular than unfair prejudice remedies and make them redundant.

Diagram plan

	Derivative action (ss 260–264)	Unfair prejudice remedy (ss 994–996)
Who can petition?	A member or a non-member to whom shares in the company have been transferred or transmitted by operation of law (s 260(5)(c))	A member or a non-member to whom shares in the company have been transferred or transmitted by operation of law (s 994(2))
On what grounds?	Directors' breach of duty(ies) (s 260(3))	The company's affairs are being or have been conducted in a manner that is unfairly prejudicial to the interests of members generally or of some part of its members. (s 994(1))
Procedure	A two-stage procedure for application for permission to continue a claim	Straightforward
Remedies	Sought on behalf of the company	Wide and flexible remedies under s 996
Costs	Indemnity order – possible	Indemnity order – not applicable

A printable version of this diagram plan is available from www.pearsoned.co.uk/lawexpressqa

Answer

[1]Your introduction should outline the main arguments and show the examiners where you are going with your answer. This sentence also indicates that you will adopt an analytical approach instead of providing a narrative account of these shareholder remedies.

The statutory derivative actions are introduced in ss 260–264 of the Companies Act 2006 and they replace the common law rules governed by the rule in **Foss v Harbottle** (1843) 67 ER 189. Whilst it can be asserted that the statutory derivative actions have some advantages over the common law rules, it is debatable whether they are more effective for shareholders and whether they overshadow the unfair prejudice remedies under s 994.[1]

Prima facie, it is an excellent idea to have various rules on derivative actions at common law consolidated into the Companies Act 2006.

There are certain obvious advantages in terms of procedure and scope of application. The new procedure may add certainty and clarity to the law. A claimant shareholder no longer has to prove fraud (**Burland v Earl** [1902] AC 83[2]) or wrongdoer control (**Prudential Assurance Co Ltd v Newman Industries Ltd (No. 2)** [1982] Ch 204. Neither the board's decision not to sue on behalf of the company (**Smith v Croft (No. 2)** [1988] Ch 114) nor the possibility of ratification of the breach of duty (**MacDougall v Gardiner** (1875) LR 1 Ch D 13) is a bar to derivative action. The court is in control of the litigation by way of the claimant's application for permission to continue the claim under s 261 and therefore the amount of vexatious litigation can be minimised and the management of a company is protected from such undue interference.[3]

The scope of derivative claims has been widened in the Companies Act 2006 as they fill up a gap at common law regarding the remedy for directors' negligence.[4] Section 260(3) clearly specifies the situations where derivative claims lie, which may help shareholders and their legal advisors make better assessments of the chances of obtaining permission to proceed. It is argued in *Gore-Browne on Companies Act 2006* that the new procedures introduce a 'welcome liberalisation' of the rules at common law.[5] Shareholders may be encouraged to use statutory derivative claims where possible, rather than the more expensive unfair prejudice proceedings under s 994.

It is, however, doubtful if statutory derivative claims are more effective weapons for aggrieved minority shareholders than those at common law.[6] Once a shareholder applies for permission to commence a derivative action, it is for the court to determine whether litigation can proceed by taking into account all the factors and circumstances and especially the list of criteria under s 263. Although the list provides some guidance for both the court and the shareholders, different interpretations of the factors such as 'good faith' and 'success of the company' may result in inconsistent exercise of judicial discretion. Most significantly, effective ratification still bars a derivative action (s 263(2)). It is possible that the restricted judicial attitudes towards derivative actions at common law may remain. Moreover, shareholders may not have the incentives to bring derivative actions as any recovery goes back to the company. The difficulties and uncertainties in obtaining a costs indemnity order, along with the inconvenience and the lack of incentives therefore still act as strong deterrents.

[7]The evaluation of the academic opinion will impress your examiners because it shows your wider understanding of the derivative actions. The phrase 'incisively argued' also demonstrates your analytical skill.

Some academics are sceptical of the success of the statutory derivative claims. As Payne (1998) has incisively argued, although the new procedure has removed the problems associated with the fraud exception, it seems unlikely to increase the use of the derivative actions in the face of the unfair prejudice remedy.[7] Both remedies are available to a member or a non-member to whom shares in the company have been transferred or transmitted by operation of law (s 260(5)(c) and s 994(2)). It is argued here that the unfair prejudice remedy is likely to remain the remedy of first choice because of its advantages over derivative claims in terms of scope of application, procedure, specific reliefs and the issue of litigation costs.[8]

[8]These phrases set a clear structure for the comparison between two remedies which are discussed in the next three paragraphs.

In terms of scope of application, unfair prejudice remedies cover a potentially wider range of wrongful conduct than derivative actions. Section 994 applies to cases where the conduct is in breach of the company's constitution, or where the conduct is consistent with the constitution but breaches the petitioner's legitimate expectations based on some informal agreements (**O'Neill v Phillips** [1999] 1 WLR 1092). Moreover, it has become more popular in the wake of the Court of Appeal's judgment in **Clark v Cutland** [2003] 4 All ER 733. It is held that minority shareholders could make use of unfair prejudice remedies to obtain a substantive remedy for the company in relation to corporate wrongs without going through the procedures in derivative actions.[9] By contrast, the scope of derivative claims is relatively narrow because they are confined to a director's breach of duties (s 260).

[9]The reference to *Clark* v *Cutland* and its implications on unfair prejudice remedies will make your answer stand out because it demonstrates your excellent understanding of the more complicated issues.

The procedures for unfair prejudice remedies are much simpler than those for derivative claims. A claimant has to go through the expenses and uncertainties of the two-stage procedure for a derivative action; by contrast, there are no such requirements for unfair prejudice claims. Moreover, the ratification principle and the decision of the independent organ do not apply to unfair prejudice proceedings.

In terms of remedies, s 996 offers a more flexible remedy in that the court can exercise discretion to choose remedies. The purchase order is the most popular remedy as an exit mechanism. The court can also allow successful petitioners to bring civil proceedings in the name of the company. As the s 994 remedy is based on the infringement of personal rights, recoveries as a result of successful litigation go to the actual claimant and are not shared by other shareholders in the company (the remedy under s 996(2)(c) would be an exception). The personal relief to the petitioners makes s 994 more attractive than derivative action where any relief goes back to the company and the claimant can only benefit indirectly. Unfair prejudice remedies are therefore powerful and preferable remedial tools for minority shareholders because of their wider scope, simpler procedures and especially the more flexible claimant-orientated remedies.[10]

Derivative actions, nevertheless, may be more attractive in certain circumstances;[11] for example, where the shareholder does not wish to sell his shares or leave the company, but needs a remedy for misconduct and the recovery of the company's assets. Moreover, the position in relation to indemnity costs orders remains slightly more favourable to shareholders in derivative actions (**Wallersteiner v Moir (No. 2)** [1974] 3 All ER 217). Despite this, it would be exceptional for a petitioner to proceed with a derivative action rather than by a s 994 petition. The Law Commission Consultation Paper (1996) argues that unless major changes were made to the unfair prejudice remedy, it would continue to offer advantages over derivative actions. Since the unfair prejudice remedy remains unchanged under the CA 2006, it can be argued that a derivative claim may not often be used in cases where an unfair prejudice remedy is available. In **Mission Capital plc v Sinclair** [2008] BCC 866 and **Franbar Holding Ltd v Patel** [2008] BCC 885, the claimant's application for permission to continue the derivative claim was refused. One of the main reasons is that the claimant could bring an unfair prejudice petition as an alternative remedy (s 263(3)(f)). It is therefore unlikely that the unfair prejudice remedies will be made redundant by the statutory derivative actions in the near or far future.[12]

[10]This sentence summarises the main points that you have made in the previous paragraphs. It reinforces your arguments and also shows a neat structure.

[11]An evaluation of the few advantages of derivative actions over unfair prejudice remedies demonstrates your sound understanding of shareholder remedies. It will gain you more marks than simply emphasising the advantages of unfair prejudice remedies.

[12]A concise conclusion should refer back to the question and strengthen your arguments.

✓ **Make your answer stand out**

■ Discuss in detail the two-stage procedure for a statutory derivative action under ss 261–263.

■ Evaluate the criteria that the courts will take into account when considering whether to grant the permission to continue a derivative claim under s 263.

■ Consider the controversial debates as to whether derivative actions and unfair prejudice remedies should be assimilated into one.

■ Make reference to academic opinions in relation to the above debates: Law Commission Report (1997), para. 6.11; Payne, J. 'Sections 459–461 Companies Act 1985 in flux: the future of shareholder protection' (2005) 64 CLJ 647; Reisberg, 'Shareholders' remedies: in search of consistency of principle in English law' (2005) 16 *European Business Law Review* 1065; Hirt, H. C. 'In what circumstances should breaches of director's duties give rise to a remedy under ss. 459–461 of the Companies Act 1985?' (2003) 24 *Company Lawyer* 100.

! **Don't be tempted to...**

■ Simply describe the derivative actions at common law and the statutory rules. You need to compare them, analyse the changes and examine the strength and weakness of this reform.

■ Discuss in detail the application of unfair prejudice remedies. This is not just a question on unfair prejudice remedies. It is essential to compare and contrast the derivative actions and unfair prejudice remedies and evaluate their differences.

Corporate insolvency

How this topic may come up in exams

Corporate insolvency is a complex area of company law. You are not required to show a detailed critical analysis but it is essential to have a clear understanding of the important statutory provisions in the Insolvency Act 1986 and apply them to problem questions. Exam questions often focus on the procedures for company voluntary arrangements, administration and liquidation. Distribution of a company's assets and the priority of creditors in an insolvent liquidation are popular topics for problem questions. Directors' liabilities in wrongful trading and fraudulent trading may also arise in corporate insolvency. This topic may overlap with directors' duties and company charges.

Attack the question

❓ Question 1

Robert Ltd manufactures HD TV screens. The sales have dropped dramatically due to the credit crunch but they are expected to recover in a few months. The directors of Robert Ltd are considering a voluntary arrangement with its creditors.

Advise the directors as to the procedure required for a company voluntary arrangement without a moratorium.

Answer plan

→ Explain the definition of a company voluntary arrangement (CVA).

→ Consider the procedures for the meetings of the company and of its creditors to approve the proposal for a CVA.

→ Discuss the effect of the approval of a CVA.

→ Examine the ways of challenging the decision to approve a CVA.

→ Discuss the procedures for the implementation of a CVA.

Diagram plan

Directors propose a voluntary arrangement (s 1, IA 1986).

⬇

Meetings of the company and of its creditors are summoned to decide whether to approve the arrangement (ss 3, 4, 4A).

⬇

The effect of approval (s 5).

⬇

Challenging the decision to approve the arrangement (s 6).

⬇

Implementation of the proposal (s 7).

A printable version of this diagram plan is available from www.pearsoned.co.uk/lawexpressqa

Answer

As Robert Ltd is only temporarily experiencing some financial problems, a company voluntary arrangement (CVA) which does not end the life of the company is more appropriate than winding up.[1] A CVA is defined as a composition in satisfaction of its debts or a scheme of arrangement of its affairs (s 1(1), IA 1986). In **Commissioners of Inland Revenue v Adam & Partners Ltd** [2001] 1 BCLC 222[2] a proposal set out the scheme that the preferential and unsecured creditors would not receive any payments while the company's main creditor would receive a better return. The Court of Appeal held that the proposal did not amount to a composition of the company's debts and therefore was not a CVA.

The directors of Robert Ltd may propose a voluntary arrangement (s 1).[3] The proposal must provide for a nominee to supervise the implementation of the CVA and the nominee must be a qualified insolvency practitioner. Directors shall submit to the nominee a document setting out the terms of the proposed voluntary arrangement and a statement of the company's affairs which contain the particulars of its creditors and of its debts and other liabilities and of its assets (s 2(3)). A director commits an offence if, for the purpose of obtaining the approval of the members or creditors, he makes any false representation, or fraudulently does, or omits to do, anything (s 6A).

The nominee shall, within 28 days after he is given notice of the proposal,[4] submit a report to the court. The report should state whether, in his opinion,[5] the proposed voluntary arrangement has a reasonable prospect of being approved and implemented, and whether meetings of the company and of its creditors should be summoned to consider the proposal, and stating the date, time and place for such meetings (s 2(2)). Every creditor of the company whose claim and address the nominee is aware shall be summoned to a creditors' meeting (s 3(3)).

The meetings summoned shall decide whether to approve the proposed voluntary arrangement, with or without modifications (s 4(1)). The proposal or modification shall not be approved if it affects the right of a secured creditor of the company to enforce his security or affects the preferential debt of the company, except with the concurrence of the creditor concerned or the preferential creditor concerned (s 4(4)). After the conclusion of either meeting, the chairman of the meeting shall report the result of the meeting to the court, and, immediately after reporting to the court, shall give notice of the result of the meeting to such persons as may be prescribed (s 4(6)).

At the members' meeting, members vote according to the rights attached to their shares by the articles; more than half in value of the ordinary shareholders is required in favour of the resolution (r 1.18 and r 1.20, Insolvency Rules 1986).[6] At the creditors' meeting, a resolution to approve the proposal or a modification can be passed when a majority of three-quarters or more in value of those present and voting in person or by proxy have voted in favour of it[7] (r 1.19, IR 1986). The decision to approve a proposed voluntary arrangement has effect if it has been taken by both the meeting of the company and the meeting of creditors. It also has effect if it has been taken by the creditors' meeting (s 4A(2)). This means that if the decision taken by the creditors' meeting is different from that taken by the company meeting, the former shall prevail.[8] A member, however, may challenge this decision by applying to the court within 28 days of the creditors' meeting (s 4A(3)). The court may order the decision of the company meeting to have effect or make such other order as it thinks fit (s 4A(6)).

Once the voluntary arrangement is approved, it binds every person who was entitled to vote at the creditors' meeting, whether or not he was present or represented at it as if he were a party to the voluntary arrangement.[9] It also binds a creditor who did not receive notice of the meeting, or if he was unknown to the nominee and a notice was not sent to him (s 5(2)).[10] After the conclusion of either meeting, the chairman of the meeting shall report the result of the meeting to court within four days (s 4(6)).

The voluntary arrangement may be challenged, upon an application to the court, by any person who is entitled to vote at either of the meetings or who would have been entitled to vote at the creditors' meeting if he had had notice of it (s 6(2)). It can be made on the ground that a voluntary arrangement unfairly prejudices the interests of a creditor, member or contributory of the company; or that there has been some material irregularity at or in relation to either of the meetings (s 6(1)).[11] In **IRC v Wimbledon** [2005] 1 BCLC 66,

Lightman J[12] considered that the unfair prejudice complained of must be caused by the terms of the arrangement itself. In determining whether there is unfairness, all the circumstances should be considered. The existence of unequal or different treatment of creditors of the same class does not of itself constitute unfairness. If the court is satisfied as to either of the grounds, it may revoke or suspend any decision giving effect to the CVA, or any decision taken by a meeting where there has been a material irregularity. It may give a direction to any person for the summoning of further meetings (s 6(4)).

On approval of the CVA, the nominee becomes the supervisor (s 7(2)) and he sets out the implementation of the CVA. He may apply to the court for directions if necessary (s 7(4)). The supervisor often holds any funds in his possession on trust for the creditors following the terms of the voluntary arrangement: **Re NT Gallagher & Son Ltd** [2002] 2 BCLC 133. If any creditor of the company or any other person is dissatisfied by any act of the supervisor, he may apply to the court which may confirm, reverse or modify the act of the supervisor, give him directions, or make such other order as it thinks fit (s 7(3)).[13] On completion or termination of the CVA, the supervisor must send notice with 28 days to all the creditors and members bound by the CVA together with a copy of a report which summaries all receipts and payments by him. Notice must also be given to the registrar of companies and to the court within the same time limit (r 1.29, IR 1986).

[13]Section 7(3) plays an important check on the supervisor's conduct and therefore it should be included in your answer.

✓ Make your answer stand out

- Briefly consider company voluntary arrangement with a moratorium which is governed by Sch A1, IA 1986. It is not popular in practice mainly due to the complex procedures, the requirement for publicity and the onerous liabilities on the part of supervisors.
- Advise the directors that, if the company has failed to pay the creditors as required by the CVA, it may be necessary to terminate the agreement and the supervisor may petition for an administration order or winding up.

Don't be tempted to...

- Focus on the procedures in relation to company voluntary arrangement with a moratorium. You must understand that there are two types of CVA and this problem question is asking you to discuss the CVA without a moratorium which is governed by Part 1 of the IA 1986.
- Make no reference to the statutory provisions. Although the subsection numbers are often not required, you should be familiar with the main provisions of the Insolvency Act 1986 in relation to a CVA.

Question 2

Critically analyse the main procedures for appointing an administrator by a holder of a floating charge, the functions of the administrator and how the administrator's conduct can be challenged.

Answer plan

→ Explain the role of administration by reference to the Cork Report 1982 and the Insolvency Act 1986.

→ Discuss who is entitled to appoint an administrator with particular reference to the holder of a qualifying floating charge.

→ Examine the objectives of an administrator.

→ Analyse the grounds for challenging the administrator's conduct.

→ Consider the effect of moratorium when the company is in administration.

Diagram plan

| Who can appoint an administrator? (IA 1986, Sch B1, para 14) |
| What are the objectives of an administrator? (para 3) |
| On what grounds can the conduct of the administrator be challenged? (para 74) |
| What is the effect of the moratorium? (paras 42–43) |

A printable version of this diagram plan is available from www.pearsoned.co.uk/lawexpressqa

¹These sentences show your good understanding of the historical background of the administration procedure. They add more credit to your answer than only focusing on the current provisions in the IA 1986.

²This sentence helps you avoid repeating the reference to Sch B1 of the IA 1986. It saves you some time in an exam.

³It shows your good knowledge of the case law and will earn you more marks.

Answer

The administration procedure was recommended by the Cork Committee on Insolvency Law and Practice Report (1982). It was designed primarily to facilitate the rescue of the viable parts of the company in financial difficulties.[1] The administration provisions have been revised by the Enterprise Act 2002 and are now set out in Schedule B1 to the Insolvency Act 1986 (IA 1986). The reference to the paragraphs in this answer is made to Sch B1 to the IA 1986 unless otherwise stated.[2]

An administrator of a company must be a qualified insolvency practitioner who is appointed to manage the company's affairs, business and property (para 1). He owes his duties to the company and not to the creditors, individually or collectively: **Kyrris v Oldham** [2004] 1 BCLC 305.[3] An administrator may be appointed by an administration order of the court, or by the holder of a qualifying floating charge, or by the company or its directors (para 2). The holder of a qualifying floating charge may therefore appoint an administrator of the company out of court. A qualifying floating charge is created by an instrument which states that para 14 applies to the floating charge, or purports to empower the holder to appoint an administrator of the company (para 14(2)). A person is a holder of a qualifying floating charge if it relates to the whole or substantially the whole of the company's property (para 14(3)).

If the floating charge is not a qualifying floating charge, the holder can apply to the court for an administration order (para 12).[4] The court may make such order only if it is satisfied that the company is or is likely to become unable to pay its debts, and that the administration order is reasonably likely to achieve the purpose of administration (para 11). In **Re AA Mutual International Insurance Co Ltd** [2005] 2 BCLC 8 the insurance company had no new business and therefore no income, the court considered that it was more likely that the company's liabilities would exceed its assets within a short period of time and an administration may achieve a better result for the creditors than a winding up.

The administrator must perform his functions in the interests of the company's creditors as a whole, as quickly and efficiently as is reasonably practicable (paras 3–4). There is a hierarchy of purposes[5] which administration is supposed to serve in para 3. The administrator must perform his functions with the objective (a) of rescuing the company as a going concern, unless he thinks either that it is not reasonably practicable to achieve this objective or that objective (b) would achieve a better result for the company's creditors as a whole. Objective (b) is achieving a better result for the company's creditors as a whole than would be likely if the company were wound up without first being in administration. The third objective, (c), is realisation of property in order to make a distribution to one or more secured or preferential creditors. The administrator can only perform objective (c) if he thinks that it is not reasonably practicable to achieve either (a) or (b), and he does not unnecessarily harm the interests of the creditors of the company as a whole.[6] It should be noted that the above objectives are based on what the administrator thinks rather than what he reasonably believes. As the courts are generally reluctant to second-guess the commercial judgements of administrators, it is almost impossible for a court to interfere with the administrator's judgements as long as they are made in good faith: **Downsview Nominees v First City Corp** [1993] AC 295.[7]

The holder of a floating charge who appoints an administrator must file with the court a notice of appointment.[8] The notice must include a statutory declaration that he is the holder of a qualifying floating charge of the company's property, that the floating charge is or was enforceable on the date of the appointment, and that the appointment is in accordance with Schedule B1. The notice must identify the administrator; it must also be accompanied by a statement by the administrator that he consents to the appointment and that in his opinion the purpose of administration is reasonably likely to be achieved (para 18(3)). The appointment of an administrator takes effect when the above requirements as to the notice and documents are satisfied. The holder of a floating charge shall notify the administrator as soon as is reasonably practicable after the notice of appointment has been filed with the court (para 20).

The administrator may do anything necessary or expedient for the management of the affairs, business and property of the company (para 59). In exercising his functions, he acts as the agent of the company (para 69). The extensive powers of an administrator are set out in Schedule 1 to the Insolvency Act 1986, including the power to take possession of, collect and get in the property of the company, sell or dispose of the company's property, raise or borrow money and grant security, bring and defend any legal proceedings, make payment and carry on the business of the company.[9]

[9]This paragraph examines the powers of an administrator. It is essential here because it leads on to the discussion in the next paragraph in relation to how the conduct of an administrator can be challenged.

A creditor or a member of the company may challenge the administrator's conduct (para 74). He may apply to the court claiming that the administrator is acting, or has acted, unfairly and harmed the interests of the applicant or the administrator proposes to act in a way which would unfairly harm the interests of the applicant. He may also claim that the administrator is not performing his functions as quickly or as efficiently as is reasonably practicable (para 74).[10] The court has extensive discretion; it may grant relief, dismiss the application, adjourn the hearing, make an interim order, and make any other order it thinks appropriate.

[10]This ground for challenging the administrator's conduct is often missing in students' exam answers. It should be included in a sound answer.

[11]A discussion of the effect of moratorium will make your answer stand out because it is a key feature of the administration procedure.

Once a company is in administration, it should be aware of the effect of the moratorium.[11] The moratorium provides a breathing space during which the company has an opportunity to make arrangements with its creditors and members. The moratorium takes effect so that no resolution may be passed or order made for the winding up of the company (para 42); no step may be taken to enforce security over the company's property or no legal process may be instituted or continued against the company or property of the company, except with the consent of the administrator or with the permission of the court (para 43).

✓ Make your answer stand out

- Consider the main changes brought by the Enterprise Act 2002. It enabled a company to be placed in administration without the need for an application to the court and therefore simplified the administration procedure. Moreover, it abolished the right of a holder of a floating charge to appoint an administrative receiver and limited the administrative receivership procedure to exceptional cases.
- Discuss the requirements in relation to the statement made by the administrator once he is appointed. The statement must set out proposals for achieving the purpose of administration (para 49). The proposals must be accompanied by an invitation to an initial creditors' meeting (para 51) and they can only be approved by a majority in value of the creditors present and voting, in person or by proxy.

! Don't be tempted to...

- Write everything you know about administration. You are not required in this question to demonstrate detailed knowledge of the complex procedure in administration. You should only focus on the issues which are related to the question.
- Assume that any holder of a floating charge can appoint an administrator. You must discuss whether the charge in question is a qualifying floating charge and whether the person is a holder of a qualifying floating charge.

📑 Question 3

Evaluate the main distinctions between different types of winding up of a company.

Answer plan

- → Consider the members' voluntary winding up (ss 91–96, Insolvency Act 1986), in particular, the requirement for the directors' declaration of solvency.
- → Examine the creditors' voluntary winding up (ss 97–106, IA 1986), in particular, the requirement in relation to the meeting of creditors.
- → Analyse the compulsory winding up by the court (s 122, IA 1986), in particular, the requirements in relation to the petitioner and the grounds for petition.

Diagram plan

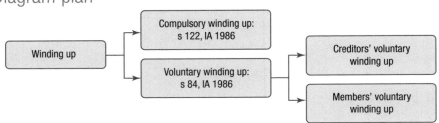

A printable version of this diagram plan is available from www.pearsoned.co.uk/lawexpressqa

Answer

¹This sentence outlines the two main types of winding up and shows the examiners that you know what this question is about.

²This sentence demonstrates that you are aware of the two types of voluntary winding up. It also shows your analytical skills by briefly comparing the two and will gain you more marks.

³Pay attention to the time limit for making the declaration of solvency.

Winding up refers to the process where the assets of the company are collected in and realised, its liabilities discharged and the net proceeds (if any) distributed to the persons entitled to it (s 107, IA 1986). Winding up may be either voluntary or compulsory (s 73(1)).¹

Voluntary winding up is the most common form, whereby members pass a resolution at general meeting that the company be wound up (s 84(1)(b)). It can be either members' or creditors' voluntary winding up; the main distinction lies in whether the company's directors are able to make a declaration of solvency.² Another difference is with respect to the appointment of liquidator. A liquidator, who must be a qualified insolvency practitioner, may be appointed by the company in general meeting in a members' voluntary winding up; the appointment may be made at creditor's meetings in a creditors' voluntary winding up.

In a members' voluntary winding up, the directors or a majority of the directors make a statutory declaration of solvency in the five weeks immediately preceding the date of the resolution to wind up the company, or on the date of the resolution but before it is passed.³ The statutory declaration must state that the directors have made a full inquiry into the affairs of the company and have formed the opinion that the company will be able to pay its debts in full within 12 months from the date of the passing of the resolution for winding up (s 89). Any director, who makes a declaration of solvency without reasonable grounds for the opinion, will be liable to imprisonment or a fine or both (s 89(4)). If in fact the debts are not paid within the period specified in the declaration, it is presumed that a director did not have reasonable grounds for his belief (s 89(5)). In the circumstances where the directors do not make a statutory declaration of solvency, it is a creditors' winding up. A meeting of creditors must be summoned to take place not more than 14 days after the members' meeting (s 98).[4] A voluntary winding up is deemed to commence at the time the resolution is passed by the members in general meeting.

[4]The requirement for the creditors' meeting must be clearly stated. You should also note the 14-day period.

In a compulsory winding up, the court orders that the company be wound up following a petition by the company, its directors, creditors and contributories (s 124(1)). In practice, most petitions are made by creditors of the company. In order to prevent individuals from purchasing shares for the purpose of winding up the company,[5] a contributory, including any present and past member of the company, can only make a winding up petition in one of the following four circumstances (s 124(2)): first, the number of members is reduced below two; secondly, the shares held by him were originally allotted to him; thirdly, the shares have been held by him for at least six months during the 18 months before the commencement of the winding up; finally, the shares have devolved on him through the death of a former holder. A contributory must also establish an economic interest in the winding up; for example, a partly paid-up shareholder remains liable to contribute the amount unpaid on his shares on winding up of the company. If the shares are fully paid up, it must be established that there is some prospect of assets available to him in the winding up.

[5]This phrase shows that you understand the rationale of the restrictions imposed on the petition by a contributory. It will gain you more marks than simply stating the law.

The grounds for compulsory winding up are set out in s 122. The most common ground is that the company is unable to pay its debts. A company is deemed unable to pay its debts in one of the following four circumstances listed in s 123. First, a creditor to whom the company is indebted in a sum exceeding £750 then due has served on the company a written demand requiring the company to pay the sum due; and the company has for three weeks thereafter neglected to pay the sum or to secure or compound for it to the reasonable satisfaction of the creditor;[6] secondly, execution or other process issued on a judgment, decree or order of any court in favour of a creditor of the company is returned unsatisfied in whole or in part; thirdly, it is proved to the satisfaction of the court that the company is unable to pay its debts as they fall due; finally, it is proved to the satisfaction of the court that the value of the company's assets

[6]Although you are encouraged to use the precise wording of the statutory provision, it is often difficult for most students to learn them by heart if a company law statute book is not permitted in an exam. You can interpret them in your own words. Here, for example, you can state that 'the creditor of the company is owed more than £750 and he has demanded the payment due in writing but the company has failed to pay the sum within three weeks'.

[7]The reference to case law makes your answer stand out from those which only describe the statutory provisions.

[8]Students are often confused with this particular area of law. Compulsory winding up starts at the time of the presentation of the winding up, not the time when the court makes the winding up order.

[9]This is an important provision because it makes any transaction which affects the company's property void. It will gain you more marks.

[10]This sentence explains the rationale of s 127 of the IA 1986. It shows your sound understanding and will add more credit to your answer.

[11]Make sure you get this right. A liquidator does not owe duties to individual contributories or creditors. You will lose some marks if it is not correctly discussed.

is less than the amount of its liabilities, taking into account its contingent and prospective liabilities.

The court has wide discretion as to whether or not to order winding up as it is a collective procedure for the benefit of creditors generally. The court may dismiss a petition if the company disputes the debt and the court accepts that the dispute is genuine: **Re MCI WorldCom Ltd** [2003] 1 BCLC 330.[7] The petition may also be dismissed if the company has a genuine and serious cross-claim for an amount which exceeds the petitioner's debt and which the company has been unable to litigate: **Re Bayoil SA** [1999] 1 BCLC 62.

Compulsory winding up is deemed to commence at the time of the presentation of the petition,[8] which takes place when the petition is delivered to the court for issue. Any disposition of the company's property, and any transfer of shares, or alteration in the status of the company's members, made after the commencement of the winding up, is void unless the court otherwise orders (s 127).[9] This is designed to avoid the risk that the property which should be available to creditors is disposed of in the period between the presentation of the petition and the making of the winding up order.[10]

The court may appoint a liquidator after the presentation of a winding up petition. The liquidator's primary duty is to collect in and realise the assets of the company and then to distribute the proceeds amongst the creditors of the company, and if any surplus remains, to the shareholders (s 143). A liquidator owes duties to the company and not to individual contributories or creditors: **Lomax Leisure Ltd v Miller** [2008] 1 BCLC 262.[11] He is in a fiduciary relationship with the company and must not place himself in a position of a conflict of interests: **Re Corbenstoke Ltd (No. 2)** [1990] BCLC 60. The exercise of power by the liquidator may be challenged by individual contributories or creditors (s 167). Furthermore, any person aggrieved by an act or decision of the liquidator may apply to court which may confirm, reverse or modify the act or decision complained of and may make such order as it thinks fit (s 168(5)).

Make your answer stand out

- Consider that a solvent company may be wound up on the just and equitable ground under s 122(1)(g) of the Insolvency Act 1986 where the relationship between the members has completely broken down.
- Discuss the role of liquidation committee in a creditors' voluntary winding up. The creditors may resolve to form a liquidation committee, which may consist of up to five creditors and, if the creditors do not object, five members of the company (s 165, IA 1986).

! Don't be tempted to...

- Use the word 'bankruptcy' to refer to winding up. Bankruptcy refers to the legal process by which the assets of an insolvent *individual or partnership* are realised and the proceeds distributed to the creditors.
- Only focus on the members' voluntary winding up. You must discuss both types of voluntary winding up in your answer.

？ Question 4

Cake Ltd is in compulsory liquidation. The proofs of debts have been submitted by creditors in relation to the following claims. The expenses for winding up are £15,000 and the interests on all the debts which are proved amount to £8,000.

1. Sugar Ltd, which is the holder of a floating charge over the entire undertaking of Cake Ltd, is claiming £100,000. Sugar Ltd still owes £40,000 to Cake Ltd in a previous transaction.
2. Cake Ltd has three unsecured creditors who are claiming £5,000, £15,000 and £20,000 respectively.
3. Five employees of Cake Ltd are claiming £5,000 each for their salaries in the six months before winding up.

Advise the liquidator in relation to the priority of payment of the above claims.

Answer plan

→ Evaluate the rules on the proof of debts and the order of distribution of Cake Ltd's assets.

→ Consider the claims by the employees: are they preferential debts?

→ Examine the claim by Sugar Ltd in relation to the rights of set-off and the prescribed part of a floating charge.

→ Analyse the claims by the unsecured creditors by reference to the principle of *pari passu*.

→ Identify that the interests on the debts are deferred debts.

Diagram plan

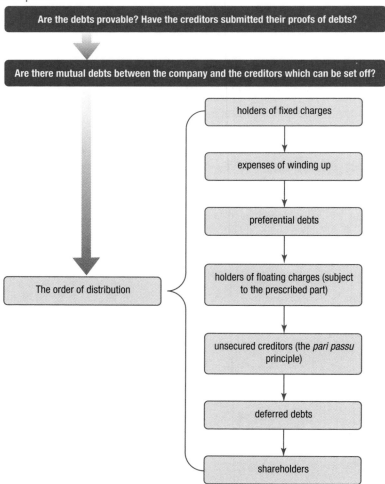

Answer

[1]This shows your good knowledge of the rules on the proof of debts. It is the basis of payment of debts in corporate insolvency and should be the starting point of your discussion.

[2]Note that the reference here is not made to the Insolvency Act 1986 but the Insolvency Rules 1986. Some students may not notice this when they are revising.

[3]Try to structure your answer clearly and use headings so that it is easier for your examiners to follow.

[4]Students are often not aware that the remuneration of the liquidator is part of the expenses of winding up. Although this particular issue does not arise in this problem question, it may be examined in other questions.

[5]The reference to the case law and the House of Lords' decision makes your answer stand out.

[6]You should pay attention to the current law in s 176ZA of the Insolvency Act 1986. This sentence demonstrates your very good knowledge of the reforms in relation to this particular area of law.

[7]The reforms brought by the Enterprise Act 2002 will gain you more marks because they show your excellent understanding of the wider context.

When a company is in liquidation, only those debts which are provable in the insolvency and which are proved will receive payment.[1] All claims by creditors are provable as debts against the company whether they are present or future, certain or contingent, ascertained or sounding only in damages (r 12.3, Insolvency Rules 1986[2]). The debt may arise at the date on which the company goes into liquidation, or after the company goes into liquidation provided that it is in respect of an obligation incurred before that date (r 13.12). In a compulsory winding up, creditors must submit their proofs of debts in writing to establish their claims (r 4.73).

1. The expenses of winding up[3]

All expenses properly incurred in the winding up, including the remuneration of the liquidator,[4] are payable out of the company's assets in priority to all other claims (s 115, Insolvency Act 1986). The controversial issue is whether the company's assets include the property subject to a floating charge. The House of Lords in **Re Leyland Daf** [2004] 1 BCLC 281 held that the expenses of a winding up were not payable out of the assets comprised in a crystallised floating charge in priority to the claims of the charge holder.[5] This ruling was reversed by s 1282, CA 2006 and is now governed by s 176ZA, IA 1986,[6] which provides that the expenses of winding up have priority over any claims to property comprised in or subject to any floating charge created by the company and shall be paid out of any such property accordingly.

2. The claims by employees – preferential debts

The claims of salaries by the employees of Cake Ltd are regarded as preferential debts, which must be paid in priority to all other debts, except the expenses of winding up (s 175, IA 1986). Preferential debts rank equally amongst them and if the assets are insufficient to meet them, they abate in equal proportions. The scope of preferential debts has been much reduced by the Enterprise Act 2002 (s 251); for example, it has removed the preference afforded to claims by the Inland Revenue.[7] Preferential debts now only refer to contributions due by employers to certain pension schemes and the limited amounts due such as remuneration of employees. Employees are entitled to claim as preferential debt salaries for services rendered in the four months before winding up but up to a maximum amount of £800 per employee (paras 9–12, Sch 6, IA 1986).[8] Thus the five employees of Cake Ltd can only claim their salaries in the four (instead of six) months before winding up and the amount is limited to £800 each.

[8]You should pay attention to the requirements of 'four months' and the amount of '£800 per employee' because they are relevant to the problem scenario.

3. The claim of Sugar Ltd

Whilst the holder of a fixed charge can look to their security for payment of the sums due, Sugar Ltd as the holder of a floating charge is subject to the prior claims of the expenses of winding up, the preferential debts and the prescribed part.

[9]This sentence identifies the legal issues in relation to the claim by Sugar Ltd. It shows where you are going with your answer.

As Sugar Ltd still owes £40,000 to Cake Ltd in a previous transaction, the issue arises as to whether the mutual debts of Cake Ltd and Sugar Ltd can be set off against each other.[9] Where, before the company goes into liquidation, there have been mutual credits, mutual debts or other mutual dealings between the company and any creditor of the company proving or claiming to prove a debt in the liquidation, the sums due from one party must be set off against the sums due from the other (r 4.90, IR 1986). In **MS Fashions Ltd v BCCI SA (No. 2)** [1993] 3 All ER 769 the company's loan from a bank was guaranteed by a director who had a deposit account with the bank. It was held that the director, as a principal debtor, could rely on the right of set-off to reduce the debt owed to the bank by him and his company by the amount in his own account with the bank. Thus, Sugar Ltd and Cake Ltd must be set off their debts against each other and Sugar Ltd can only claim the balance of £60,000.[10]

[10]It is important to relate your discussion back to the question and apply the law to the problem scenario. You will lose marks if there is insufficient application to the question.

Another issue arises in relation to the prescribed part of a floating charge which should be set aside for unsecured creditors. The liquidator shall make a prescribed part of the company's net property available for unsecured debts. They shall not distribute that part to the holders of a floating charge unless it exceeds the amount required for the satisfaction of unsecured debts (s 176A, IA 1986). The prescribed part of the company's net property shall be calculated according to Art 3 of the Insolvency Act 1986 (Prescribed Part) Order

[11] The legal issue in relation
to the prescribed part of the
company's property is often
missing in the exam answers.
An excellent understanding
of this area of law will make
your answer stand out.

2003:[11] where the company's net property does not exceed £10,000 in value, 50% of that property; where the company's net property exceeds £10,000 in value the sum of 50% of the first £10,000 in value; and 20% of that part of the company's net property which exceeds £10,000 in value, subject to a maximum of £600,000. The requirement for setting aside the prescribed part does not apply if the company's net property is less than £10,000, and the liquidator thinks that the cost of making a distribution to unsecured creditors would be disproportionate to the benefits (s 176A, IA 1986). The claim of Sugar Ltd therefore may be subject to the prescribed part depending on the value of the company's net property.

4. The claims by the unsecured creditors

When the company goes into liquidation, its assets, after paying the expenses of the winding up and the preferential debts, form a common fund which is subject to a statutory trust for the benefit of all the creditors: **Webb v Whiffin** (1872) LR 5 HL 711. The unsecured creditors must be paid in accordance with the principle of *pari passu*, which requires that all creditors participate in the pooled assets in proportion to the size of their claim. Where the assets are insufficient to meet all the claims, they abate proportionately (s 107, IA 1986).[12]

[12] The principle of *pari passu* is one of the most important rules in insolvency law. It must be included in a sound answer.

5. The interests on all proved debts – deferred debts

The interests on all proved debts from the company going into liquidation until the date of actual payment are considered as deferred debts. Deferred debts refer to the debts which are deferred by statute until all the other debts of the company have been paid (s 189, IA 1986).

In conclusion, the assets of Cake Ltd should be distributed in the following order: the expenses of winding up, the employee's salaries (subject to the maximum amount), the claim of Sugar Ltd as the holder of a floating charge (subject to the rights of set-off and the prescribed part), the claims of the unsecured creditors (according to the principle of *pari passu*) and the interests on all proved debts.[13]

[13] Your conclusion should clearly address the question by summarising the order of payment in relation to the claims against Cake Ltd.

✓ Make your answer stand out

- Discuss the position of shareholders in an insolvent liquidation. If there are insufficient funds to pay the creditors in full, no funds will remain for the shareholders. You can point out that shareholders' losses are only limited to their capital and they are not liable to pay the creditors because of the principle of limited liability (the *Salomon* principle).

- Consider the no-deprivation rule which is also known as 'the rule in *Ex p Mackay*'. It provides that any contractual provision designed to defeat the *pari passu* distribution of the insolvent's assets is void.

! Don't be tempted to...

- Only focus on the claims by the creditors and employees. You must also discuss the expenses of winding up and the payment of interests on the proved debts.

- Get the order of priority of payment wrong. This is a very important area of law in corporate insolvency and is also a very popular exam topic. Make sure you know the order of payment of debts when the company is in liquidation.

❓ Question 5

John and Sam were directors of Fresh Fruit Ltd since January 2009. Fresh Fruit Ltd traded at a loss from May 2009 and its position gradually got worse. John and Sam did not take any professional legal or financial advice; instead, they falsified the company's accounts to show inflated profits in order to obtain additional overdraft facilities from the bank.

Fresh Fruit Ltd went into insolvent liquidation in December 2009. Two years later, both John and Sam were appointed directors of Tasty Fruit Ltd and directly took part in its management.

Advise the liquidator of Fresh Fruit Ltd in relation to the conduct of John and Sam.

Answer plan

→ Examine whether John and Sam are liable for fraudulent trading.

→ Analyse whether John and Sam are liable for wrongful trading.

→ Apply the law in relation to the prohibition on the re-use of company name.

→ Consider director's general duties in the Companies Act 2006.

Diagram plan

Should John and Sam be held liable for fraudulent trading? (s 213, IA 1986)

Should they be held liable for wrongful trading? (s 214, IA 1986)

Did they breach the rules on the prohibition of the re-use of company name? (s 216, IA 1986)

Did they breach their fiduciary duties to Fresh Fruit Ltd? (ss 170–177, CA 2006)

A printable version of this diagram plan is available from www.pearsoned.co.uk/lawexpressqa

Answer

[1]The introduction should identify the main issues that you are going to discuss in your answer. It also indicates that your answer is well structured.

The liquidator needs to consider the conduct of John and Sam as directors of Fresh Fruit Ltd in three main aspects:[1] first, whether they should be liable for fraudulent trading or wrongful trading; secondly, whether they breached the rules on the prohibition of the re-use of company name; and, thirdly, whether they breached their fiduciary duties owed to Fresh Fruit Ltd.

Civil liability may be imposed on John and Sam for fraudulent trading according to s 213 of the Insolvency Act 1986 (IA 1986). If, in the course of the winding up of a company, it appears that any business of the company has been carried on with intent to defraud creditors of the company or for any fraudulent purpose, the court, on the application of the liquidator, may declare them liable to make such contributions (if any) to the company's assets as the court thinks proper. The conduct must involve actual dishonesty: **Re Patrick and Lyon Ltd** [1933] Ch 786;[2] for instance, where directors allow a company to incur credit when they have no reason to believe that the creditors will ever be paid: **Re William C Leitch Bro Ltd** [1932] 2 Ch 71. Fraudulent trading is also a criminal offence under s 993, CA 2006.[3] As John and Sam falsified the company's accounts with

[2]The reference to case law adds more credit to your answer than simply stating the statutory provision in s 213.

[3]Students often forget to discuss the criminal offence for fraudulent trading in their answers.

[4]As this is a problem
question, you need to apply
the relevant law to the
problem scenario.

the intention to defraud creditors, it is clear that they should be held
liable for fraudulent trading.[4]

Section 214 of the IA 1986 on wrongful trading applies if the
company has gone into insolvent liquidation and, at some time
before the commencement of the winding up of the company,
the director knew or ought to have concluded that there was no
reasonable prospect that the company would avoid going into
insolvent liquidation. The court, on the application of the liquidator,
may declare that a director or shadow director is to be liable to make
such contribution (if any) to the company's assets as the court thinks
proper. The court shall not make such declaration if it is satisfied
that the director took every step to minimise the potential loss to the
company's creditors as he ought to have taken (s 214(3), IA 1986):
Re Brian D Pierson Ltd [2001] 1 BCLC 275.[5]

[5]This is an important
exception to the liability for
wrongful trading and should
be discussed in a good
answer.

The director's obligation to predict insolvency is assessed both
subjectively and objectively. The facts which a director ought to
know or ascertain, the conclusions which he ought to reach and
the steps which he ought to take are those which would be known
or ascertained, or reached or taken, by a reasonably diligent person
(s 214(4), IA 1986). The reasonably diligent person should have the
general knowledge, skill and experience that may reasonably be
expected of a person carrying out the same functions as are carried
out by that director in relation to the company, and the general
knowledge, skill and experience that that director has.[6]

[6]You can point out here that
the objective and subjective
standards of care and skill
for directors in s 214(4) of
the Insolvency Act 1986
have been adopted in s 174
of the Companies Act 2006
(director's duty to exercise
reasonable care, skill and
diligence).

The crucial issue is how to establish that directors knew or ought to
have concluded that there was no reasonable prospect of avoiding
insolvent liquidation.[7] In **Official Receiver v Doshi** [2001] 2 BCLC
235 it was held that a director who knew that his company could
only continue to trade as a result of fraudulent invoicing ought to
have concluded that there was no reasonable prospect that the
company would avoid going into insolvent liquidation. When Fresh
Fruit Ltd was trading at a loss and the situation got worse, John
and Sam ought to have concluded that there was no reasonable
prospect of avoiding insolvent liquidation. The claim for wrongful
trading, however, is unlikely to succeed where directors have acted
responsibly: **Re Continental Assurance Co of London plc** [2007]
2 BCLC 287. It appears that John and Sam did not take necessary
steps to minimise the loss by seeking professional advice or act

[7]You need to show your
knowledge of the statutory
provisions in s 214 of the
Insolvency Act 1986 and,
more significantly, analyse
their application by reference
to case law. The latter will
gain you more marks.

[8]Try to refer back to the problem question after analysing the relevant area of law.

[9]The latter part of the sentence will gain you more marks because it shows your sound understanding of the purpose of s 216.

[10]Note the requirement of the period of '12 months' before the liquidation.

[11]The prohibited names in s 216 not only include the name of the company in liquidation but also the name which is similar to it. Students are often not aware of the latter.

[12]You need to pay attention to the requirement as to the length of time for the application of s 216 because it affects your advice to the liquidator.

[13]The reference to the case law and the judgment of the Court of Appeal shows your excellent understanding of s 216. It will improve your grade.

responsibly and therefore it is mostly likely that they will be held liable for wrongful trading.[8]

The re-use of the name of the company which has been wound up is prohibited in s 216, IA 1986 in order to prevent any exploitation by the directors of any remaining goodwill in the insolvent company.[9] Where a company has gone into insolvent liquidation, a director of the company, who was in post at any time in the 12 months preceding the liquidation,[10] shall not be a director of any other company under a prohibited name, or in any way, whether directly or indirectly, be concerned or take part in the management of any such company (s 216(3)). A prohibited name is a name by which the liquidating company was known in the 12 months preceding liquidation or *a name which is so similar to it as to suggest an association with that company*[11] (s 216(2)). The prohibition on the use of the name lasts for *five years*[12] (s 216(3)). If a person acts in contravention of this prohibition, he is liable to imprisonment or a fine, or both (s 216(4)). In **Ricketts *v* Ad Valorem Factors Ltd** [2004] 1 BCLC 1 the defendant was a director of Air Component Co Ltd, which went into insolvent liquidation in February 1998. One month later he became a director of Air Equipment Co Ltd, which also traded in air compressors. The Court of Appeal compared both names in the context of all the circumstances in which they were actually used or likely to be used. It was held that the two names suggested an association and the second company's name was a prohibited name.[13]

These prohibitions do not apply where re-use of the name is permitted with the leave of the court or in the circumstances prescribed in the Insolvency Rules 1986 (rr 4.228–4.230). John and Sam were directors of Fresh Fruit Ltd since January 2009, which is within the 12 months before it went into liquidation in December 2009. Thus, they shall not be directors of Tasty Fruit Ltd or take part in the management in it within five years of the liquidation because Tasty Fruit Ltd suggests an association with Fresh Fruit Ltd, unless the above exceptions apply.

In conclusion, it can be argued that John and Sam should be liable for fraudulent trading as they falsified the accounts with the intent to defraud its creditors. They should also be liable for wrongful trading as they ought to have concluded that there was no realistic prospect

[14]Your conclusion should specifically address the issues that arise in the question. Your answer will benefit from a sound conclusion.

of Fresh Fruit Ltd avoiding an insolvent liquidation. The rules on the prohibition of the re-use of company name were infringed. Moreover, they have breached their fiduciary duties to promote the success of Fresh Fruit Ltd and to have regard to creditors' interests in case of insolvency (s 172, CA 2006).[14]

✓ Make your answer stand out

- Consider that a director of an insolvent company may be disqualified under s 6 of the Company Directors Disqualification Act 1986 if the court is satisfied that his conduct as a director makes him unfit to be concerned in the management of a company.
- Discuss the exceptions to the prohibitions on the re-use of a company's name in the Insolvency Rules 1986. For instance, re-use of the name is permitted where the successor company acquires the whole or substantially the whole of the business from the liquidator and notice is given to the creditors that the director will be acting in that capacity of the successor company (r 4.228).
- Comment on the practicalities of challenging directors' conduct for fraudulent trading and wrongful trading. The liquidator may face difficulties in trying to bring litigation against the directors due to a lack of funding.

! Don't be tempted to...

- Jump straight to the conclusion that John and Sam are liable for wrongful trading and fraudulent trading. You must analyse the relevant statutory provisions and then apply them to the problem scenario.
- Forget to discuss the prohibition on the re-use of the company's name. You need to show a good understanding of the key provisions in the Insolvency Act 1986 and the Insolvency Rules 1986.

❓ Question 6

Tomato Ltd specialised in the production of tomato soup. In May 2010, the directors of Tomato Ltd sold the company's computers to their family members at £2,000. The computers were worth £20,000. In July 2010, Tomato Ltd, which was solvent, sold its factory which was valued at £100,000 to Butternut Squash Ltd for £30,000. It was still able to pay its debts in consequence of this transaction.

In October 2010, Tomato Ltd went into compulsory liquidation. After the commencement of the winding up, the directors sold its remaining stock to Swede Ltd.

Advise the liquidator as to the validity of the above transactions.

Answer plan

→ Examine whether the sale of computers and the sale of the factory were transactions at an undervalue under s 238, IA 1986.

→ Discuss whether the sale of computers and that of the factory were transactions defrauding creditors according to s 423, IA 1986.

→ Evaluate whether the sale of the company's stock to Swede Ltd was valid after the commencement of winding up according to s 127, IA 1986.

→ Consider the misfeasance procedure in s 212, IA 1986.

Diagram plan

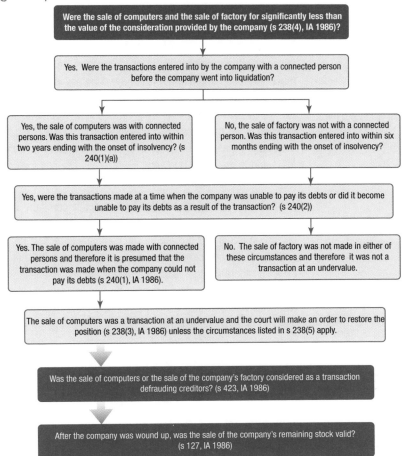

A printable version of this diagram plan is available from www.pearsoned.co.uk/lawexpressqa

Answer

[1]This paragraph identifies the legal issues that arise in the problem question. The last sentence shows that you understand the significance of the time when the transactions were made.

This question concerns the validity of three transactions: the sale of computers to the directors' family members, the sale of factory to Butternut Squash Ltd and the sale of the company's remaining stock to Swede Ltd. The first two transactions took place before Tomato Ltd went into liquidation whilst the third took place after it went into liquidation.[1]

[2]You should pay attention to the time limit here because it is one of the main conditions for the application of s 238.

[3]This is another key requirement for the transaction to be caught in s 238. You will lose some marks if it is not included in your answer.

A liquidator can challenge a transaction previously entered into by the company at an undervalue under s 238 of the Insolvency Act 1986 (IA 1986). He may apply to the court for an order where the company has entered into a transaction with any person at an undervalue at a time in the period of two years (six months for unconnected persons) ending with the onset of insolvency,[2] which is defined as the commencement of the winding up. The transaction must have been entered into when the company was unable to pay its debts or it becomes unable to pay its debts in consequence of the transaction (s 240(2)).[3] This requirement is presumed to be satisfied when the transaction was entered into by a company with a connected person. The court shall make such order as it thinks fit for restoring the position to what it would have been if the company had not entered into that transaction (s 238(3)).

[4]The reference to case law demonstrates your sound understanding of this area of law. It will gain you more marks than simply stating the statutory provision in s 238.

A transaction at an undervalue arises if the company makes a gift to that person or otherwise enters into a transaction with that person on terms that provide for the company to receive no consideration, or the company enters into a transaction with that person for a consideration the value of which is significantly less than the value of the consideration provided by the company (s 238(4)). In **National Westminster Bank plc v Hones** [2002] 1 BCLC 55, the court, in determining whether the transaction was at an undervalue, identified the consideration of the transaction and compared the value obtained by the company and the value of the consideration provided by the company.[4] In **Re MC Bacon Ltd** [1990] BCLC 324 Millett J held that both the consideration provided and that received must be measurable in money or money's worth; both must be considered from the company's point of view; and a comparison must be made between two figures representing the actual value of the consideration. The court shall not make an order if it is satisfied

[5]Some students do not discuss the exceptions in s 238(5) in their answers. As they directly affect your conclusion as to whether the sale was a transaction at an undervalue, failure to discuss them will adversely affect your mark.

[6]The definition of the connected person demonstrates your detailed knowledge and adds more credit to your answer. Some students may take it for granted that family members are connected persons without any application of the statutory provisions.

[7]The specific examples of the court orders help your answer stand out from those which only state that: 'The court will make an order to restore the position.'

both that the company which entered into the transaction did so in good faith and for the purpose of carrying on its business, and that at the time it did so there were reasonable grounds for believing that the transaction would benefit the company (s 238(5)).[5]

As the company's computers were sold to the directors' family members, who were considered as connected persons under s 249 and s 435,[6] within two years of the commencement of the liquidation, it is presumed that the transaction was entered into when the company was unable to pay its debts or it became unable to pay its debts in consequence of the transaction. Moreover, the transaction was made for a consideration which was significantly less in value. It is very unlikely that the directors could convince the court that the transaction was entered into in good faith or that the transaction would benefit the company. Thus, the court will make an order to restore the position it would have been in if the company had not entered into that transaction, for example, by ordering the property to be vested back in the company and ordering the directors' family members to make payments to the liquidator in respect of benefits received by them from the company: **Re Paramount Airways Ltd** [1992] 3 All ER 1.[7]

In relation to the sale of the factory, it was entered into with Butternut Squash Ltd (which was an unconnected person) within six months before the commencement of winding up and the value obtained by Tomato Ltd was significantly less than the value of the consideration provided by it. This transaction, however, was entered into when Tomato Ltd was able to pay its debts and it was still able to pay its debts after the transaction. It therefore was not considered as a transaction at an undervalue under s 238, IA 1986.

[8]Some students are not aware of the provision in s 423. As the problem question is essentially concerned with transactions at an undervalue, a discussion of s 423 adds more credit to your answer.

The court may also make an order under s 423, IA 1986 in relation to transactions at an undervalue.[8] If the court is satisfied that the transaction was entered into with the purpose of putting assets beyond the reach of the creditors or of prejudicing the interests of the creditors, the court may make such order as it thinks fit for restoring the position to what it would have been if the transaction had not been entered into, and protecting the interests of persons who are victims of the transaction. Section 423 covers a broader range of circumstances than s 238; for instance, it applies even when the company is not in liquidation or administration; there is no

[9]The comparison between s 238 and s 423 shows your excellent understanding of the relevant law with regard to transactions at an undervalue. It will make your answer stand out from those which only state the provisions of s 238 and s 423.

[10]Note that s 127 applies to transactions *after* the commencement of the winding up of the company. You will lose some marks if this legal issue is not clearly addressed.

[11]The misfeasance procedure in s 212 is another power that the liquidator may exercise against directors. A discussion of s 212 may impress your examiners.

time limit in relation to the transaction in s 423, unlike the two-year limit in s 238.[9]

The transaction in relation to the company's remaining stock is governed by s 127 of the IA 1986 on the avoidance of property dispositions. In a winding up by the court, any disposition of the company's property, and any transfer of shares, or alteration in the status of the company's members, made after the commencement of the winding up[10] is, unless the court otherwise orders, void. Thus, the disposition of the company's remaining stock is void without the court's permission.

The liquidator can also apply to the court according to s 212, which provides a summary remedy against delinquent directors.[11] The court may examine the conduct of the director if, in the course of the winding up of a company, it appears that the director has misapplied or retained, or become accountable for, any money or other property of the company, or been guilty of any misfeasance or breach of any fiduciary or other duty in relation to the company. The court may compel the directors of Tomato Ltd to repay, restore or account for the money or property or to make contribution to the company's assets as the court thinks just.

 Make your answer stand out

- Examine whether directors are liable for fraudulent trading (s 213, IA 1986).
- Discuss whether directors are liable for wrongful trading (s 214, IA 1986).
- Analyse briefly whether directors have breached their general duties (ss 170–177, Companies Act 2006).

! Don't be tempted to...

- Provide a common sense answer that the transactions were void without any application of the relevant statutory provisions. A good analysis of s 238 and s 127 of the IA 1986 is required.
- In your discussion of transactions at an undervalue under s 238, make no distinction between transactions with connected persons and those with unconnected persons. This distinction is important because a different time limits apply.

Bibliography

Abarca, M. L. de E. (2004), 'The need for substantive regulation on investor protection and corporate governance in Europe: does Europe need a Sarbanes-Oxley?' *Journal of International Banking Law and Regulation* 419

Almadani, M. (2009), 'Derivative actions: does the Companies Act 2006 offer a way forward?' 30 *Company Lawyer* 131

Armour, J. (2000), 'Share capital and creditor protection: efficient rules for a modern company law' 63 *Modern Law Review* 355

Attenborough, D. (2006), 'The Company Law Reform Bill: an analysis of directors' duties and the objective of the company' 27 *Company Lawyer* 162

Berle, A. A. (1931), 'Corporate powers as powers in trust' 44 *Harvard Law Review* 1049

Berle, A. and Means, G. (1932), *The Modern Corporation and Private Property*. New Brunswick, NJ: Transaction Publishers

Boros, E. (1998), 'Altering the articles of association to acquire minority shareholdings', in B. A. K. Rider (ed.), *The Realm of Company Law*. London: Kluwer Law International, p.116

Boyle, A. and Birds, J. (2007), *Boyle & Birds' Company Law*, 6th ed. Bristol: Jordans

Burke, P. (2003), 'The Higgs Review' 24 *Company Lawyer* 162

Cadbury Report (1992), *The Financial Aspects of Corporate Governance*. London: Gee

Capper, D. (2003), 'Fixed charges over book debts – the future after Brumark' 24 *Company Lawyer* 325

Clark, T. (2004), *Theories of Corporate Governance*. London: Routledge

Clarkham, J. and Simpson, A. (1999), *Fair Shares: The Future of Shareholder Power and Responsibility*. Oxford: Oxford University Press

Cork Committee (1982) Cork Committee on Insolvency Law and Practice Report (Cork Report), Cmnd 8558

Davenport, B. J. (1993), 'What did Russell v Northern Bank Development Corporation Ltd decide?' 109 *Law Quarterly Review* 553

Dedman, E. (2002), 'The Cadbury Committee Recommendations on Corporate Governance – a review of compliance and performance impacts' 4 *International Journal of Management Reviews* 335

Dignam, A. and Lowry, J. (2009), *Company Law*, 5th ed. Oxford: Oxford University Press

Dodd, E. M. (1932), 'For whom are corporate managers trustees?' 45 *Harvard Law Review* 1145

Drury, R. R. (1986), 'The relative nature of a shareholder's right to enforce the company contract' *Cambridge Law Journal* 219

DTI (1999), *Modern Company Law for a Competitive Economy: The Strategic Framework.* URN 99/654, February

DTI (2000), *Modern Company Law for a Competitive Economy: Completing the Structure.* URN 00/1335, November

DTI (2000), *Modern Company Law for a Competitive Economy: Developing the Framework.* URN 00/656, March

DTI (2001), *Modern Company Law for a Competitive Economy: Final Report.* URN 01/942 and 01/943, July

DTI (2005), White Paper

Ferran, E. (1994), 'The decision of the House of Lords in Russell v Northern Bank Development Corporation Ltd' *Cambridge Law Journal* 343

Ferran, E. (2004), 'Corporate transactions and financial assistance: shifting policy perceptions but static law' *Cambridge Law Journal* 225

Finch, V. (1992), 'Company directors: who cares about skill and care?' 55 *Modern Law Review* 179

Freedman, J. (1994), 'Small businesses and the corporate form: burden or privilege?' *Modern Law Review* 555

Goldberg, R. (1985), 'The controversy on the section 20 contract revisited' 48 *Modern Law Review* 158

Grantham, R. (2003), 'Can directors compete with the company?' 66 *Modern Law Review* 109

Greenbury Report (1995), *Directors' Remuneration.* London: Gee

Gregory, R. (1981), 'The section 20 contract' 44 *Modern Law Review* 526

Griffin, S. (1991), 'Holding companies and subsidiaries – the corporate veil' (1991) 12 *Company Lawyer* 16

Griffin, S. (2003), 'Corporate collapse and the reform of boardroom structures – Lessons from America' 6 *Insolvency Law Journal* 214

Griffiths, A. (1993), 'Agents without principals: pre-incorporation contracts and section 36 C of the Companies Act 1985' *Legal Studies* 241

Gross, J. (1971), 'Pre-incorporation contracts' *Law Quarterly Review* 367

Hampel Report (1998), *Committee on Corporate Governance: Final Report.* London: Gee

Hannigan, B. (2007), 'Altering the articles to allow for compulsory transfer – dragging minority shareholders to a reluctant exit' *Journal of Business Law* 471

Hannigan, B. (2009), *Company Law,* 2nd ed. Oxford: Oxford University Press

Harris, J. (2006), 'Law Society issues criticisms of company law Reform Bill at Second Reading' 27 *Company Lawyer* 95

Hicks, A. (1997), 'Corporate form: questioning the unsung hero' *Journal of Business Law* 306

Higgs Review (2003), *Review of the Role and Effectiveness of Non-executive Directors.* London: DTI

Hirt, H. C. (2003), 'In what circumstances should breach of director's duties give rise to a remedy under ss.459-461 of the Companies Act 1985?' 24 *Company Lawyer* 100

Hirt, H. C. (2004), 'The scope of prohibited financial assistance after *MT Realisations Ltd v Digital Equipment Co Ltd*' 25 *Company Lawyer* 9

Ho, L. C. (2003), 'Financial assistance after Chaston and MT Realisations' *Journal of International Banking Law Regulation* 424

Kahn-Freund, O. (1944), 'Some reflections on company law reform' 7 *Modern Law Review* 54

Keay, A. R. (2006), 'Enlightened shareholder value, the reform of the duties of company directors and the corporate objective' *Lloyd's Maritime and Commercial Law Quarterly* 335

Keay, A. R. (2007), 'Section 172(1) of the Companies Act 2006: an interpretation and assessment' 28 *Company Lawyer* 106

Keay, A. R. and Loughrey, J. (2008), 'Derivative proceedings in a brave new world for company management and shareholders' *Journal of Business Law* 151

Kiarie, S. (2006), 'At crossroads: shareholder value, stakeholder value and enlightened shareholder value: which road should the United Kingdom take?' *International Commercial and Company Law Review* 329

La Porta, R., Lopez-de Silanes, F. and Shleifer, A. (1999), 'Corporate ownership around the world' *Journal of Finance* 54

Law Commission (1996), *Shareholder Remedies: A Consultation Paper* (No. 142). London: The Stationery Office

Law Commission (1997), *Shareholder Remedies* (No. 246, Cm 3769). London: The Stationery Office

Law Commission, *Company Directors: Regulating Conflicts of Interests and Formulating a Statement of Duties* (Consultation Paper, No. 153). London: The Stationery Office

Linklater, L. (2006), 'Piercing the corporate veil – the never ending story?' 27 *Company Lawyer* 65

Little, B. (1992), 'How far does shareholder's freedom of contract extend? – *Russell v Northern Bank Corporation Limited* and other recent cases' *International Commercial and Company Law Review* 351

Lowry, J. (2008), 'Judicial pragmatism: directors' duties and post-resignation conflicts of duty' *Journal of Business Law* 83

Lowry, J. and Edmunds, R. (2000), 'The no conflict- no profit rules and the corporate fiduciary: challenging the orthodoxy of absolutism' *Journal of Business Law* 122

Luxton, P. (1991), 'Financial assistance by a company for the purchase of its own shares – the principal or larger purpose exception' *Company Lawyer* 18

Ma, F. (2011), 'Removal of directors: Lord Morris in Bushell v Faith [1970] AC 1099' in Geach, N. and Monaghan, C. (eds) *Dissenting Judgments*: with a Foreword by Lord Nicholls of Birkehead. London: Wildy, Simmonds and Hill.

MacNeil, I. (2000), 'Shareholders' pre-emptive rights' *Journal of Business Law* 78

MacNeil, I. and Li, X. (2006), '"Comply or explain", market discipline and non-compliance with the Combined Code' *Corporate Governance* 486

Mallin, C. A. (2007), *Corporate Governance*, 2nd ed. Oxford: Oxford University Press

Millett, Lord, Alcock, A. and Todd, M. (2007), *Gore-Browne on Companies Act 2006*. Bristol: Jordans

Milman, D. (2007), 'Share capital maintenance: current developments and future horizons' *Company Law Newsletter* 1

Moore, M. (2006), 'A temple built on faulty foundations: piercing the corporate veil and the legacy of Salomon v Salomon' *Journal of Business Law* 180

Myners Report (2001), *Institutional Investment in the UK: A Review*. London: HM Treasury

Ottolenghi, S. (1990), 'From peeping behind the corporate veil to ignoring it completely' 53 *Modern Law Review* 338

Payne, J. (1998), 'Bigger and better guns for minority shareholders' *Cambridge Law Journal* 36

Payne, J. (2005), 'Sections 459-461 Companies Act 1985 in flux: the future of shareholder protection' 64 *Cambridge Law Journal* 647

Pennington, R. (2009), 'Recent developments in the law and practice relating to the creation of security for companies' indebtedness' (2009) 30 Company Lawyer 163.

Poole, J. and Roberts, P. (1999), 'Shareholder remedies – efficient litigation and the unfair prejudice remedy' *Journal of Business Law* 38

Prentice, D. (1974), 'The corporate opportunity doctrine' *Modern Law Review* 464

Prentice, D. and Payne, J. (2004), 'The corporate opportunity doctrine' 120 *Law Quarterly Review* 198

Reisberg, A. (2005), 'Shareholders' remedies: in search of consistency of principle of English law' 16 *European Business Law Review* 1065

Reynolds, B. (1996), 'Shareholders' class rights: a new approach' *Journal of Business Law* 554

Riley, C. A. (1993), 'Vetoes and voting agreements: some problems of consent and knowledge' 44 *Northern Ireland Legal Quarterly* 34

Riley, C. A. (1999), 'The company director's duty of care and skill: the case for an onerous but subjective standard' 62 *Modern Law Review* 697

Rixon, F. G. (1986), 'Competing interests and conflicting principles: an examination of the power of alteration of articles of association' 49 *Modern Law Review* 446

Rixon, F. G. (1986), 'Lifting the veil between holding and subsidiary companies' 102 *Law Quarterly Review* 415

Savirimuthu, J. (2003), 'Pre-incorporation of contracts and the problem of corporate fundamentalism: are promoters proverbially profuse?' *Company Lawyer* 196

Scanlan, G. (2004), 'The Salomon principle' 25 *Company Lawyer* 196

Sealy, L (1997), 'Shareholders' remedies in the common law world' *Company Financial and Insolvency Law Review* 172

Sealy, L. (1992), 'Shareholders' agreements – an endorsement and a warning from the House of Lords' *Cambridge Law Journal* 437

Sheehan, D. and Arvind, T. T. (2006), 'Prospective overruling and the fixed-floating charge debate' 122 *Law Quarterly Review* 20

Smart, P. (2004), 'Fixed or floating? Siebe Gorman post-Brumark' 25 *Company Lawyer* 331

Smith Report (2003), *Audit Committees Combined Code Guidance*. London: Financial Reporting Council

Smith, A. (1776), *The Wealth of Nations*. London: Random House

Sugarman, D. (1997), 'Reconceptualising company law: reflections on the Law

Commission's Consultation Paper on Shareholder Remedies: Part 1' 18 *Company Lawyer* 226

Sykes, A. (2002) 'Overcoming poor value executive remuneration: resolving the manifest conflicts of interest' 10 *Corporate Governance: An International Review* 256

Sykes, A. (2010), 'The continuing paradox: a critique of minority shareholder and derivative claims under the Companies Act 2006' *Civil Justice Quarterly* 205

Times, The (1994), 'What a way to run the DTI', 1 November

Turnbull Report (1999), *Internal Control: Guidance for Directors on the Combined Code*. London: Accountancy Books

UK Corporate Governance Code (2010). London: Financial Reporting Council

UK Stewardship Code (2010). London: Financial Reporting Council

Walker Review (2009), *Review of Corporate Governance of UK Banking Industry*. London: HM Treasury

Wedderburn, K. W. (1957), 'Shareholders' rights and the rule in *Foss v. Harbottle*' *Cambridge Law Journal* 194

Worthington, S. (2000), 'Corporate governance: remedying and ratifying directors' breaches' *Law Quarterly Review* 638

Yap, J. L. (2010), 'Considering the enlightened shareholder value principle' 31 *Company Lawyer* 35

Index

administration 179, 223–7
agency 226
    company and shareholders 6, 30, 35–6, 37, 39–40, 41
    monitoring costs 92, 108, 117
    pre-incorporation 12, 15–16, 18, 19–20, 21
    theory 107–10, 121, 130
annual report 112, 118, 126–7
articles of association 9, 11, 131, 148, 205
    allotment of shares 151
    alteration of 52, 54–61, 64, 65, 66, 121, 152, 167–8
    enforcement of 45–9, 51–2, 64
    entrenchment 56
    general management clause 83, 116, 145
    removal of directors 49–53, 65–6
    shareholders' agreements versus 62–6
    transfer of shares 143, 145
audit committee 112

bankruptcy 231
book debts: charges over 175–6, 179, 182–6
bribes 99
business judgement 76

Cadbury Report 1992 107, 111, 112, 121
capital maintenance 145–9, 163, 169–70
    purchase of own shares 148–9, 158–66
chairman 126, 131
charges
    fixed 5, 173, 174–86
    floating *see separate entry*
charities 5
chief executive 126
Combined Code 109, 110, 111–14, 127
    directors' remuneration 125–6, 130–1
    institutional shareholders 120, 121, 127, 128

    non-executive directors 116–18, 125, 126–7, 130–1
company secretary 9
company voluntary arrangement (CVA) 219–23
company's constitution 46, 70, 75, 109, 205
    articles of association *see separate entry*
conflicts of interest 117, 122, 130, 190, 230
    authorisation (s 175(4)) 71, 89–90, 93, 200
    declare interest in existing transaction (s 182) 98, 100, 102, 104, 200
    declare interest in proposed transaction (s 177) 72, 95–8, 100, 102, 104, 109, 200
    director's duty to avoid (s 175) 71–2, 86–95, 100, 104, 109, 161, 190, 200, 210
    third party benefits (s 176) 71, 99, 109
connected persons 90, 94, 102–3, 201, 242
    floating charges 179–80, 188, 189–90
constructive notice: charges 180–1
contracts 98, 131
    pre-incorporation 15–16, 17, 19–21
    shareholders' agreements 62–6
    statutory 46, 51, 54, 59, 64
Cork Committee 1982 224
corporate governance 84, 133–7
    agency theory 107–10, 121, 130
    Combined Code *see separate entry*
    institutional shareholders 108, 112, 119–28, 132
    non-executive directors *see separate entry*
    remuneration committee 125, 129–31, 132
corporate personality 5, 6, 25–7, 28, 29, 34
    lifting corporate veil 6, 27–41
costs 197, 213–14, 215
creditors
    directors and interests of 101
    unsecured 179, 234–5
    voluntary winding up 228, 229, 231

criminal offences 113, 143, 148, 156, 179, 239
  financial assistance 148, 161, 165
  fraudulent trading 237
  reduction of capital 147, 169
  solvency 147, 228

derivative actions 109, 144, 161, 193–8, 199
  institutional shareholders 122
  only available to members 81, 136
  two-stage procedure 196, 201–2
  unfair prejudice claims and 144–5, 161, 195, 202, 211–16
directors
  agency problem 107–10, 121, 130
  appointment of 117, 121
  board of 107, 108, 116–18, 119, 121, 126, 130, 131, 132
  business judgement 76
  chairman and chief executive 126
  definition 69–70
  disqualification 104, 190, 240
  dual board structure 119
  fraudulent trading 28, 31, 104, 237–8, 240
  misfeasance procedure 103–4, 244
  non-executive *see separate entry*
  prohibited company names 239, 240
  public companies 9, 70
  removal of 49–53, 65–6, 121, 206, 209
  remuneration 59–60, 112, 123, 125–6, 129–33
  right to nominate 59, 62
  service contracts 53, 59, 60, 97, 211
  solvency 147, 169, 228
  wrongful trading 28, 32, 104, 190, 238–9, 240
directors' duties 36, 37, 108–9, 116, 205
  allotment of shares 74–6
  care, skill and diligence (s 174) 71, 82–6, 99, 109
  codification of 69–73
  common law 70, 71, 72, 75, 79, 83, 84, 91, 93, 97, 102, 135
  conflicts of interest (s 175) 71–2, 86–95, 100, 104, 109, 161, 190, 200, 210
  declare interest in existing transaction (s 182) 98, 100, 102, 104, 200
  declare interest in proposed transaction (s 177) 72, 95–8, 100, 102, 104, 109, 200
  delegation of power 85
  exercise powers for proper purposes (s 171) 53, 70, 75–6, 109, 153, 161
  financial assistance for purchase of own shares 160, 161, 165
  independent judgement (s 173) 71, 109
  promote success of company (s 172) *see separate entry*
  ratification of breaches 90, 93–4, 195, 196–7, 201, 213, 214
  special knowledge and reasonable care 99
  substantial property transactions 98, 102
  third party benefits (s 176) 71, 99, 109
disclosure of directors' remuneration 131–2
disqualification of directors 104, 190, 240
distributions 147
dividends 144, 147, 157

employees 81, 136, 137, 233–4
enlightened shareholder value 71, 77, 78–82, 109, 135–7, 200
Enron 113, 126

fiduciary relationships 122, 230
  directors and company 70, 83, 92, 109
  promoters 14–15, 18
financial assistance for purchase of own shares 148–9, 158–66
fixed charges 5, 173, 174–81
  book debts 175–6, 179, 182–6
floating charges 5, 174–81, 186–90
  appointment of administrator 224–6, 227
  avoidance of (s 245) 179–80, 181, 187, 188
  book debts 175–6, 182–6
  priority of payment 233, 234–5
  registration 187–8
  voidable preference (s 239) 180, 187, 188–90
Foss v Harbottle, rule in 47–8, 56, 109, 194, 195, 199

fraud 195, 196, 213
fraudulent trading 28, 31, 104, 237–8, 240
free-riding problem 122, 123, 197

general meetings
    alteration of articles 59, 64
    annual 9, 121, 127
    ratification of misconduct 90, 93–4, 201
    variation of class rights 168
    voting 50–1
    winding up 228
Germany 119, 134
good faith
    administrators 225
    altering articles: *bona fide* for benefit of
        company as whole 52, 54–6, 57, 60–1
    derivative actions 196, 197, 201, 213
    financial assistance for acquisition of own
        shares 160, 164
    non-cash consideration for share allotment 155
    promote success of company: acting in *see
        separate entry*
    registration of share transfer 144
    undervalue transactions 103, 243
    unfair prejudice 209
Greenbury Report 1995 112, 130
Greene Committee (1926) 163
groups and lifting corporate veil 30–1, 37–41
guarantee companies 5, 11

Hampel Report 1998 112
Higgs Report 2003 112, 116–17

incorporation
    advantages and disadvantages of 3–7
    from private to public company 10
    names 8, 9, 10–11
    private companies 8–10
    promoters 12–21
information
    asymmetry 108, 120
    price-sensitive 123
injunctions 161

insider dealing 123
insolvency
    administration 179, 223–7
    CVA 219–23
    liquidation *see separate entry*

Japan 134
Jenkins Committee 1962 204
joint and several liability 4, 31, 151, 156, 157

limited liability 5, 6, 7, 25, 27, 29, 34, 236
limited liability partnerships (LLPs) 4–5, 6
limited partnerships 4
liquidation
    compulsory winding up (s 122) 211, 229–30,
        231
    creditors' voluntary winding up 228, 229, 231
    deferred debts 235
    duties of liquidator 230
    expenses of 233
    floating charges, avoidance of (s 245) 179–80,
        181, 187, 188
    floating charges: voidable preference (s 239)
        180, 187, 188–90
    members' voluntary winding up 228
    misfeasance procedure 103–4, 244
    pari passu principle 235, 236
    priority of payment 179, 180–1, 231–6
    prohibited names 239, 240
    property dispositions after start of 244
    set-off 234
    statutory declaration of solvency 228–9
    undervalue transactions 102–3, 240–4
listed companies 113, 132
    Combined Code *see separate entry*

market abuse 123
meetings *see* general meetings
memorandum of association 9
Myners Report 2001 112

names 8, 9, 10–11, 239, 240
negative pledge clauses 175, 176, 180–1

negligence 99, 195–6, 213
non-executive directors 111, 112, 115–19, 125,
    126–7, 130–1, 132
notice and negative pledge clauses 180–1
novation 21

partnerships 4
performance-related remuneration 126, 131
personal guarantees 6, 27
pre-emption rights 53, 75, 143, 151–2, 162
pre-incorporation contracts 15–16, 17, 19–21
preference shares 152, 166–70
preferential debts 233–4
priority of payment 179, 180–1, 231–6
private companies 8–10, 143, 147, 148, 156,
    163, 169
promote success of company (s 172) 70–1, 72,
    76–7, 90, 190, 210
    allotment of shares 153
    creditors 101
    derivative claims 196, 201
    enlightened shareholder value 71, 77, 78–82,
        109, 135–7, 200
    executive and non-executive directors 116
    intelligent and honest director 76–7, 79,
        200–1
    registration of share transfers 144
    unlawful financial assistance 161
promoters 12–21
property transactions, substantial 98, 102
public companies 8–9, 70, 147, 148–9, 156–7,
    158–66, 205
purchase of own shares 148–9, 158–66

quasi-partnership companies 205–6, 209–10

rectification 143
registration 9–10, 64
    charges 178–9, 187–8
remuneration committee 125, 129–31, 132
resolutions 9, 121, 221, 228
    ordinary 50–1, 65–6, 75, 209
    ratification of misconduct 90, 93–4

special 10, 11, 46, 52, 54, 57, 59, 60, 64, 66,
    147, 151–2, 163, 167–8, 169

Salomon principles 25–8, 29, 32, 34, 40
    lifting corporate veil 6, 27–41
Sarbanes-Oxley Act 2002 113–14
secret profits 12, 14–15, 18–19, 33–5, 36
    codification of directors' duties 71, 88
set-off 234
share capital 151
    authorised 9, 10
    capital maintenance see separate entry
    class rights see variation
    purchase of own shares 148–9, 158–66
    reduction of capital 146–8, 169–70
    shareholders' agreements and increase in 65
shareholder remedies
    derivative actions see separate entry
    personal actions 196, 201, 211
    unfair prejudice see separate entry
shareholders
    activism 112, 122
    agency: company and 6, 30, 35–6, 37, 39–40,
        41
    agency problems: directors and 107–10, 121,
        130
    enlightened shareholder value 71, 77, 78–82,
        109, 135–7, 200
    institutional 108, 112, 119–28, 132
    non-executive directors' remuneration 131
    pre-emption rights 53, 75, 143, 151–2, 162
    remedies see shareholder remedies
    repayment of dividends 157
    shareholder primacy 79, 80, 81, 134, 135, 136
    shareholders' agreements 62–6
    substantial property transactions 98, 102
shares 142–3
    allotment of 74–6, 150–3, 154–8, 205
    bonus 151
    company limited by 5, 6, 7, 11
    discount to nominal value 155
    equitable and legal title 143–4
    non-cash consideration 151, 154–7

preference 152, 166–70
prices 112, 122
redeemable 148
transfer of 141–5
short-termism 122, 134
Smith Report 2003 112
sole traders 3–4
solvency
statement 147, 169
statutory declaration of 228–9
stakeholder theory 79–80, 81, 134–5, 136
Hampel Report 1998 112
substantial property transactions 98, 102

third party benefits (s 176) 71, 99, 109
time limits
compulsory winding up 229
CVA 220, 221, 222
floating charges 179–80, 188, 189
members' voluntary winding up 228
names 10, 239
non-cash consideration for shares 156
non-executive directors 117
preferential debt salaries 234
reduction of capital 147, 169
registration of charges 179, 187–8
transfer of shares 143
undervalue transactions 102, 103, 242
Turnbull Report 1999 112

UK Corporate Governance Code 2010 110, 113, 114
UK Stewardship Code 2010 120, 121–2, 127–8
undervalue transactions 102–3, 240–4
unfair harm and administrators 226
unfair prejudice 53, 75, 81, 109, 161, 203–16
articles of association 48, 61
class rights 153, 168
derivative actions and 144–5, 161, 195, 202, 211–16
institutional investors 122
locus standi 204, 209
petitioner's own conduct 61, 210–11
purchase order: shares 206, 210, 211, 214
quasi-partnership companies 205–6, 209–10
unfair prejudice challenge to CVA 221–2
United States 108, 113–14, 134, 135
unlimited liability 4, 5

variation of class rights 52, 56–7, 59, 152–3, 166–8, 169–70
voting 50–1, 52, 65–6, 127, 128, 144
shareholders' agreements and 64–6

winding up *see* liquidation
wrongful trading 28, 32, 104, 190, 238–9, 240